HIGH LIFE 'N' LOW DOWN DIRTY

D1419993

ALSO AVAILABLE FROM EBURY PRESS

Was There Then: Oasis – A Photographic Journey
by Jill Furmanovsky

Primal Scream: Higher Than The Sun
by Grant Fleming

The Prodigy: Adventures With The Voodoo Crew
by Martin James

The Stone Roses and the Resurrection of British Pop
by John Robb

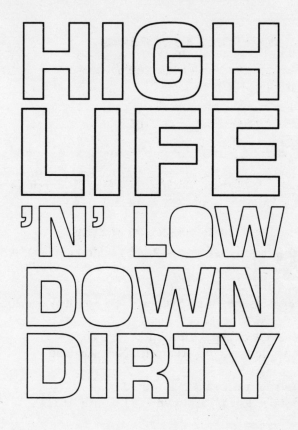

HIGH LIFE 'N' LOW DOWN DIRTY

The Thrills and Spills of Shaun Ryder

Lisa Verrico

EBURY
PRESS

First published in Great Britain in 1998

1 3 5 7 9 10 8 6 4 2

© 1998 Lisa Verrico

All rights reserved. No part of this publication may be reproduced, stored in a retrieval system, or transmitted in any form or by any means, electronic, mechanical, photocopying, recording or otherwise, without prior permission from the copyright owners.

Ebury Press
Random House, 20 Vauxhall Bridge Road, London SW1V 2SA

Random House Australia Pty Limited
20 Alfred Street, Milsons Point, Sydney, New South Wales 2061, Australia

Random House New Zealand Limited
18 Poland Road, Glenfield, Auckland 10, New Zealand

Random House South Africa (Pty) Limited
Endulini, 5A Jubilee Road, Parktown 2193, South Africa

Random House UK Limited Reg. No. 954009

A CIP catalogue record for this book is available from the British Library

ISBN 0 09 185419 9

Cover design by Push

Cover photograph by Davies and Davies

Printed and bound in Great Britain by Mackay's of Chatham plc

Papers used by Ebury Press are natural, recyclable products made from wood grown in sustainable forests.

Introduction

When I was 15, *The Stones* biography by Philip Norman came out for the first time. It is still the only hardback book I own. When I read it, I couldn't believe that people really lived their lives like that. Even with the stories down in black and white, fixed by dates and places and different versions of events, some of it was hard to swallow. To this day, I'm not sure how much of *The Stones* is fact and how much was hype.

As a journalist with the boredom threshold of a three-year-old, I have never wanted to spend months on a book about someone else. I always thought it would be a waste of time. When I was asked to write about Shaun Ryder, however, I realised that his was the only rock'n'roll story in my experience to rival what I had read when I was 15. There are currently hundreds of much better-known, far more successful musicians, but this was the only biography I could write which might make the same impact on someone else that Norman's *The Stones* had made on me.

High Life 'n' Low Down Dirty is not Shaun Ryder's story in his own words. It is not even simply his story. Based on several first-hand accounts from musicians, producers, journalists, photographers and industry figures who have all at some stage worked with Shaun, this is a tale that takes in a culture which was raised in clubland, but is rooted in rock'n'roll. If events range only from the far-fetched to the blatantly bizzarre, bear in mind that even Shaun called himself a cartoon-style character. The cover of this book, he reckons, makes him look like Dennis The Menace. Having learnt a lot about his life, I would say the description is spot-on. This is certainly a story of comic-strip proportions.

Lisa Verrico

Part One

ONE

Waiting For The Mail Man

Shaun Ryder stumbled into music. He didn't plan to be in a band. He didn't dream of life as a rock'n'roll star. Growing up, he hadn't even idolised any singers. Sure, he admired David Bowie, liked John Lennon and thought Johnny Rotten was cool – but he didn't want to *be* them. Shaun was never sure what he wanted. He just knew he hated being bored.

As a teenager, Shaun William Ryder could have stumbled in several different directions. Few of them were legal, none involved a nine-to-five. He was smart but badly-educated, wise but unambitious. If something caught his interest, however, Shaun quickly became a self-taught expert on the subject. For as long as he can remember, his life has been about entertaining and educating himself. If that turns other people on in the process, all the better. If it doesn't, too bad.

The Ryder family home was at 53 Conniston Avenue, Little Hulton, north Manchester. A council estate of a thousand or so grey semis, Little Hulton was a place purpose-built to take some of Salford's overspill, after much of the district was knocked down to make way for tower blocks in the early 1960s. Not as rough as inner-city areas such as Moss Side, the estate's rows of quickly run-down houses, which lined rather desolate streets, was nevertheless a grim place to grow up. No attempt had been made to make Little Hulton attractive. Instead of parks, there were stretches of wasteland, sometimes strewn with industrial waste. Amenities were all but unheard of, unless you counted the corner shops and pubs, filled with locals who marked their fortnights by dole days, having given up hope of ever finding a job. For the kids, it was a case of making your own entertainment. Behind the Ryders' road was a sewage works.

Just for fun, Shaun and his mates would often hang out there, shooting at rats with a stolen air pistol.

Little Hulton was also, however, a typically tight community. Ever since unemployment had begun to rise sharply at the start of the 1980s, residents had learnt to rely on one another. The kids may have hung out in gangs, strolling the streets looking for mischief or trying to spot stereos in parked cars, but at least they knew their neighbours. Endless arguments, usually fuelled by local gossip, might have been resolved by a public brawl, but one could rest assured that everyone shared the same problems. Poverty was rife, and so too were drink and drug addictions. Few people lived in Little Hulton without wanting to leave.

Unlike his son Shaun, Derek Ryder grew up with stars in his eyes. In early 1960s Manchester, Derek was a regular in his hometown's most infamous nightspots. During that decade, the city boasted some of the country's finest clubs with Rowntree's Sound, Jackie's Explosion, Nice'n'Easy and the legendary Twisted Wheel. It was, however, a live band venue called Oasis (which had evolved from a jazz haunt known as 2 J's) which particularly appealed to Derek. Oasis played host to the new breed of beat groups – including The Beatles – and, between live sets, employed local pop DJs like Dave Lee Travis to play the latest singles by both British and American groups.

Seeing unknown acts start out at places like Oasis and Rowntree's Sound and end up earning a living from music – or better still, making their fortune from it – gave Derek Ryder a goal in life. His ambition, he decided, was to succeed as an entertainer. To be lead singer in his own band was his first choice, although a gig as bassist in someone else's outfit always looked more likely. Derek even tried his hand as a stand-up comic. Depressingly, he never progressed beyond the local pub or Manchester Mecca circuit. Maybe the time wasn't right or perhaps, as he would later claim, the lucky breaks never came his way. The chances are though that Derek simply wasn't talented enough.

Derek was married to Linda, a nurse. A strict Roman Catholic, she went to church every Sunday and even attended anti-abortion rallies in town. On 23 August 1962 Linda gave birth to Shaun, the couple's first child. Determined to have kids of a similar age, less than a year later she was pregnant with a second son, Paul.

As the 1960s progressed into the 1970s, Derek's musical aspirations began to fade. He still liked to sport outlandish hippy clothes, let his greying hair curl down to his shoulders and hang out in happening clubs, but he also slowly adapted to his increasingly settled home life. He resigned himself to his proper job as postman on a neighbouring estate. He thought he ought to settle down. After all, he now had two young sons to look after. But just how much trouble they would turn out to be not even Derek could have guessed. Nor could he have known that, in the years to come, the pair would provide him with the chance to finally fulfil his rock'n'roll ambitions.

The earliest tale of mischief ever recounted by Shaun Ryder concerns an incident at school when he was only four years old. Having been ignored for months by a class teacher who would reward her favourite pupils with toffees, Shaun decided to spend breaktimes stealing sweets for himself. He claimed he would climb from the playground through an open window, break into his teacher's desk and help himself to toffees. Until, that is, he got caught. Doubtless the story has in its origins at least a grain of truth. The reality, however, is that both Shaun and his younger brother Paul were pretty good primary school pupils. It's little wonder. The pair attended St Marks school in Wardley, where Sue Ryder – their aunt – was not only a Junior 3 teacher, but also headmistress.

Outside school, Shaun wasn't as well-behaved. At the age of seven, he began committing acts of petty theft and vandalism, stealing from shops and from friends' parents' homes. He and Paul hung out in a group of around a dozen kids, several of whom were their slightly older (and hugely influential) cousins, the Carrolls. Before returning home to Little Hulton in the evenings, or on Sunday mornings when Shaun and Paul said they were at church, the gang would make their own entertainment by lobbing bricks through office windows or exposing themselves to the irate shop keepers they had robbed earlier in the day.

Thanks, no doubt, to his aunt's presence at primary school, Shaun started Swinton's Catholic secondary school, St Ambrose Barlow, in the top stream for several of his subjects. By the end of his first year, however, he had slipped into the lowest of four sets for every class.

Not that Shaun attended many lessons. In fact, he was very rarely ever at school after the age of eleven. He preferred to sneak off to the cinema, go window-shopping or, he reckons, take his girlfriend for lunch in town. When he did turn up at school, he was often assigned rubbish duty in the playground as a punishment. He didn't mind. Sauntering around outside smoking fags seemed better than having to pretend to study. To this day, Shaun swears he can barely recite the alphabet, although he does recall flicking through his dad's Sven Hassel books, if as much for their wacky covers as for the text.

'I never had the patience to read,' he says. 'I always got words mixed up. I'd have to read the same line three times over before I got what it meant.'

Shaun did persevere, however, with Richard Allen's *Skinhead* and *Suedehead* novels.

'They were the only books I ever read,' he says. 'That's because they were full of "fuck this" and "fuck that". There was tons of shagging in them too.'

Throughout their years at St Ambrose Barlow, both Shaun and Paul Ryder continued to commit petty crimes, which they did well to conceal from their parents. The two even sought out and shared the ideal hiding place for their ill-gotten gains – a large gap beneath the bottom drawer of a dressing table in their bedroom. Shaun's space was on the left, Paul's on the right. Predictably, Shaun's haul was always the most impressive and certainly the more stylish. At one stage, alongside the money, cigarettes and the starting pistol he had nicked from school, Shaun had four pairs of brand new patchpocket flares and some expensive leather Mod-style shoes. Of course, he could never risk his mum catching him in the clothes. Consequently, he had either to wait until she had gone out in order to leave the house in them, or hide the articles in a bag and change at a friend's.

Shaun would subsequently claim that the worst of his crimes as a kid came about because he was led astray by a boy two years above him at school. He said he was sent into houses through open windows to steal money and valuables. If he came back empty-handed, he was beaten up. Once, he reckons, he was even dangled upside down out of a window.

Although Shaun would later play up his childhood mis-demeanours, the truth was that the vast majority were relatively trivial offences. Unlike a lot of kids from his neighbourhood, Shaun was always scared of having to face up to his mother, should he or his brother be caught. It may have been Derek who administered the punishment – once allegedly chasing Shaun out into the street mid-argument in only his underpants – but it was Linda who suffered the shame. When Shaun was aged eleven, both he and Paul broke into a warehouse to steal crates of Carlsberg. They were caught selling the cans at closing time outside their local pub.

The only serious incident in which a pre-teenage Shaun took part involved the torching of his school's expensive new science lab – the day after it officially opened. At the least, Shaun was there. And the story made the local paper. But to be honest, he wasn't entirely up for hardcore crime. It was too much trouble. Silly stunts were just as entertaining and a lot less hassle. He had witnessed what the worst of the Swinton kids his age were already getting up to and tried to steer clear. He thought they were psychotic and cruel. He knew most would waste their youth in juvenile detention centres and borstals. Shaun was too smart to spend time inside. Besides, the boredom would have driven him round the bend. To Shaun and Paul, misbehaving meant a quick fix of fun. It was simply something to do, a way to pass the time until a more interesting diversion ambled on to the horizon. In this instance, that took the pin-thin shape of a gawky kid two years Shaun's junior. His name was Mark Berry, but everyone knew him as Bez.

Shaun and Bez first met through mutual mates, who had insisted for months that they would be ideal best friends. The rumours they had heard about each other made them initially wary on the night they finally met, but after several hours spent sat together talking and smoking hash, the pair forged a strong bond. For the following decade, they would be inseparable.

Bez was born in Liverpool on 18 April 1964. His father was a strict CID police officer whose job took the family to Manchester when Bez was only a few years old. Skinny but athletic, with a severe crop verging on a skinhead, throughout his pre-teens Bez was heavily into sport. Particularly talented at football, he even played briefly for Prestwich Heyes.

Just like Shaun, Bez started getting into trouble around the age of eleven. He would hang out on the streets with older kids until very late at night, often not coming home at all. He committed petty theft and, when he was disciplined for regularly playing truant from school, decided not to bother attending at all. Instead, Bez began to seek out unusual and increasingly outlandish ways to misbehave. Unlike Shaun, however, his illegal antics weren't so much an attempt to stop himself being bored, but rather part of a continual quest for kicks. Bez was after a buzz, the bigger the better. He built his own bike from stolen parts and rode it recklessly around his estate. He spent his days stealing, quickly graduating from stuffing handfuls of sweets into his pockets to burgling houses while the owners were at work. In spite of his age, Bez was wise enough to know that his life was rapidly heading in a dubious direction. Then he met Shaun Ryder.

What Shaun and Bez shared was self-confidence. Both had blind optimism for the future. But of course, while they waited for whatever momentous event was on its way to change their lives, they were going to have a good time.

The first song ever to have an effect on Shaun Ryder was David Bowie's 'Life On Mars'. He heard it played on the radio.

'I still can't explain why it meant so much to me,' he admits. 'It was just the groove. I already liked The Rolling Stones and The Beatles, but only because I'd been hearing their albums in our house since I was a kid. Bowie was the first musician I discovered on my own, which made him sort of special to me. I've no idea why I liked him, I just thought he was cool.

'I saw him performing "Starman" on *Top Of The Pops*. He was playing this amazing blue guitar. He was double-thin, with spiky orange hair. I remember thinking he looked like he was whizzing his tits off. After that, someone gave me a Bowie T-shirt. It was blue, with a picture of his face made up as Ziggy Stardust on the front. I wore it all the time.'

David Bowie's albums were among the first in Shaun's record collection. 'I didn't buy though,' says Shaun. 'I stole them. It was when Salford got its first big superstore. It was massive, big as a football pitch. We'd never seen anything like it before, but they treated it like it was just a little Tesco. There were no cameras and no security men, only a few stupid little mirrors and a bunch of old grannies on the tills. You could march in there and pinch anything you wanted. The first things I nicked were *Pin-Ups* and *Hunky Dory* and that Rod Stewart album with "Mandolin Wind" and "Maggie May" on it.'

Music, however, wasn't too important to Shaun. Sex and drugs already seemed a lot more appealing. He was thirteen when he lost his virginity in an underground car park in Manchester's city centre. All he remembers is that he kept on a pair of eight-hole Doc Martens throughout the event. Fortunately, he was wearing a pair of conveniently wide parallel trousers at the time. Oh, he also recalls that he enjoyed it more than almost anything else in his life.

It was the same year that Shaun did his first drugs. He took a microdot acid trip with Bez. Subsequently, the pair would regularly drop a few tabs over an afternoon, before wasting the day wandering aimlessly around the Arndale Centre, a huge shopping precinct in town. Shaun also claims to have seen his first syringe at thirteen. He was on a fairground ride with his girlfriend, he recalls, when she shoved one down her jeans when she noticed the police approaching.

During the following summer, when he turned fourteen, Shaun took his first job, on a neighbouring council estate. It involved stripping wallpaper and removing the window frames from empty properties. He was paid £30 a house. After a couple of weeks, Shaun sussed that it was quicker to knock the walls down completely, rather than fiddle with the furnishings. He got fired. Returning to school for what was to prove his final year already seemed pretty pointless.

'If I did go to school, I was the class clown,' he says. 'I'd spend most of my time in the playground, rhyming sentences and making up songs. It was all stupid, juvenile stuff, coming up with daft names for my mates and talking like I was reciting nursery rhymes. I probably pretended it was some sort of code, made out I knew what I was doing.'

Shaun didn't mind missing classes. They didn't interest him. Besides, he had discovered a far more satisfying way to pass the days – shagging lonely thirtysomething housewives in Little Hulton. Already, he says, he loved sex, the dirtier the better. Just before he finally quit school, Shaun was sent to an interview with a careers adviser. He said he wanted to move to Amsterdam and earn his living making porn films. The adviser didn't object.

Bez seemed less obsessed by sex. He was probably too busy

experimenting with drugs to bother much with women. By the age of thirteen, Bez was regularly taking speed and acid, not to mention selling the stuff to his schoolmates. By fifteen, he says, he had tried almost every drug on the market, including heroin and cocaine.

On leaving school, Bez took a job moving boxes in a warehouse. It was to be the only regular employment he would ever have. He lasted five months before being sacked for consistently failing to turn up. He didn't have to; he was already making more money dealing drugs.

Shaun left school at fifteen. He wasn't interested in passing any exams, so there was no reason for his teachers to try to persuade him to stay. Outside school, he was falling into increasingly serious trouble. The final straw, as far as the authorities were concerned, was a badly botched joyride. Intoxicated, Shaun stole a brand new Ford Granada. Minutes later, with the police in pursuit, he drove straight through an elderly couple's front hedge, over their lawn and into their just-built extension. It wasn't Shaun's day as the couple's son was a local copper, and as a result he was sent to a detention centre.

If Shaun's incident-strewn adolescence sounds extreme, it was only typical of his environment. In fact, his antics seemed tame when compared to those of some of the kids on the Salford estates. The Ryder family's reputation certainly didn't match that of their relations, the Carrolls, who were well known on the Salford pub scene.

'My grandfather, Big Billy Carroll, was a big Irish motherfucker,' Shaun claimed. 'He was cock of the estate, a bit of a spiv. He'd go to church every fuckin' night, say a prayer, then go right back to his bad ways. Lorry drivers round our way lost their jobs because Big Billy turned their wagons over, off his head on Newcy [Newcastle] Brown. He always had crates of the stuff in his shed.'

Shaun's numerous Carroll cousins were a big influence on his teenage years. They played him Roxy Music records and introduced him to northern soul. He admired their standing in Salford and envied the respect they commanded within the community, regardless of how they had earned it. Shaun grew up quickly because of his cousins – Paul Carroll, who was only a couple of years above him at school, was killed in an after-hours fight in a pub.

On Shaun's release from the detention centre, in an attempt to keep him out of trouble, he was sent to work as a messenger boy at the Post Office where his dad was employed. His task was to deliver telegrams to the estate. Shaun didn't want the job, of course, but he had little choice. He was too young to sign on and had yet to come up with an alternative of his own. Besides, being a messenger boy did have its benefits.

'I used to hang around waiting for the man with the mail to arrive in the morning,' he says. 'Then I'd keep an eye out for the envelopes from banks with cash cards in them. In those days, they used to send the cards and the numbers out together. I could go out and get whatever I wanted. What did I buy? Clothes mainly. Oh, and I'd get some perfume for my mum.'

TWO
Holdalls And Handbags

A curious Shaun Ryder snuck into his first club when he was eleven. The venue was the Wishing Well in Salford's Swinton and the year was 1973. The music policy was northern soul and funk, as opposed to the lightweight pop of Mud and Showaddywaddy that most places in Manchester played at the time. Shaun reckons you only had to be thirteen to get past the bouncers and buy alcohol at the bar. Maybe he looked or acted older; more likely he was let in because of his big cousins.

Manchester's obsession with dance music dates back to the 1950s. The first American R&B and soul records to be shipped to Britain soon found their way to the city, after arriving at docks in nearby Liverpool. Then came Merseybeat. When that scene began to decline in the mid 1960s, however, soul once again became Manchester's dominant club music, and was reflected in the growing popularity of venues like Oasis and Nice'n'Easy.

Northern soul took hold in the early 1970s. Predominately a Midlands movement (taking in industrial areas from Lancashire in the north to the edge of East Anglia), northern soul grew out of an underground scene based on imported 1960s soul singles, the rarer the better. The scene took off in Manchester at a club called the Twisted Wheel. In fact, the very term 'northern soul' is said to have been coined by magazine journalist Dave Godin following a trip to a Twisted Wheel all-nighter in 1970. Northern soul referred to much more than the uptempo American R&B tunes that filled the dancefloors of working-class clubs. It summed up a lifestyle. Northern soul fans were obsessed by music, fuelled by amphetamines and dedicated to being different. They had their own dress code – smart but casual, sticker-covered holdalls instead of handbags, wide trousers with optional embroidered patches. They even developed their own style of dancing.

Northern soul was to prove the biggest influence to date on both Shaun and Bez. Shaun connected with the scene. He loved the fact that it was about more than just music. It was a way of life, one which encompassed style, illicit substances and all-night parties – three of his favourite things. For the first time in his life, Shaun was also exposed to people who lived for something that they enjoyed, as opposed to just enduring a dull job.

Shaun and Bez's first experience of a northern soul all-nighter was at Wigan Casino – by then, the Twisted Wheel had been shut down by the drug squad. The speed-crazed Casino was responsible for lifting northern soul out of the underground, and attracted busloads of party-goers from all over the country. The Casino was also where Bez claims to have leant to dance. He first went there at the age of thirteen, although only by sneaking in through the fire doors. Like Shaun, he didn't initially go for the music. Bez was there to sell speed. That first night, he went in with a bagful of amphetamine tablets known as chalkies.

By the late 1970s, when Shaun was almost legally allowed into clubs, northern soul had been eclipsed by punk in most Manchester clubs. Notably, R&B venue Nice'n'Easy had been transformed into a place called Pips, which was soon to be a massive influence on the city's music scene. Tucked behind Manchester Cathedral, beneath the old Corn Exchange, Pips boasted nine separate rooms, several bars and an unprecedented seven dancefloors, each of which played a different style of music. Consequently, Pips attracted an odd cross-section of clubbers. Secretaries and office workers, still in their suits, would get drunk and dance to chart tunes in one room, while students would groove to either standard disco or indie guitar groups such as Echo And The Bunnymen in another. Along a corridor, even hardened northern soul and funk fans would be kept happy.

It was the Roxy room at the back of the labyrinth-like club, however, which was always the most interesting. The Roxy room was full of punks who wanted to hear Iggy Pop and The New York Dolls, as well as glam-rockers into Bolan and Gary Glitter. It also appealed to Roxy Music romantics and ardent Bowie fans, many of whom made themselves up to look like their idol, despite knowing that they were likely to be beaten up on the way home. Pips soon became Shaun Ryder's favourite club.

'In Pips, you could hear reggae, funk, northern soul, punk, ska, Bowie and bands like The Buzzcocks and Joy Division,' says Shaun. 'You could walk from one room where everyone was dancing to The Specials, to another where a load of punks were jumping about to The Sex Pistols' "Pretty Vacant". Then all the Mods and Perry Boys with their Slazenger jumpers and side partings started coming down. I was always into all those different types of music.

'At that time in Manchester, a lot of our mates would only listen to The Specials and Selector, or Joy Division and New Order, or whatever. But Bez and I just loved tunes. We liked Tom Jones and Johnny Cash and The Bay City Rollers, on top of everything else. That's why Pips was the perfect place for us to hang out.'

Pips had one further, important influence on Shaun – it attracted lots of well-known musicians. Joy Division, A Certain Ratio and Orange Juice could all regularly be spotted speeding away their evenings in the shadows of the Roxy room. Shaun realised that some musicians were really no different to him and his mates. In fact, Pips' mix of musical styles probably persuaded established bands to experiment just as much as it influenced the likes of Shaun and Bez. Significantly, the catholic blend also encouraged an emergent new breed of club DJs to forgo musical categories and focus instead on the impact of a specific track on an audience.

Shaun Ryder's taste grew increasingly haphazard as he continued to soak up myriad influences from his immediate environment. His head filtered out occasional interesting events in his generally dull daily life, muddled them with cheap drugs and late nights in clubs, then mixed them up in a fantasy world poached from music, movies and TV. Shaun was hooked on Granada TV's daytime re-runs of 1960s detective series *Randall And Hopkirk Deceased*, and he was intrigued by the style of new British bands like Roxy Music and obsessed by the dress sense of the Mods and Perry Boys he saw around town.

He adored New Order's nonchalant attitude, but hated the students who were into their music. He loved the energy of punk, but didn't want to dye his hair. He liked the hippy lifestyle, but couldn't stand the ideals. His mind was becoming a jumble of whatever took his fancy. The line between fantasy and reality was beginning to blur. Shortly after he started work at the Post Office, Shaun would claim to have been watched early one morning on his way to the bus stop by aliens in a UFO. He swore then that it had nothing to do with drugs.

Despite his new job, Shaun couldn't keep out of trouble. In 1979, aged seventeen, he and a friend made local news headlines and were even mentioned in the *Daily Mirror* when they fed contaminated bread to pigeons in the centre of Manchester. Laced with poison, the bread multiplied in size inside the birds' stomachs. The following day, the local paper branded Shaun 'the sick face of Britain' and reported that up to 3000 pigeons had literally exploded throughout the city.

'I absolutely hated those bloody pigeons,' says Shaun. 'You couldn't even sit down in Piccadilly Gardens and eat your lunch without the things landing all over you. Me and a mate were just walking round with these boxes of rat poison pellets one day. We decided to put them inside bits of bread and feed them to the birds. It was great. They were dropping out of the skies.'

The following year, Shaun moved out of his parents' house and in with his girlfriend, whom, it's claimed, he married briefly 'because that's just what everyone in our area did'. Shaun claims to have been stoned and tripping on acid on his wedding day. Not surprisingly, the relationship didn't last long. Eighteen months later, Shaun was separated and sharing a house with his brother and Bez. He had also quit his job as a Royal Mail messenger boy.

'Working is all right if you're sixteen,' he says. 'You get a decent amount of money for that age, but you never earn much more. You work every day for most of your life. Then they pay you off when you're fifty and you look back and you have nothing.' Shaun signed on. It was certainly better than being promoted to a proper postman, which was due to happen any day. There was no way he was working all hours for hardly any money. Having no job was without doubt better than that. Life on the dole, however, had one big drawback. It was boring. For the first few months, it was good to be able to lie in, albeit in a succession of grim, council-paid places in Salford .

'We had a couple of flats that were just fuckin' horrible,' he says. 'I don't look back at that time with the slightest sense of nostalgia.

Sometimes when we had no money, the only buzz we could get was from a cheap tube of gas.' Nevertheless, Shaun finally had the freedom to do as he pleased. Except that neither he nor Bez had much to do, bar go out at night and queue up at the dole office every other week. Shaun even got to the stage of refusing to discuss how he spent his days, in order to make his life appear more interesting than it really was.

Eventually, in order to fill in the hours, he and Bez decided to form a band. 'We were getting older and we felt like we should have something more to do than just take drugs,' says Shaun. 'We listened to music all the time anyway, so starting a band seemed like an obvious idea. It wasn't that important to us as taking drugs though. Drugs were part of our lives, just like eating food or drinking.'

Shaun and Bez began Happy Mondays by first roping in Shaun's brother Paul on bass, the instrument the pair's father had previously played. The trio were then joined by three vague acquaintances, whom Shaun had seen knocking about his estate for over a decade. All three had also attended Wardley High, the same school as Bez. In fact, two of them were still there. Gary 'Gaz' Whelan was only fifteen years old and training to be a professional footballer when he became Happy Mondays' drummer, albeit one with a very basic kit.

Immediately after Shaun and Bez had accepted Gaz into the band, his best friend from school, Paul Davis, approached the pair to take him on instead. 'I remember Paul D coming up to me in the street and asking if Gaz Whelan was in our band,' says Shaun. 'I went, "Yeah, why?" and he goes, "Well, he's my best friend, but he's shit. He shouldn't be in your band. What does he do, play the drums? I'd be much better."'

Shaun wasn't sure. Eventually, he said that if Paul had a different instrument, he was in. Paul couldn't actually play anything, but turned up at an informal rehearsal several days later with a little, toy-like keyboard. The following week, however, he changed his choice of instrument, after someone he knew offered him use of a bass guitar. Shaun was furious. His brother played bass. By the end of the day, Paul Davis was back on keyboards, albeit ones with the notes handwritten on the keys.

The sixth Mondays member, Mark Day, was the eldest of them

all. He had been three years above Bez at school and, at twenty, was a full five years older than both Gaz Whelan and Paul Davis. A Hendrix obsessive, he would prove to be a gifted, if unusual, lead guitarist.

'No specific musicians ever made me want to be in a band,' explains Shaun. 'They may have got me into tunes, but I never joined any groups at school or anything. Even after I left, the only things I knew for sure were that I liked smoking dope and that I didn't want a job. If any group inspired me to start writing songs, I guess it was Joy Division. I never actually saw them play, but I always thought they were cool. That was down to the way they looked more than their music though. At the time, everyone else seemed to have punky, spiky hair and be wearing safety pins. Joy Division just looked like me and my mates, all in V-neck sweaters with Fred Perry shirts and their hair in side partings.'

Certainly, the nascent Happy Mondays shared Joy Division's talent for burying a melody deep in the mix of their music. However, they had none of that band's sense of purpose. In fact, they owed more to another Manchester band, A Certain Ratio, which was then doing well locally with its rhythmic, punk-influenced funk. At least, Happy Mondays sounded as though they might appeal to a fraction of A Certain Ratio's audience, should they ever graduate from loose grooves to proper tunes. It looked unlikely. Despite fairly regular rehearsals (or more precisely, smoking sessions) in the gym hall of a Swinton primary school or in guitarist Mark Day's attic most Wednesday and Thursday evenings, the band had yet to write a single song.

'We really only formed as an excuse to skin up and get pissed with a few other people,' says Shaun. 'I don't think we even imagined ever playing any gigs. If I had to sum us up at the start, I would say we were a punk band. In those days, every band our age played punk. It was 90% front, 10% talent, or maybe 10% chance. You just had to have the balls to carry it off. You imagined you were as good as fuckin' Buddy Rich on drums ... and suddenly you were.

'I'm not trying to pretend we were proper punks though. None of us ever had any coloured hair. I had a skinhead most of the time. And a goatee beard. We were just lads who liked the Buzzcocks. I guess you'd call us casuals, although I don't mean that in a bad way.'

Almost as soon as they formed, the Happy Mondays established their own code. It began by giving each other nicknames. Shaun's was X.

'That was a piss-take,' he says. 'I used to get really paranoid about people calling out my name in clubs and in the street when I was selling draw. I kept thinking I'd get caught. My mates started calling me X instead. It wasn't to disguise my identity, it was to freak me out more. Imagine you're sorting someone out with some dope and a bunch of nutters start screaming X at you. It doesn't help.'

Before X, Shaun had been called Horse because of his surname Ryder/rider, but Horse now moved to brother Paul, while their dad, Derek, was referred to as Horseman. Gaz Whelan was briefly called Ronny, after Liverpool football player Ronny Whelan. More crudely, Paul Davis became Knobhead, later changed to Penis, while Mark Day was Cow, although he also answered to Daisy, Moose or just plain Bastard.

In 1981, Wigan Casino, which had been out of favour for years, finally closed down. Manchester's nightlife had lost its edge and straight-laced, atmosphere-free clubs such as bank-clerk haunt Rotters were the only venues making any money. Suddenly, you had to dress smart or wear a shirt and tie to stay out after closing time. Shaun, of course, hated such clubs. Well, he knew he would have hated them, had the bouncers ever let him in to take a look.

That summer, though, plans were already in the pipeline for a boost to local nightlife. The directors of Manchester's leading independent record label, Factory, were scouring the city for a suitable venue in which to open a revolutionary new club. Factory Records had established itself at the tail end of the 1970s by releasing the records of Joy Division, and was currently enjoying by far its greatest commercial success to date with New Order. The idea of opening a club came originally from company director, New Order manager and former DJ, Rob Gretton. Gretton was disillusioned with the mainstream clubs on offer at the time and thought that a purpose-built venue would prove a good investment for the newly flush Factory. His partner, Tony Wilson, agreed. Wilson, then best known locally as a pop TV presenter on ITV channel Granada (his 1970s rock series *So It Goes* had showcased the likes of The Clash, The Jam, The Sex Pistols and Magazine), had recently spent some time in New York, where he had been inspired by venues such as the hip and phenomenally successful Danceteria.

The pair reasoned that a club which operated as both a cutting-edge disco and a credible live venue could refresh the city's flagging nightlife. Although it clearly wasn't a new concept, what was to make their project different was its design. Other places mixing DJ sets with live bands were all dark and dingy, traditional indie venues. Like Danceteria, Factory's club was to look like a hi-tech disco. The label bought and converted a derelict yacht marina on the corner of Whitworth Street West, in a rather grim area not far from the city centre. The building's multi-level, super-spacious interior was given an arty, minimalist look by designer Ben Kelly, who painted the brickwork, placed zebra-striped pillars along the side of the dancefloor and hung speakers from the ceiling. The club was called the Hacienda (Spanish for Factory) and opened for business on 21 May 1982.

Shaun and Bez became instant regulars. They liked the club because it looked better than any other in Manchester. Moreover, they could go in wearing whatever they wanted, then get stoned and misbehave without being thrown out. They were, however, dubious about a lot of the clientele. Because it was owned by Factory, the club quickly became a magnet for the moody raincoat brigade and serious students who bought records of local bands on the label. On some nights though, the club would copy the eclectic music policy of Pips, which particularly appealed to Shaun.

With Bez in tow, Shaun would walk to the Hacienda from Little Hulton. The two liked to set off early in the evening, stopping off for a drink several times on the way. They would go into pubs, sit across the table from groups of girls and make idle chat. Meanwhile under the table, Shaun claimed years later, he would slip off his shoes, open the girls' handbags with his feet and try to nudge out their purses without being noticed. If he succeeded, he'd head off to the toilets to take out the money. They would then leave as quickly as possible. How much they stole dictated how many pubs they had to hit before going to the club. If the two spent all the money before the end of the evening, they would start stealing from the students inside the Hacienda, nicking their handbags, taking out the cash, then chucking the rest off the balcony on to the dancefloor.

Shaun, Bez and a couple of mates moved into a house not far from the centre of Manchester. Having found a new club in which to hang out at night, they were living to party. So too, it seemed, was the rest of the band. Shaun later revealed that Paul Davis, then still fifteen, overdosed on heroin in their flat. Shaun says he thought that at one stage Paul had died. He bundled him into the back of a car, then drove round Manchester for hours wondering what to do with the body.

'Everything in all of our lives was secondary to having a good time, all the time,' says Shaun. 'The band wasn't even on our list of priorities. Going out, doing drugs and having a laugh with our mates was all we really thought about.'

Nevertheless, Shaun had started writing his first songs and was developing a distinctive lyrical singing style. Happy Mondays were also amassing a few proper instruments, usually by offering weed as an exchange. Shaun and Bez were both dealing soft drugs from the house, which may have been why – not for the first time – Bez was arrested. He had drugs in his possession and was subsequently sent to Strangeways. When he got out, he went travelling for almost a year. He visited the Middle East and Africa and ended up living in a cave in Morocco with a university professor. He returned to Manchester with a massive mop of curly hair and edited highlights of his travels. According to Shaun, however, Bez wasn't revealing the best of his stories. Over the following months, Shaun would frequently suggest that Bez had enjoyed a rather unconventional relationship with his professor friend. Bez ignored his jibes. Perhaps Shaun was just joking. Shaun would also imply that Bez had been given an easy ride in Strangeways, thanks to his not unattractive features and youthful physique. Bez didn't even bother to respond. He did, however, announce that he was never, ever going back to prison. For the first time in his life, Bez seemed determined to make something of his future.

THREE

The Sound Of Salford

How apt that the first person to see a spark of something special in Happy Mondays had as much of an eye for style as for songs. Former northern soul DJ Phil Saxe ran a clothes stall called Some Wear in the Oasis market in Manchester city centre when he literally stumbled across the band.

'Shaun tripped me up on purpose in the Hacienda in order to get my attention,' says a lisping, typically enthusiastic Saxe.

Coincidentally, that night Saxe was actually looking for musicians to manage. He had turned up at the club's regular local bands talent contest, to check out a guitar group which he thought showed some promise. Saxe already knew individual members of Happy Mondays; he recognised them all from around Oasis and the Arndale Centre, but had recently seen Shaun and Bez loitering a lot at his stall. The pair had already decided to ask Saxe to maybe manage the band or just offer them some advice, but were unsure of how best to approach him.

Despite being in his mid thirties, Saxe had gained an enviable reputation among Manchester's style-setters. He was obsessed by the city's youth culture and constantly had an eye on the next new trend. In part, of course, it was for business reasons. Saxe is said by some to have kick-started the late 1980s fashion for ridiculously-flared jeans, after discovering an entire warehouse full of them for sale for next-to-nothing. It was more than making money that interested him, however. He genuinely hoped to help some of the city's charismatic, working-class kids channel their creative energies into activities which would improve their lives.

Shaun admired Saxe for his street suss. More importantly, he identified with his interest in clothes. For as long as he could remember, Shaun had been obsessed by style. He judged people by their dress sense. It was a mark of their taste, their favourite music and their lifestyle. Shaun himself loved designer labels, even if he couldn't afford to buy them. He had an idea of how he wanted to dress, although he often decided it was too much effort and ended up just as scruffy as Bez, who wasn't really bothered about clothes.

Saxe spotted something special in the Happy Mondays' ramshackle make-up, if not in their music at this early stage. Together, they had an endearing, honest attitude which conflicted with the increasingly staid mainstream. Manchester's clubs had grown stale since the demise of northern soul, a movement which had once so excited Saxe. The majority of guitar groups were dull and uninspiring, preferring to ape the style of successful local outfits like The Smiths and New Order than create their own sound. By not trying to be anyone other than themselves, Happy Mondays had unconsciously filtered all their influences into a unique mix which could have originated from nowhere other than the estates of Salford. It was that unforced street sense which attracted Saxe, although he admits that he never initially imagined that would succeed outside Manchester, assuming they were simply too steeped in local colour to appeal to outsiders. Nevertheless, he did believe that they could help precipitate change in the city.

For their part, Happy Mondays desperately needed someone like Phil Saxe – and they knew it. Not that any of them would admit it, of course. Shaun had decided to try and make a go of the band. Not for the sake of fame or even money – he didn't anticipate either. But after a couple of years spent practising intermittently and writing the occasional tune, it was time to either jack it in or move it on. Otherwise, there just wasn't any point. Turning up to rehearse the same songs in the same grotty school was beginning to get boring.

Although they had the talent, and they were teaching themselves the technical knowhow, what Happy Mondays lacked was the ability to sell themselves. They were six sullen individuals. They couldn't be any other way, even if they tried. That gave them attitude, but it didn't get them gigs. Phil Saxe's boundless enthusiasm, gift-of-the-gab and industry contacts were what they needed now. Tripping him up was their way of asking for his assistance.

Saxe agreed immediately to help the Happy Mondays, and gradually grew into the role of band manager. He began by setting up their first ever gigs in a variety of small and less than salubrious local venues.

Their debut appearance took place at a tiny converted theatre called the Gallery in Manchester's Peter Street. Predictably, the audience numbered only a few of their mates. It was just as well. Shaun spent most of the short set shouting at the rest of the band. None of the others could play their instruments properly. No one knew a thing about sound on stage. It wasn't simply shambolic, it was a mess. Shaun was singing out of time and out of tune, tracks would slow down or speed up at random, and, even in so intimate a venue, Happy Mondays managed to misplace their natural charisma. The truth was that Shaun had no idea how to perform in front of an audience. He felt awkward and inhibited. There was no room beside him for Bez, who instead jerked frantically along to the songs from the floor in front of the band.

Happy Mondays' second show marked their debut appearance on stage at the Hacienda, on a 'battle of the bands' night just like the one at which, several months earlier, Shaun had first approached Phil Saxe. The contests were organised by club booker and DJ Mike Pickering, a former punk who had fallen for northern soul and was always in and out of bands of his own. Pickering also worked informally as an A&R man for Factory Records, and reasoned that he could combine the role with his Hacienda job. Consequently, once a week for over a year, he chose several bands from the piles of demo tapes he had been sent to compete against each other in the club. Pickering put on Happy Mondays as a favour to Phil Saxe, whom he had first met in the late 1970s at northern soul all-nighters in Blackpool. Saxe, however, didn't attempt to push the band on to Pickering. He felt that they first needed to play more live shows. He was right. Despite Happy Mondays' increasingly coherent – if still utterly chaotic – set, they came last in the contest.

The Happy Mondays quarrelled all the time. Gaz Whelan and Mark Day said Shaun and Bez weren't taking the band seriously enough. Shaun reckoned they should learn to play properly before they criticised anyone else. Paul Ryder never knew whose side to take, while Paul Davis seemed to think everyone was against him. Gaz and Mark were right about Shaun though. He did like the idea of being in a band and he enjoyed having something to do with his days, but it was still little more than a sideline in his life. He didn't consider music as a career. He certainly wasn't making any money from it.

In 1984, Phil Saxe secured Happy Mondays a deal with Factory Records. It was in fact Mike Pickering who persuaded label directors Tony Wilson and Rob Gretton to sign them. Pickering had been impressed by vast improvements in the band's increasingly funk-led live sets. He organised a gig for them in the Hacienda, invited Wilson and Gretton down, then tried to convince them that this ramshackle outfit were worthy of at least a little investment. Despite what Tony Wilson would later claim, he was far from impressed. He thought Happy Mondays sounded too messy to succeed. Nevertheless, he conceded that their Salford sound might go down well in Manchester and was swayed by the enthusiasm of both Saxe and Pickering. He was also intrigued by the fact that Rob Gretton, whom he didn't imagine would be impressed, thought that the band showed promise. Factory were in.

'We thought it was great when Factory signed the Mondays,' says New Order singer Bernard Sumner, whose band were then literally funding the label.

'Ever since Joy Division went with Factory, we had been mixing with a lot of middle-class people like Tony, Mike Pickering, Vini Reilly and virtually all the other acts on the label. Suddenly this band appeared who were on the same wavelength as us. We were both from poor backgrounds and lower-working-class families. Actually, the Mondays weren't lower-working-class, they were the underclass. I think they invented that term.

'New Order and the Mondays had the same attitude too. Like us, they weren't musos. A lot of Manchester bands at that time were very po-faced and pretentious. The Mondays couldn't have cared less about writing proper songs or showing people how well they could play their instruments. They didn't give a damn about musicianship or competing with other bands. All they really wanted to do was take loads of drugs, shag tons of girls and have a laugh. Hooky and I thought that was an admirable outlook on life. It was certainly the same reason we were both in New Order.'

Bernard had first seen Shaun at a mutual friend's New Year's Eve party two years earlier, where he reckons one of Shaun's mates pulled a razor on Rob Gretton for supporting Manchester City rather than Manchester United. Being a United fan himself, he thought the guy made sense. Shaun refutes the accusation. No one he knows has ever used a razor as a weapon. If Bernard meant a Stanley knife, however, he thinks he can recall the event.

Within six months of signing to Factory Records, Happy Mondays found themselves on stage in front of thousands of people. At Bernard and Peter Hook's request, the band was invited to support New Order on a couple of dates of their forthcoming Low Life tour of the UK.

'That was when we got to know the Happy Mondays,' says Sumner. 'We'd only really seen them in clubs before that, although Paul Ryder did used to be Hooky's postman. Following that tour, we hung out together all the time.

'On a personal level, Hooky and I clicked with them immediately. Socially-speaking, they were exactly the same as us. There's a massive north/south divide in Manchester. We were all from the north. It really does make a big difference. Our sense of humour – hard-edged and very dry – is completely alien to them. People from the north of the city entertain themselves by sitting round insulting their friends all day. If you did that in the south, everyone would get very offended. It's all wit and repartee down there. So that was the initial connection with the Mondays – we laughed at each other.'

While the Happy Mondays went down well with New Order themselves, the band's audiences weren't as impressed. Even in front of a hometown crowd at a show in Macclesfield Leisure Centre, few people paid any attention, assuming that New Order's choice of support was simply a favour to Factory. It was little wonder. The huge, hangar-like venue didn't suit the Mondays at all. They still weren't playing proper songs, but rather trying to lock on to a groove, which seemed to grind to a halt almost as soon as it got going. Shaun in particular looked out of place. His lyrical rants had little link to the basic tunes the band was playing. Moreover, he was intimidated by the situation. He felt paranoid in front of so many people. He felt as though he should be putting on a performance, but couldn't bring himself to fake it. Not that he was bothered after the event. Just being able to say Happy Mondays had played with New Order and to have made some famous new mates was enough. To be honest, it was more than he had expected.

'I don't like to see our audience before I go on stage,' says Sumner, 'it gives me the willy-nillys. I prefer to sit backstage and chill out. But that night I stuck my head out to see a bit of the Mondays' set. I remember thinking, "What the fuck is this?" It was mad, a total mess. Then I went back to the dressing room for a beer.'

In September 1985 the EP 'Forty Five' became Happy Mondays' debut record release. It was a twelve-inch with three tracks: 'Delightful', 'This Feeling' and 'Oasis'. Recorded in Manchester's Strawberry studios, the trio of tracks was produced by Mike Pickering. Initially, Tony Wilson had asked his good friend Vini Reilly (the man behind Durutti Column, the first act ever to sign to Factory) to take charge. Reilly, however, spent only a few hours in Strawberry studios before concluding that he most definitely wasn't the right man for the job. Despite his usually open-minded approach to music making, Reilly found it impossible to communicate with a band who couldn't play their instruments properly. He himself was an incredibly accomplished, classically trained guitarist. He didn't know how to deal with Happy Mondays' punky playing and, to be honest, he despised their unprofessional attitude, reputedly calling them scumbags in the studio and telling Factory that they were the worst bastards ever to walk the face of the earth.

For a fan of Happy Mondays' chaotic, loose-limbed live sets, Pickering's production seemed strange. He tightened up the band's sound and turned the EP's title track, 'Delightful', into a jangly, sub-Smiths style indie tune. What Pickering gained by making the track more palatable, he lost in terms of the Mondays' humour and natural charm. In truth, the track 'Oasis' was a far better representation of the band.

'"Delightful" should have been a slow, spacey, disorientating track,' says Shaun. 'But we knew nothing about recording – in fact, none of us had ever seen the inside of a studio before – so we just let Mike do whatever he wanted to the song. I guess we didn't help. We all did loads of whizz so our playing kept speeding up. It was out of synch. It was wrong. In the circumstances, Mike got a good sound, but it just wasn't us. From that moment on, we realised that as soon as you go into a studio, everything is literally taken out of your hands. That's why you have to be double sure that you're in there with the right person. It has to be someone you totally trust.'

Although Tony Wilson would later claim that he had been hugely disappointed by Pickering's production, and that he had spotted something special in Happy Mondays' wah-wah guitar sound and had hoped that the Hacienda DJ would transform the band into a club act, in truth he didn't pay much interest to 'Delightful'. PR man Dave Harper, who had recently started doing Factory's press, after working for Factory's European sister-label Benelux, recalls that Wilson rarely mentioned Happy Mondays at all.

'Factory had recently signed a group called The Railway Children,' says Harper. 'Despite what Tony would tell you now, he was convinced that they were the great white hope. Many people, including me, said that he was backing the wrong band. The Railway Children were okay, but pretty bland and a bit passé. No one bar Tony was particularly interested in their type of music at the time, whereas it was obvious that the Mondays had something special. Anyway, Tony kept banging on to me about getting press for The Railway Children, insisting that they should be huge. If a paper didn't want to write about them, he wanted to know why. I don't think he ever asked how I was doing with the Mondays. As far as I was concerned, he didn't take them seriously at all.'

'It was probably a good sign that Tony didn't have high hopes for the Happy Mondays,' notes Sumner. 'When Tony is mad for a band, it usually means you'll never hear from them again. He has a knack for signing acts that are bound to bomb. He always liked the Mondays a lot as people though, regardless of what he thought of their music. From the very beginning, he totally loved their irreverence. Tony regards an irreverent attitude as a priceless quality, which I think is to be admired. It's certainly unique among record company executives.

'The Mondays really liked Tony too, no matter what they might have said over the years. The band was never anti-middle-class. They weren't inverted snobs. Neither was New Order. We all thought Tony was a chap. It was mainly middle-class people who didn't like him. They thought he was a bit of a clever dick, probably because he was on TV a lot at the time. But working-class people love that. It gives them a buzz to be friends with someone who is famous. And Tony was never boring. What's more, he had a good job at Granada. He didn't have to get involved in music. We all knew that he was doing it because he wanted to, not just to make money. Whatever you thought of Tony Wilson, you had to admit that he was massively enriching the music and club culture of Manchester. You had to admire him for that.'

Wilson, however, wasn't the only person to dismiss Happy Mondays' debut. 'Delightful' was ignored by the music press and rejected by radio. Like the band's support slots with New Order earlier in the year, their first single may have marked a step on in their musical career, but it could scarcely be considered a success.

Shaun Ryder saw out 1985 in the company of one of his favourite singers, former Specials frontman Terry Hall. Post Fun Boy Three, Hall had moved to Manchester with his latest project, The Colourfield.

'I first met Shaun in the Hacienda at a New Order gig,' recalls Hall. 'We were introduced by someone from Factory. We said hello, chatted for a bit and he seemed nice, but I knew nothing at all about his band or their music.

'At the time, Colourfield was rehearsing for a UK tour in some run-down building in the city centre. The Happy Mondays were in the room next door. They were still trying to get it together at that stage. Anyway, Shaun and I got on really well and started hanging out a lot. I suppose initially it was because we were both big football fans. Then I found that I had much more in common with him than any of the studenty musicians around Manchester, so I asked his band to support The Colourfield on tour. I think we played about ten dates together in clubs and universities around the country.'

The experience taught the Happy Mondays a lot about the mechanics of being in a band.

'It was good for us to go on the road with Terry,' says Shaun. 'It was a real education to see how professional he was. Up until then, we never actually knew how proper bands worked, because even our supports with New Order had been one-offs. Touring with The Colourfield, watching Terry and learning how he controlled an audience gave us our first real insight of what being a musician was all about. Also, Fun Boy Three had been one of our favourite bands when we were younger, so it was a boost for us. Plus Terry was dead cool.'

'I'm not sure that Shaun was really a fan of my music,' says Hall. 'He just understood where I was coming from. I have to admit that I very rarely have anything at all in common with other artists or musicians.

'I don't get off on all that working-class crap, but there was a level of understanding between us that was rooted in our backgrounds. We both knew why we were doing it. The motivation we shared may have manifested itself in music, but it had nothing to do with how well you could play an instrument. It had much more to do with attitude. It was about how you felt and what you considered to be precious and not precious.

'My attitude to being up on stage in front of an audience was that you didn't have to *do* anything. There wasn't a need to perform or entertain people with some sort of act. You could actually say exactly what you needed to say to people without having to fake it. I'm sure that's what intrigued Shaun.'

Hall admits that although he did quite like their music, it was largely the fact that Shaun wore flares that made him ask Happy Mondays on tour.

'Shaun was very into his clothes,' says Hall. 'He wore flares long before anyone else, which really impressed me. His sense of style was great. You know how some people join groups or go to the football to dress up, like they need that excuse in order to think about their image. Well, you could tell that, whether or not he was in a band, Shaun would have been just as concerned about how he looked. That's why he was a natural on stage. He didn't bother about how he looked any more than if he had been out in the crowd. He didn't change into stage gear or anything. He didn't psyche himself up or calm himself down. It didn't matter whether he was straight or off his head. Actually, I don't ever remember Shaun being straight when he went on stage. In fact, I don't ever remember Shaun being straight.'

Touring with Terry Hall taught Shaun not to feel awkward in front of an audience, regardless of whether or not they were enjoying the show.

'By the end of the tour, Shaun was much more confident on stage,' says Hall. 'All of the band were, and believe me, there were a hell of a lot of them. There was definitely at least ten of them up there on one occasion. They still couldn't actually play very well, but that never seemed to worry them. They just got on with it, and sometimes they hit the mark. Their music was really rough, like punk rock, and also very funny and chaotic. I'm sure the crowd thought they were taking the piss but I found it very refreshing. I liked the fact that no one appeared to be in charge. Shaun's dad Derek used to try to inject some order, but really he had no idea how to control them.

'The Happy Mondays reminded me of being in The Specials, and of the gigs we played before our first album came out. They were great. Bands have a natural optimism at that early stage in their career that they can never recapture. I specifically remember one show that the band did with us. Their set was longer than ours. With The Colourfield, we hardly ever used to finish the gig. Why not? Because we couldn't be bothered. I never knew just how abrupt our performances were though, until I realised that we were on stage for less time than the Mondays. I was shocked. I'd always thought their sets were incredibly short.'

Already, Happy Mondays boasted a huge travelling entourage, which would colonise The Colourfield's dressing room, before, during and after the shows.

'You could see how they might really piss people off,' says Hall. 'I remember at one gig not being able to get into the dressing room at all because there was so many of them in there doing drugs. But I quite admired that attitude. Plus, they were very entertaining people to be around. Bez would sometimes run right off stage after their show, straight into the dressing room and collapse on top of a load of people. He seemed to be the maddest of the lot, but he was always very funny.'

Terry Hall and Shaun Ryder got on so well that, following the tour, Hall even considered working with Happy Mondays.

'There was a point at which I was going to produce the band,' he says. 'Shaun gave me a tape of some songs which I thought were fantastic. I even took the tape to a couple of record companies, although I knew they were involved with Factory. No one was interested in them though. In fact, everyone said they were shit, which really pissed me off.'

Hall didn't produce the songs, but his experience backs up Tony Wilson's claim that no other record company in the country at that time would have touched Happy Mondays.

'I reckon Tony was right about that,' says Factory PR Dave Harper. 'Record labels always look for bands with drive to invest in.

The Mondays had no drive whatsoever. At the start, it was solely Phil Saxe who made anything happen for them. Happy Mondays would never have got anywhere without him. To be honest, I often wondered why they had bothered to form a band in the first place.'

FOUR

Looks Like Freaky Dancin'

A slightly shabby, otherwise unassuming little office block at 83 Clerkenwell Road, EC1, London, used to be shared by a number of small, independent music businesses. A nascent Creation Records occupied one of the floors there. Dave Harper was based in the building too, splitting his space with an American woman called Nicki Kefalas, whose promotions company also counted Factory among its clients. Upstairs was a sixty-year-old radio plugger, who had totally lost the plot after taking too many drugs.

'It was a very vibrant little place,' recalls Harper. 'It was quite a scene in its own right. Everyone there was a real music fan. It wasn't like a record company, full of office types, in it for the money. We were outside of the mainstream, but all working with a lot of good bands.'

It was to 83 Clerkenwell Road that Happy Mondays came on their first official trip to London.

'Phil had decided the band needed to come to London so that I could write a biography for them, which I was then to send out to the press,' says Harper. 'That was the first time I met the Mondays. Not that they said much. Phil did all the talking; they just sat there looking really suspicious. Phil was very funny, full of life and a great salesman. He literally never shut up. The Happy Mondays didn't say a word. They seemed to be trying to hide in the corner, but my office was so small that they could scarcely all get in the door. So they just sat muttering to each other and skinning up.

'Phil introduced me to each member of the band in turn, then told me all their nicknames. He took total charge of the situation. I think I'd had a bit of blow by then, so I just let him. He told me to ask the band some questions. So I did. Immediately, Knobhead started accusing me of being the devil. Then the rest of them said I was talking shit. That went on for a while. We were obviously getting nowhere, so Phil decided I should tape-record the band just as they were.

'It turned out to be a genius idea. I got a microphone, plugged it into the office stereo and taped an entire hour's worth of this complete gibber-gabber. I have to admit I was a little dubious at first, but I was also pretty desperate. In the end, I didn't edit their conversation at all. I just transcribed it and sent the highlights out to the music press. That was the biography. It ran to six or seven pages of them simply telling funny stories about their lives and describing Little Hulton. It was the perfect way to capture them and their strangeness. It was the only way. It went down really fuckin' well with the press though. It caught everyone's attention. To this day, it's by far the best biography I have ever written, except of course that I didn't write it.'

Dave Harper's biography was designed to introduce the national music press to Happy Mondays prior to the release of a second single. The band had been rehearsing – albeit infrequently – in a tiny, dark, graffitied room at Manchester's Boardwalk, a converted Victorian schoolhouse where the bulk of the city's new young indie bands used to practise. Combined with a succession of pub and club gigs and – for the first time – a few pieces of proper equipment (acquired from social clubs by newly-recruited sound man, Derek Ryder), the rehearsals had perceptibly improved both the band's playing and performance. Moreover, Shaun had started to write what could almost be termed proper songs. At last, Happy Mondays were beginning to build up a small following. In the audience at one local show, at the Ritzy, as support for Factory labelmates A Certain Ratio, was New Order's Bernard Sumner.

'It was the first time I had actually watched one of their gigs from the crowd,' says Sumner. 'It was brilliant. I really enjoyed myself. The Mondays didn't look or sound like anyone else I had ever seen on stage. They were so funny, just a bunch of scruffy lads off council estates. In fact, they sounded exactly as they looked – bloody shambolic. You'd probably call them scallies now, although that was never a Manchester term. They were casuals.

'I remember feeling incredibly pleased that they were on our label. They reminded me so much of all the people I had grown up with.

That was a really strange thing to get my head round. They were exactly like me and my mates, but I'd never seen anyone like us up on stage before.'

Sumner's obvious enthusiasm for the band prompted Phil Saxe to ask him to produce Happy Mondays' second single, the double A-sided 'Freaky Dancin'/The Egg'.

'Because Phil speaks with a lisp,' says Sumner, 'I spent two years thinking his name was Phil Phax. I wrote it down in my phone book like that. When I told people he had asked me to produce the Mondays' single, they kept laughing at me. Every time I brought it up, the whole room would dissolve into fits of hysterics. That went on for ages. I was getting pretty paranoid about it. I had already produced a couple of other local bands so I didn't see why I couldn't cope with the Mondays. Then one day I saw Phil's name written down in full and realised that the joke had nothing to do with me working with the band.'

Happy Mondays' second single was a revelation. Both 'Freaky Dancin'' and 'The Egg' were loose, rhythmic, sexy songs that swayed between classic American 1970s funk and 1980s Salford. Tony Wilson now credits Bernard Sumner's production with exposing the dance element to the band's music that he had previously expected Mike Pickering to pick up on.

'I was getting heavily into dance at the time,' says Sumner, 'but I don't think that single was a particularly dancey record. If it was, it had nothing to do with me. It was a neutral production on my part. What I did was take a snapshot of the Happy Mondays exactly as they were – utterly chaotic and shambolic. Often when you do that, you get a brilliant artifact that captures the moment perfectly.

'I was really only in the studio as a favour to Phil. I knew I wasn't going to be producing the Mondays for ever, so I didn't want to come in and impose a direction on them. Besides, the band was at such an early stage in their career that it wouldn't have been right for me to push any ideas on them or put a clean polish on their sound. They were still developing and that had to happen naturally. Subsequent producers did change their sound and it worked. But I think if I had tried that, the band would have rebelled. If suddenly I had introduced drum loops and sequencers, Shaun would have walked out. That wasn't what he wanted at the time.

'Could they play? Mark Day, the guitarist, definitely had his own sound. They could play enough, but not well. It was loose, shall we say. The funniest thing was that they would all speed up after every drum fill, then gradually slow down, then speed up again. Shaun was constantly shouting at the others. He was definitely in charge, with a little help from Bez maybe. To be polite, I'll say Shaun dished out friendly guidance. He certainly knew how to kick the band into the right mood. Literally.'

Despite Happy Mondays' technical ineptitude, Sumner recalls that they treated their songs seriously. 'They didn't take anything every day seriously, but they did take a lot of care over their music, in a mad sort of way. Shaun certainly knew what he wanted. He realised that the band had something special and didn't want an outsider to come in and interfere with their sound. "Freaky Dancin'" worked so well because both Shaun and I were after the same thing. For all of Shaun's apparent indifference, he has always harboured a secret agenda, albeit only in his own head. That has proved to be his passport to success. It's why he's very careful about the people he chooses to work with.'

Shaun, however, still had a lot to learn about the recording technique.

'Shaun didn't seem to have a clue how a studio worked,' says Sumner. 'He kept shouting at the rest of the band down the vocal mike. He'd be screaming at the drummer, "Faster you cunt, fuckin' speed up!" Then he'd start ranting that everyone was crap and that they should learn to play their instruments properly. It was all going down on tape. The only one he didn't shout at was Bez, who was always standing there shaking his maracas.

'Listening back to that session was one of the funniest things I have ever heard. It was just so natural and brilliant. You could hear the fights coming at you from all over the place, through the drum mikes and everything. Between recording and mixing the single though, my poncy muso engineer wiped off the background noise. I remember walking into the studio and hearing the track being played back. I was like, "Where has all the shouting gone?" He said, "I wiped it all off, of course." Fuckin' idiot. I was furious. There's actually still some shouting on there though. Listen to "Freaky Dancin'" closely and you'll hear it. It's them, just as they were. Loose with a capital L.

'The odd thing is, I don't remember any of the band doing drugs the entire time we were in the studio. They may have smoked a little pot, but I was definitely taking more drugs than the lot of them put together. They preferred to go upstairs and watch porn videos. I even remember offering Shaun some drugs and him saying no. It was just a line of speed or something, but his dad was around at the time and Shaun didn't want him getting the wrong idea. He was afraid Derek would think he was doing smack.'

Shaun didn't mind sharing Sumner's food though. Used to stealing from the supermarket when they wanted to eat, Happy Mondays couldn't believe Bernard when he threw out a Chinese take-away he had hardly touched, just because he thought it tasted horrible. Seconds later, they were all fighting for the food, eating it with their fingers from the bin.

Packaged in a simple but bright sleeve (at the time, Factory bands tended to ape New Order and opt only for sombre colours), Happy Mondays' second single attracted the attention of a handful of significant music industry figures. First, Radio 1's John Peel invited the band to record their first ever session. Then, in September, Happy Mondays received their first piece of national press, albeit written by Hacienda DJ and Manchester fanzine editor Dave Haslam.

In an attempt to convey the fact that an exciting new music-based scene was emerging from the city, for a feature in *NME*, Haslam grouped together four local bands – The Railway Children, Tools You Can't Trust, The Weeds and Happy Mondays. The Mondays themselves, however, insisted that they didn't want to be labelled alongside any of the other acts, saying that all they shared with the city's host of Joy Division and James wannabes was a rehearsal room at the Boardwalk. In fact, that was the only thing they said. The rest of the article was filled with quotes from Phil Saxe, explaining that he was on 'a moral crusade' with the Mondays, and coming out with admirable comments such as 'this band is all about making money and securing a job, because otherwise these kids are on the dole'.

'Early on, it was impossible to persuade Phil not to sit in on the interviews,' says Dave Harper. 'He said he had to because the band were a bunch of plebs. But he was an absolute motormouth. Phil is brilliant , but the band literally couldn't get a word in edgeways when he was there. He just wouldn't shut up.

'Of course, in one sense that was a good thing. Phil was involved because he believed in the Mondays. He was utterly convinced that something would happen to them in years to come and his enthusiasm was infectious. His connection to Manchester's rag trade and street culture intrigued people too, particularly because The Smiths' manager Joe Moss had also been in the clothing business. Shaun would never have admitted it, but he really appreciated what Phil was doing for them.'

One of the rooms on Creation Records' floor of the offices at 83 Clerkenwell Road was occupied by independent PR man Jeff Barrett, who would soon start his own label, Heavenly, to release records by Manic Street Preachers and a band called Flowered Up, often considered to be London's equivalent of Happy Mondays. At that time, Barrett was doing press for Creation bands such as Primal Scream, as well as working freelance as an agent and tour manager. He had moved recently to London from Plymouth, where he had run a record shop.

'I had always been a fan of Factory releases,' says Barrett. 'I remember being sent "Delightful" when I lived in Plymouth and thinking it was really good. After I came to London, Dave Harper gave me a white label test pressing of "Freaky Dancin'", which became my favourite single for a long time. "Freaky Dancin'" was the sound of a revolution. It was mad and exciting and funny. It was also utterly unlike anything else.

'A few weeks later, I was looking for a support act for a band called The Weather Prophets, who were playing a gig at the Clarendon in Hammersmith. They were doing pretty well at the time. I had already booked a main support, but not a first-on. I suggested the Mondays to The Weather Prophets, then played them "Freaky Dancin'". They were well up for it, so I set it up with Harper.

'I remember the day. It was a Saturday, and I was tour managing. The venue was this huge old Irish dance hall on Hammersmith Broadway with a shitty little pub underneath. It's now a bus station. Anyway, you used to get loads of dodgy winos coming out of the pub and sitting at the side of the dancefloor in the venue with their bottles of sherry. I arrived late in the afternoon for The Weather Prophets' soundcheck. The band were having a nightmare and insisted on clearing the venue while they tried to sort out some problems.

'I looked around the hall and there was this big bunch of blokes sitting slumped against the wall with dozens of tins of beer and bottles of cider. Most of them had hoods up over their heads. I thought they were bums who had come in to hear the music. I went over and asked them to move outside. They just stared up at me and said, "But we're Happy Mondays." Jesus Christ, I was shocked. I mean, as soon as I got up really close, I realised that they did actually look quite cool. Odd, but quite cool, and Shaun was wearing this great snorkel parka. What really amazed me though, was that they looked exactly as "Freaky Dancin'" had sounded. It was bastardised Northern punk rock. They were skinny white boys, but their attitude – like their music – was black and funky. It was also very trippy. One look at them and it was obvious that they did shitloads of hallucinogenics.'

Barrett was also booking pub gigs in London at the time, and decided to arrange some shows for the band.

'I got them a gig a few weeks later at the Black Horse in Camden,' he says. 'It was on a Sunday afternoon. The Mondays turned up and there were literally dozens of them, plus Shaun's dad. They had no idea who I was. I told them and they half pretended to remember me from Hammersmith, but really they didn't have a clue.

'No one in London gave a fuck about the Mondays at this stage. In fact, no one even knew who they were. But Shaun walked straight into the venue, took one look around and announced that the band weren't fuckin' playing there because there wasn't a proper stage. I told him they didn't need a stage, they could just stand in the corner. It was a pub, for heaven's sake. Meanwhile, Derek was saying, "It's a gig. It's in London. Do it!" Then Bez said he'd play anywhere if it meant getting free beers, so we were on.

'After the show, Shaun came over and asked if I could sort him out a draw. It was an expression I'd never heard before. Spliff or puff I would have understood. The scene was getting better and better by the minute. I realised they had their own language to go with the nicknames. It was brilliant. While I was still trying to figure out what a draw was, Derek came over. He said, "I'm not going to ask what Shaun wants from you. But if it's acid he's after, don't get it for him." Then he walked off. I was thinking, "Wow, that's the bloke's dad." It was so cool.

'I ended up putting the Mondays on at the Black Horse a couple more times after that. When they played, the place literally didn't know what had hit it. Not that anyone in the pub had actually come along to see them. But I thought they were brilliant, easily the best new band around at the time. The Weather Prophets really liked them too, so they gave them quite a few support slots. The two bands just smoked tons of pot together.'

Although 'Freaky Dancin'' had been well-received in certain quarters on its release in the summer of 1986, by autumn, most people had yet to hear of Happy Mondays. Not even Phil Saxe's gift-of-the-gab, it seemed, could convince most London-based magazine editors that there was better music being made in a city such as Manchester than there was in the capital. This was, after all, an era which belonged to established stadium acts such as Simple Minds, Genesis and U2. Fortunately, however, Dave Harper's unusual biography was beginning to arouse a little press interest, albeit in the band as bizarre, drug-addled, working-class characters, as opposed to their songs or live sets.

'With the help of that biog, I managed to persuade *Melody Maker* to review a gig that the Mondays played in a club called the Cricketers, by the Oval cricket ground in London,' says Harper. 'There were eight people in the audience and the show was completely and utterly shambolic. I thought at one point it was going to end before it had even started. But it was obvious that the band had something special and they were certainly unlike anyone else around at the time. In fact, they weren't like anyone else *ever*. *Melody Maker* gave the gig a great review. That slowly started the ball rolling.'

For several months, however, Happy Mondays' shows continued to attract only a handful of people, usually hardcore footballs fans, some of whom would start fighting before the gig had even begun.

'If they played in Manchester,' recalls Harper, 'they would occasionally get a reasonable turnout. Because of the band's big network of friends there, though, local gigs tended to turn into a private party. If you weren't one of the gang, no matter how small the venue was, you probably wouldn't have got into it. I remember a couple of times seeing that bald bloke Cressa, who later became the dancer for The Stone Roses, but was then a Mondays' roadie, get up on stage to dance beside Bez. Obviously the rest of the crew and all their mates would start cheering and shouting at him. No one else knew who he was, so they couldn't understand what was going on.

'No matter where they played, it was very rare for any women to be in the audience. Even if only ten people turned up to a show, at least eight of them were bound to be sad indie blokes. There was quite a strong rad fem movement going on at the time, which didn't help. Not that the crowd – or should I say lack of it – ever seemed to bother the band. I never once saw any of the Mondays get depressed when they turned up at a gig and no one was there. They just went on, played the same set and had a laugh. In fact, they never seemed to be depressed about anything.

'It was obvious that they were still treating the group as little more than an excuse to drink and smoke and go out in a gang. The gigs were almost an interruption to their social lives. They didn't care about the money or the size of the crowd, as long as there was a pub or a club nearby. As soon as they were out at night with their mates, they forgot all about the band.'

The shows remained riotous.

'Technically, the Mondays didn't seem to be getting any better,' says Harper. 'Gaz, the drummer, could still scarcely play, although Paul was a pretty good bass player and Mark – or Cow or whatever he was called at the time – was a really interesting guitarist. As for Knobhead's keyboard playing, I couldn't work it out at all. It was very abstract, as though he was playing a different tune to everyone else. Actually, I could never work out Knobhead himself. He was well weird. He was the one who had initially shouted at me in the office. He was convinced I didn't like him and kept telling the others not to listen to me.

'Shaun was a real Dickensian, dodgy-looking character on stage. Actually, he was pretty much the same off stage. He was really skinny, with a shaved head and this little goatee beard. He was neat and tidy though. His T-shirts would always be pressed and he'd make sure his gold chain was pulled out over the top. He liked that Perry Boy/Mod style and he loved labels. He didn't try to look like anyone in particular though, except maybe Shylock. At the time, he was wearing a Star Of David round his neck, which was pretty odd, considering his family is Catholic.

'During the gig, he would hunch up over the microphone for most of the set and amble aimlessly about the stage, often bumping into Bez. Bez's role in the band was rather ill-defined, but he was paid the same as the others and there was definitely something missing when he wasn't with them. He was like a point of contact between the band and the audience. The Mondays needed that because crowds are used to connecting with the singer, and sometimes Shaun wouldn't look at the audience once during the show. If he did lift his head up, it was usually to shout in the direction of the ceiling. He never put anything on though. That's what was so great about him. At first, people thought he was just acting like that for a laugh. Then they met him and realised that was in fact his natural persona.

'It was always clear that Shaun was the leader of the band. He's one of those people born to be in charge. He could be incredibly sulky though, unlike Bez who is very friendly and physical and chatty. Despite the general opinion that Bez was mad, he very rarely seemed off his head. Paul Ryder was the most apparently normal of the lot, Knob bloke was hardly on this planet and Gaz was just this chirpy little lad. Cow was forever having the piss taken out of him because he was meant to be a real mummy's boy, although it was only really Knobhead who Shaun would keep threatening to sack.'

Happy Mondays as a collection of oddball individuals – rather than musicians – was the angle which intrigued the London press. In October 1986 *NME* gave the band their first national live review. It was of a show in the capital's Bay 63 club, on a bill split with two other bands, Blurt and Young Gods. Fifty people were in the audience. Happy Mondays warranted only one sentence in the article. 'Happy Mondays get into being a menagerie,' noted *NME*, 'dangling a loose, scraped-back funk in front of the diminutive audience.'

'The music papers were definitely more into the Mondays' attitude than their music,' says Harper. 'Personality-wise, the band weren't like any other that London journalists had ever come across. They had their own language, for a start. Also, of course, they were completely out there, off their heads on drugs most of the time, which was absolutely unheard of back then.

'It became apparent to me very quickly that journalists were intimidated by them. I remember one writer interviewing them for *Sounds*. He got in the back of their tour van and the band were all doing blow from a bong they had made by punching a hole in the bottom of an empty beer can. He didn't know what to make of them and later told me he was quite scared by the experience. He did a brilliant PR job though, because he subsequently told everyone how frightening the Mondays were, which naturally resulted in a little flurry of interest. Personally, I never found them scary at all. I always thought they were really friendly and funny and actually quite sweet. They were one of my favourite bands from the first day I met them.'

The Hacienda had been haemorrhaging money since the day it opened. Factory's initial aim – to create an energetic, new musical scene from within the confines of the club – had always been ambitious. Not only was the venue horrendously expensive to both build and run, but economic recession across the UK was hitting the entertainment industries hard. In Manchester, a city which didn't encourage use of its centre, with poor public transport from the suburbs and almost no late-night services, there simply weren't enough punters out at night to fill the numerous clubs, not even on a Saturday night, never mind during the week. New laws had also stopped all of the city's venues from opening on Sundays.

The Hacienda's hangar-like interior compounded its problems. Even when the club managed to attract a couple of hundred punters (which it did more often than its rivals), the place looked deserted. It was impossible to create any sense of an atmosphere. Consequently, any of the groups of office workers, lone punks or indie music fans that did wander in usually didn't stay long. Ironically, the Hacienda was also suffering from a terrible reputation as a music venue. Its state-of-the-art sound system, which had cost a then staggering £40,000 to install in 1982, suited neither the size nor shape of the club. Sound bounced around the interior, echoing in some places, deafening in others, but it wasn't loud enough on the dancefloor.

Tony Wilson was contemplating closing the venue when one of his Factory co-directors, Alan Erasmus, suggested poaching Paul Mason, manager at Nottingham's successful Rock City venue, to inject some new ideas into the club. It worked. Promoter Mike Pickering had already shelved his talent contests (he may have had an eye for promising new bands, but no one pays to see a group they have never heard of) and was cutting back in general on the number of live acts he booked. In a revolutionary move at that time in Manchester, he also began a regular Friday night club with no live music at all. It was called Nude – because there was nothing on – and the music policy was predominately black American dance, from James Brown through to hip hop.

In late 1986, Dave Haslam, then a DJ at the Boardwalk, was invited to promote his own weekly club at the Hacienda. He named the night Temperance, aimed it at students, and employed DJs who mixed the new wave of American electronic dance acts like Mantronix with the usual indie guitar fare. Within weeks, Temperance was pulling in 600 people. Pickering, too, was attracting larger and larger audiences. He was flying regularly to the US, checking out what was happening in the clubs as house music spread from Chicago and Detroit to cities like Boston and New York, and buying up as many singles as he could afford. As 1986 drew to a close, house music – already established in London clubs and at warehouse parties throughout the south-east – was finding its feet at the Hacienda.

FIVE
No More Heroes

Factory sidestepped its usual practice of recruiting from within its ranks when it came to hiring a producer for Happy Mondays' debut album. The decision to use former Velvet Underground member John Cale was down solely to Tony Wilson.

According to Wilson now, he recognised in Happy Mondays the same poetic punk style that had made Patti Smith's *Horses* one of his all-time favourite albums. Dave Harper believes however that employing John Cale was simply a publicity stunt on the part of the Factory director. Either way, it had the potential to be a brilliant marketing ploy. It was obvious that not enough people were into the band for the album to sell well, and by boasting someone as well-known – not to mention as unlikely – as John Cale as producer, the record was bound to attract considerable additional press attention.

As Velvet Underground fans, both Shaun Ryder and Bez knew all about John Cale, although the rest of the band had perhaps only heard his name. Shaun reckoned that Wilson had chosen Cale because of the drugs connection. The truth was that, just a couple of months earlier, Cale had taken part in the Festival Of The Tenth Summer, an event organised by Wilson at Manchester's massive G-Mex centre. Supposedly a celebration of a decade of post-punk music, the festival featured appearances by predominately local acts like New Order, The Smiths, The Fall, Pete Shelley and A Certain Ratio. John Cale was among the line-up, doubtless in an attempt to promote *Artificial Intelligence*, the latest in a long line of solo albums to be released largely to indifference.

Having been a massive Velvet Underground fan, Wilson was delighted to meet (not to mention slightly in awe of) John Cale and found the prospect of him working with a Factory band extremely exciting. Happy Mondays themselves didn't much care who was at the helm of their debut album. Their only preference had been for Bernard Sumner, whose work on 'Freaky Dancin'' they admired. They had also liked working with Bernard because, according to Shaun, he hadn't rushed the band or forced them into anything in the studio. Bernard, however, was busy with New Order, who had recently released *Brotherhood* and was due to begin an extensive world tour.

'There were other reasons besides my commitments with New Order,' says Sumner. 'I didn't want to continue working with the Mondays mainly because I don't believe you can be a part-time producer. You can play at it, but eventually you have to choose between being a musician or a producer. At the time, I'd just finished doing a few remixes and I had also mixed an LP for a band called Section 25. That had made me realise just how much time and energy it takes to work on someone else's record. If I was going to put so much effort and so many ideas into something, it was going to be my own songs. Plus, it was a bit close to home. It was an inside job, what with us both being on Factory. I was worried that, eventually, I'd make them end up sounding like New Order.'

In December 1986, John Cale spent two weeks with Happy Mondays at Fire House studios in London.

'I didn't really give a toss about recording an album,' says Ryder. 'All I wanted from the band was to make some quick money. We didn't have a professional attitude to music in those days. If recording an LP meant spending weeks on end in some studio, grafting away and not being able to do what we wanted, when we wanted, we'd rather not have bothered. We didn't form a band so that we could be told what to do by someone else. That was the whole point of avoiding a proper job. All that mattered to us was us having a good time. The Mondays was just a big game. John Cale was actually all right, but he got on our nerves a bit because he kept wanting us to work.

'We always had real battles in the studio, fist fights and everything, but recording that album was the worst. There was even a stabbing involved, although I'm not sure who did who. I know I smashed bottles over Gaz's head and he bit me a couple of times. The problem was that all of us were into different drugs. There was the speed and coke part of the band, the trippy part of the band and the part that was on downers and spliff. It was like that for years. A lot of the time, in the studio or on tour, we couldn't stand the sight of each other. It can be really annoying when you're cooped up with someone who is on a totally different trip to you. But as soon as we were apart, we'd realise those differences were part of our characters, so it would all be okay the next day.'

Wilson now claims, in retrospect, to have regretted his choice of producer for the album. Certainly Cale didn't have a clue what Happy Mondays were about. Middle-class and well-educated, he had never even met people from their background before. He couldn't connect with the band's attitude or understand their sense of humour. Moreover, despite his punk credentials, like Vini Reilly, Cale was classically trained and unused to working with musicians who couldn't play their instruments properly. Worst of all, perhaps, the former heroin addict was then struggling to stay off drugs and had found that eating a piece of fruit (usually a tangerine) at twenty-minute intervals helped keep his cravings at bay. John Cale and Happy Mondays could hardly have been more ill-suited to one another.

Two years later, in *NME*, Tony Wilson would salaciously recall a story concerning Cale's introduction to the band.

'When John first asked me what the Mondays were like,' noted Wilson, 'I said, "The best way I can describe them, so you know what you're letting yourself in for, John, is scum. They are fuckin' scum."'

Wilson then claimed that, when Happy Mondays had protested at his description, he had reminded them of the day that Dave Harper was wandering down the street with two of the band, looking for the studio, when one of them insisted that it had to be close by because he had spotted a pile of Bez's vomit. Harper denies that the incident ever took place and attributes the story to Wilson's imagination.

'I did go to visit the band in the studio,' he says. 'I was told it was in Kentish Town, north London, roughly opposite what was then called the Town & Country club. I couldn't find the fuckin' place though, so I never went. I soon wished I had, I wouldn't have been so disappointed when I heard the album. I remember getting the tapes back and being stunned by how incredibly lame the songs were. They sounded really thin and amateur. I'd hoped for so much more. There were some good bits in there, but overall I thought it was a bit of a shambles.'

Cale had failed to capture either the loose sway of the Mondays that Sumner had exposed on 'Freaky Dancin'' or the groove of the band playing live. Instead, he tightened the tangle of influences in their slightly askew style and lifted Shaun's vocal clear out of the messy mix. The result was a tough, bleak, basic collection of tracks, topped by vitriolic, nonsensical shouting from Shaun. Sometimes, it sounded as though several songs were being played at the same time. It certainly wasn't an easy record to listen to. Nor was it commercial. Nevertheless, when occasionally Happy Mondays did come together on a groove, they hit harmonies which were strangely appealing and oddly unique. The record also boasted the bones of most of what were to become Happy Mondays' trademark musical elements, notably Paul Ryder's deep dance basslines, largely stolen from northern soul standards.

'House was just happening for us when we made that album,' says Shaun. 'We were all sloping off to the Nude nights and obviously that influence was sinking in. We definitely had ideas in our heads when we were writing and recording the songs which we couldn't apply to the music, just because we weren't good enough musicians. It's like when you see something you like the look of, then you try to draw it on a piece of paper to show someone else, but you can't. That was our problem. We knew what we wanted the songs to sound like, but we were still at the stage of learning how to put them together. The reason there were a lot of gaps on the album, was because that was us trying to get a Doors-like groove going. Looking back, it may sound like basic indie rock, but it wasn't. At that time, indie meant tight, fast, neat music and we were aiming for a really spacious, trippy sound.'

In line with Happy Mondays' love of nicknames and largely meaningless banter, the album was given a suitably obscure and entertaining title. After endless arguments, Shaun declared that the LP was to be called *Squirrel And G-Man Twenty Four Hour Party People Plastic Face Carnt Smile (White Out)*.

'Squirrel is the name of Knobhead's mum, because she looks like a squirrel,' explained Shaun. 'G-Man is Bez's dad because he's a cop. Twenty Four Hour Party People is what we used to call ourselves even before the band. It's like a title for whizz freaks. Plastic Face and Carnt Smile are just two mad sayings stuck together. When I came up with the title, the rest of the band were going, "No way, you're off your head. You can't call it that." But they like it now for the same reason I liked it then – it sounds mental.'

The release of *Squirrel And G-Man Twenty Four Hour Party People Plastic Face Carnt Smile (White Out)* in mid-April 1987, was preceded by the double A-sided single 'Tart Tart/Little Matchstick Owen's Rap'. At the tail-end of February, Tony Wilson commented on the release in an interview in *Sounds* on the apparent rebirth of Factory Records, following a substantial increase in interest from the media in the label's latest signings.

'Our current release schedule is very promising,' noted Wilson. 'This week sees a new single from the Railway Children, next week comes one from Miaow, and two weeks after that, one from Happy Mondays. All three groups are poised to become major Factory acts. Certainly, Happy Mondays should succeed as a cult band, while Miaow and Railway Children should become Smiths and New Orders.' In March, 'Tart Tart' was made one of three Singles Of The Week in *Melody Maker*, alongside Tom Jones and Throwing Muses. 'Far more brusque than last year's primitive funk classic, "Freaky Dancin'",' noted the review, which also described the couplet, 'Now maggot sleeps on a desk, he wears a sleeping bag as his vest' as perhaps the perfect pop lyric: 'This is romance, this is corruption, this is a terrible temptation. Unless my ears are in collusion, Happy Mondays do it again.'

Not everyone, however, was as impressed. In *NME*, journalist Steven Wells slated the single. 'Now I get to review one of Happy Mondays' songs,' he wrote. 'Dross. "Tart Tart" is someone shouting in a Manchester accent over a weak and watery foonk like nearly everything else on Factory. Isn't it time we stopped the hype?'

Despite split opinions on the musical merit of the insistent rhythms and scary shouting that collided on 'Tart Tart', the single was a success. It didn't sell well, but it did significantly raise awareness of Happy Mondays.

'The press was particularly intrigued by the lyrics of the songs,' says Harper. 'To the band's credit, they did try to explain what they meant in interviews, but not so that anyone could understand. It wasn't normal English. It was just their slang, their own little language. You could recognise the words, but you couldn't make sense of the order they were in. Shaun didn't write like that on purpose. That's how the whole band actually spoke. It's why a lot of people, including journalists, didn't feel comfortable in their company. The band would rapidly gibber away to each other and exclude anyone who didn't understand, which meant everyone bar their friends. They were a real gang, which is exactly what came across in the songs.'

'If a line sounds good on record,' says Shaun, 'I'll sing it. It doesn't have to mean anything, and I don't have to mean it either. I'm quite happy to sing lyrics that mean fuck all, just as long as they're witty.

'We didn't want the songs on *Squirrel And G-Man* to be proper and we didn't expect them to be taken seriously. Most of the lyrics came from comments Bez and I had made to each other. I picked out words and one-liners that sounded good, then jumbled them all up together. We were trying to make a completely corny album. It just didn't turn out like that. Nothing ever went the way we planned it.' Touchingly, Shaun explained to the press at the time of its release that 'Tart Tart' was dedicated to a girl called Dinah, who had looked after him and Bez when they had found themselves homeless. She was a drug dealer who had been really into the band before recently dying of a brain haemorrhage.

'Shaun told me "Tart Tart" was about dirty women in Little Hulton,' says Harper. 'If it was dedicated to anyone, it was thirty-five-year-old divorcees on council estates, the sort of women he always used to say gave him warts. At the time, Shaun was obsessed by venereal diseases. He talked about them constantly in interviews. I eventually found out why.

'We were in a Portakabin backstage at Finsbury Park, where Happy Mondays were playing some festival, when Shaun asked if I wanted to see his wart. Before I could answer, he pulled his trousers down, held his knob out in his hand and about halfway down there was this huge wart. You know what a Victory V lozenge looks like, it was exactly the same shape and size as that. He started rabbiting on about how he had started to get it treated, but the hospital he had to attend was in the middle of Manchester and the DSS had stopped paying the bus fare there, so he had given up going. Apparently, he'd had it for ages. He didn't seem the slightest bit embarrassed about showing it to me. As for me, I was proud to have seen it. It was a fine specimen.'

Squirrel And G-Man Twenty Four Hour Party People Plastic Face Carnt Smile (White Out) was released in a brash, brightly-coloured, cartoon-style sleeve depicting a spread of ice-cream sundaes and birthday cake. Factory Records' staunchly indie agenda – to give their audiences value for money – meant that neither 'Delightful' nor 'Freaky Dancin'' appeared on the album, although it did contain a reworked version of 'Oasis', from Happy Mondays' debut 'Forty Five' EP. Song titles such as 'Olive Oil', 'Kuff Dam' and 'Weekend S' continued the band's tradition of nicknames, while every track boasted bizarre lyrics, black humour and a seedy side. Album opener 'Kuff Dam' took its cue from a porn film called *Mad Fuck* (the song title is the film title spelt backwards, almost), while '24 Hour Party People' was about northern soul fans shooting up speed in order to stay up dancing all night. It was the track 'Desmond', however, that proved to be the most contentious. In ripping off a line from The Beatles' 'Ob-la-di, Ob-la-da', Shaun ensured that 'Desmond' landed Factory with a writ from the lawyers of Michael Jackson, owner of The Beatles' back catalogue. The label diffused the situation by promising to destroy all copies of the initial pressing of the album.

Despite the threat of legal action making for an interesting angle from which to draw attention to the record's release, *Squirrel And G-Man* sold incredibly badly. Only a few thousand copies were bought within the first few months.

The reaction from the press, however, was on the whole very positive. *Melody Maker* even called the album 'the most shambolically lovable record of the year'. 'If Mike Leigh had written all his plays on speed and set them to music,' said the paper's reviewer, 'he might have come close to Happy Mondays' brutal charm. Astounding.'

For six weeks following the release of *Squirrel And G-Man*, Happy Mondays went on tour across the UK. Support for the band was picking up principally in London, where people had begun to appreciate their maverick attitude and individual style. *Melody Maker* even awarded Happy Mondays their first front cover, claiming that the country needed radical acts of their ilk, what with the indie charts mellowing out of late to music by the likes of The Darling Buds and The House Of Love.

The cover shot showed Shaun in a parka, hood up, howling at the sky. The singer's swagger and the band's collective dress sense – slightly flared jeans, muddy trainers, anoraks and T-shirts – were duly noted. 'Happy Mondays are unusual because they just go on stage,' was one observation in the article. 'They don't do it 'cos they look good.'

'Most bands are a million miles away from where we are,' was Shaun's retort. 'In every sense. Those people don't look right, they just happen to be in the right place or know someone. We laugh at bands like that, but they have nothing to do with us.'

'A lot of journalists loved Shaun's anarchic attitude,' says Harper, 'whether or not they liked Happy Mondays' music. I remember him berating one writer virtually before he had asked a single question. For some reason, Shaun had decided he didn't like the guy. He was going, "Am I supposed to thank you for turning up to interview us? Do you want me on bended knees, pleading with you to write something nice about my band? Well, no chance."

'Shaun told most journalists that he never read their stupid papers, although he always did when he was in them. He didn't seem to care what they wrote though. He wasn't bothered about other bands either. Shaun would rather watch *Tomorrow's World* on TV than *The Tube*. He certainly didn't feel in competition with anyone and he never went out of his way to find out about other musicians, unless he'd heard a song of theirs that he really liked. It was a very refreshing, very unusual attitude.'

Without Phil Saxe in tow to monitor what came out of their mouths, Happy Mondays proved to be hugely entertaining interviewees.

'Phil is stupid, we're going to sack him,' Shaun told *Melody Maker*. 'Write in your article that we're going to sack him. He's got too much money, Phil. He's dead mean with us though. All he gives us are tapes because he's trying to educate us about music. He gives us Philip Glass albums and stuff like that. They're hopeless. We don't listen to them. We use them for scraping the ice off the windscreen.'

Shaun Ryder's lack of formal education also gave journalists the chance to take the piss. The singer claimed in one interview that he wanted the band to make lots of money so that, ultimately, he could do nothing 'like Princess Caroline of Morocco'.

In May 1987, Happy Mondays played what was to prove their final appearance at Camden's Black Horse pub. In a spot-on live review, *Sounds* journalist Roy Wilkinson perfectly summed up the frenetic, insular live show. 'Stumbling on like a misdirected sextet of Stretford End psychopaths who have come down for the match,' he noted, 'Happy Mondays look like no band you or I have ever seen. Clad in their designer-horrible jeans (individually tailored for that baggy-arsed bastard look) and their footie anoraks, the fearsomely insular Mondays gang sprawl, slob and slide about the "stage" before launching into their sardonic, insistent rumble of Manc northern soul.

'Fronted by the stubble-faced, hunched-hobbit figure of Shaun Ryder, a man whose eyes blear a myopic, vaguely-defined threat and whose mouth spouts a street-battered jargon of its own, Happy Mondays are a conundrum. Looking at this rag-bag collection – and particularly the insane, autopilot dance mechanics of freelance percussionist Mark Berry – you wouldn't credit them with a great deal of creative impulse. But lurking beneath this hooligan exterior lies a bizarre world view and a blundering muse that have united to bring forth the band's quite unique, shifting funk grooves. Happy Mondays make the sound of days spent in bed and in shopping malls.'

The strangeness of the Mondays' live experience, however, excluded anyone not on their wavelength. *NME* were at the same show, but came to a strikingly different conclusion about the band. 'Grunginess abounds,' began the review. 'Beside a Pan's Person maracas player, singer Shaun Ryder looks like Scooby Doo's Shaggy doing a passable impression of a stage-struck orangutan in labour. The sound is criminally-awful and even the audience grimace in despair.

'I'm bowled over by the coldness of it all. What variety and originality there is in Ryder's vocal style disappears tonight, the songs' already obscure lyrics are lost and the experience becomes pointless. Carnt smile. Won't.'

'The band did read their reviews,' says Harper, 'but they didn't seem to care if they were good or bad. Shaun was certainly more bothered about being called badly-dressed than being told he couldn't sing. I guess it was because they didn't think they were any good themselves. For Shaun at least, it was as though he was playing at being in a band. Writing songs and performing them on stage was something that singers did, and he was just copying them. He didn't actually realise he was a singer in his own right.'

'The Mondays were the first band I'd met that were hugely into The Beatles and didn't mind talking about it. Gaz was like an obsessive fan. He really did believe he was related to Ringo. Gaz did have that same loose drumming style – he was always ahead of or behind the beat. Sometimes at rehearsals, Shaun and Bez would pretend to be Lennon and McCartney. They would swap over which Beatle they were on different days, depending on their mood. What with old Ringo behind the drums, it could all get a bit surreal.'

At gigs, Shaun was often more interested in making money than entertaining the audience. After the show, both he and Bez would wander about the crowd, offering dope or speed for sale.

'Because we had an album out and we were being written about in the press,' says Shaun, 'people imagined we were doing really well. They thought us selling drugs at the gigs was some sort of act. In their position, I would have thought the same. But nothing had changed for us. We still had no money. We'd look at some of the lads that had started to follow the band who were dressed in really smart gear and wish we could have afforded it. Well, we couldn't, so we sold them stuff instead.'

'The Mondays were always ranting on about how all six of them worked for the Royal Mail,' says Harper. 'I thought that meant they all had jobs at the post office, and I knew a couple of them definitely did. It turned out the others just ripped off mail bags. They didn't seem to differentiate between the two. They always had cash on them anyway, and they certainly wouldn't have got that from record sales.'

Six months after the release of *Squirrel And G-Man*, '24 Hour Party People' became the second (and final) song to be lifted from the album and put out as a single, albeit as a twelve-inch only. Backed by two previously unreleased tracks, 'Yahoo' and 'Wah Wah (Think Tank)', the brash, rowdy '24 Hour Party People' received almost exclusively positive reviews. Not that Shaun was the slightest bit bothered. His life had moved on immeasurably since *Squirrel And G-Man*. '24 Hour Party People' may have been written about northern soul devotees, but it now perfectly described its authors.

On an early summer trip to Ibiza that year, Shaun had taken Ecstasy for the first time. Happy Mondays went on hold for over a year.

SIX

Ecstasy Daze, Ibizan Nights

Ecstasy first filtered into Britain from the US in 1985. The drug's chemical compound, MDMA, was formulated in Germany at the start of the century as an appetite suppressant, then later used by doctors to treat patients with psychological problems. In the early 1980s, Ecstasy – then legal in the US – was commonly used as a recreational drug in cities such as Austin, Texas, where it could be bought over the counter in chemists for around $20 a tablet. In the summer of 1985, alerted to MDMA's new use by a phenomenal increase in demand for the drug, the US government declared Ecstasy illegal.

Ecstasy's arrival in UK clubland – or more precisely, London clubland – was all but unremarkable. Very few people indulged in the new drug and there was no buzz on the street about its effects. Even at the capital's warehouse parties, speed, cocaine and LSD staunchly stayed the substances of choice. It took house music to launch MDMA in the UK. The repetitive rhythms and tribal percussion of trance-inducing electronic music emanating mainly from Chicago provided the perfect catalyst to propel Ecstasy into its current position as by far Britain's biggest dance drug.

Ecstasy first caught on in Europe in 1987 on the nightlife-orientated holiday island of Ibiza. All-night parties at venues like Ku Club, Pacha and Club Amnesia had already earned the island a tabloid-friendly reputation for hedonism. Throw in the warm weather, beautiful scenery and a big British local community, and it's hardly surprising that, by the mid 1980s, Ibiza had become a popular summer holiday destination for thousands of UK clubbers.

The licensing laws and twenty-four-hour entertainment also made the island the ideal location for Ecstasy abuse to thrive. By 1988, thanks to Brits back from abroad, MDMA had infiltrated every major city in the UK.

Like many Ecstasy users, Shaun Ryder would insist in later years that he had first taken the drug months before he even knew of its existence. He would claim that he had spent much of 1986 in Amsterdam experimenting with E. In fact, as anyone involved with Happy Mondays that year will attest, the singer's Class A intake amounted predominately to speed and cocaine.

Looking back, it's simple to spot when Shaun discovered Ecstasy. It was on a break in Ibiza in the spring of 1987. The singer recalls taking the drug for three days solid, crashing out for the following forty-eight hours, then starting all over again. For the next twelve months, Happy Mondays would vanish from the musical map. There would be no new recordings, no appearances in the press and no news stories on the scheduled second album.

'Shaun did literally disappear for a lot of that year,' says Harper. 'Not that anyone at Factory noticed. The label had no idea what he was up to. Besides, the whole band had always been into taking trips abroad without any warning. I remember Horse telling me once about how he had recently been mugged in Algeria. I hadn't realised he had even left Manchester.'

'Ever since we were kids, we looked at travelling as an education,' says Shaun. 'We liked to get away as often as possible. I'd go to Germany just so I could get Adidas trainers no one had back home. When I was sixteen, me and our kid managed to get to Spain on a mad coach ride that cost us £60. We landed on the beach with 50p in our pockets and a bit of weed. But that was okay. When I had no money at all, I'd hitch to Amsterdam. That was always my favourite city.'

'All of the Mondays were involved in a big scene of ligging and travelling,' says Harper. 'They'd head off to football matches in Bulgaria when they only had £5 or try to blag a tenner so they could get together with some mates in Spain. They had this huge network of friends from Salford that they would hook up with all over Europe. I guess when they got to places, they would make money by selling drugs or stealing wallets. I'm not sure. I know some of their mates sold pirated posters or T-shirts or cassettes. The connection wasn't music though, it was football. Happy Mondays didn't hang out with any other bands. And the fact that they were signed to Factory didn't seem to matter to their mates. It was just some little detail of their lives. That was such an unusual attitude in Manchester at the time. Most people in bands would be holding down proper, sensible jobs, while desperately trying to make a go of their music in their spare time. The Mondays couldn't have been more different.'

True to form, having discovered Ecstasy, Shaun spent most of the summer of 1987 in Amsterdam. He shaved off his goatee beard, all but gave up alcohol and began to grow his hair. He hung out in the city's clubs and coffee bars and frequented its red light district. If a British band he liked played in town, Shaun might blag it in for free, but live music was no longer high on his agenda. Bez, meanwhile, was back and forth between Salford and Ibiza, where the members of New Order were installed in a hilltop studio, recording tracks for the album *Technique*.

'We went to Ibiza to record *Technique* because of a studio we'd heard about, not because of the drugs,' says Sumner. 'I remember Hooky went over there to check the place out. He phoned to tell us that the studio was shit and that the acoustics were fuckin' terrible. Then he said the place had a massive swimming pool and its own bar. We were straight there.

'A few weeks later, Bez – who had heard all about the studio – came over with a load of his mates from Manchester. We got a phone call from them about an hour before they arrived. I'd read in the *NME* the previous day that Bez had just written off four cars outside the Hacienda. The very first thing he asked me when he got to the studio was if he could borrow my driving licence. For some totally mad, inexplicable reason, I gave it to him. I guess I regretted it even as I handed it over.

'Bez and his crew were staying on the other side of the island from the studio. He said he was going to go hire a car, and that he would come pick me up to go out at about 7pm. Hours later, I'm still waiting, really annoyed with him. At 10.30pm, this bloke called Jeff the Chef runs into the studio, gasping for breath and absolutely dripping with sweat. The studio was pretty far up a hill and he had just run all the way from the bottom. It turned out Bez had written off the hire car. Jeff the Chef is shaking as he tells me the story.

Apparently, it had been raining and Bez couldn't see the road signs. So he had driven right over to one sign, then crashed right into it.

'I headed off down the hill to find him. The car was totally fucked. One front wheel had buckled completely and the bonnet had kind of crushed in on top of it. Bez was saying, "Don't worry, it's fine. We can still go out. The car's okay in reverse."

'I eventually went out later that night with Bez and someone – well, I strongly suspect it was Bez – slipped something in my drink. I blacked out and had to be carried home. All I remember is lying in bed, throwing up all night. When I woke up in the morning, there was puke all over the floor and there was Bez, lying in the bed right beside me, trying to shag his girlfriend.

'I was supposed to be flying back to Britain that day at 10am. When I woke up, it was one in the afternoon. What's worse, I had no means of transport and the rest of the band had all gone home. The only way to get back to the studio was to get Bez to drive me in the hire car. When we got there, some lad who was working as an engineer had loads of E. There was nothing to do but take it. I felt horrible, just horrible.

'Later that day, one of Bez's mates wrote off a hire motorbike. He hadn't even got it on the road. He crashed it right there in the shop, fractured his skull and had to be taken to hospital. Then he did a runner from the hospital and got arrested at the airport. Believe it or not, Bez's mates made him look like a kind of together guy.'

After the pair's adventures in Ibiza, Bernard and Bez became firm friends.

'The two of us even got in synch over certain things, including throwing up,' says Sumner. 'I remember once, when the Mondays supported New Order at Birmingham NEC, I ran into the toilets to throw up, and Bez did exactly the same. We were puking into sinks side-by-side. That started to happen a lot. I guess it had a lot to do with the amount of E we were taking. We never fought over the toilet though. It was always neighbouring sinks. That time at the NEC was particularly odd. I started coughing and Bez started coughing, I started retching and Bez did the same. As soon as I puked, he did too.

'Bez came on the road with New Order a couple times that year. His presence compounded my bad habits. At the best of times on tour, you don't eat properly and you're constantly drinking and taking drugs. The lifestyle in itself grinds you down. In one sense, having Bez around was good for me. I thought, "At least I'm not the only person puking every night at 8 o'clock."

By the end of 1987, both Shaun and Bez were spending at least some time back in Britain. In Manchester, the pair shared a shabby, converted Victorian house with Happy Mondays' tour manager Muzzer – an acquaintance of Shaun's since their teens – and one of his friends. Outside, the gravel path was overgrown by an unkempt garden. Inside, piles of videos, lots of records and Rizla papers were scattered across the floor.

'My mate and I used to buy all the bog rolls and milk and stuff,' says Muzzer. 'Shaun and Bez didn't know what shopping was. They lived to party.

'It was Bez who gave me my first E. I had the flu and he told me taking half a tablet would make me feel better. I asked him what would happen when it wore off. He told me to keep taking them. He said to always stay ahead of the comedown and you'd never feel ill. At least, that's what seemed to work for him.'

Like Bernard Sumner and Peter Hook (who were now mixing *Technique* at Peter Gabriel's Real World studios outside Bath), Shaun and Bez split their social lives between the Hacienda back home and acid house parties and clubs such as Shoom and Spectrum in London.

'When we were all in Manchester,' says Sumner, 'we would all meet up early at the Hacienda, in the bottom alcove on the left, every Wednesday, Friday and Saturday evening. The we would stay out all night. We'd go on to house parties after the club closed. It was brilliant for about eight months. Then it became hugely popular and a very straight crowd turned up and spoiled it.'

Financially-speaking, Sumner should have been pleased. With resident DJs such as Mike Pickering, Dave Haslam and Graeme Park filling the Hacienda with house music, the club was doing good business for the first time in its troubled five-year history. When Ecstasy arrived on the scene, queues to get into the venue stretched way down Whitworth Street.

One of Shaun Ryder's most infamous claims is that Happy Mondays' introduced Ecstasy to Manchester.

'The Hacienda didn't change the Mondays,' says Shaun, 'the Mondays changed the Hacienda. I'm sure no one was using Ecstasy in Manchester until we brought it into the city. We got in touch with twenty or so of our mates who were bringing the drug into the country from Valencia and Ibiza. It was all going straight to London, so we bought a load and brought it up to flog in the Hacienda. We sold it from our regular corner under the balcony on the left-hand side of the club. We created a vibe which spread out across the dancefloor from there. All the clubbers wanted to know exactly what our mates were on and why they were dancing so strangely. We actually started out giving the tabs away. Groups of people would split one between three or four of them. After two weeks, everyone wanted to buy E from us. Then they found out we kept the stash in our house. On some nights, the queues at our front door were longer than they were at the Hacienda.'

'Shaun may have been selling a lot of Ecstasy,' says Sumner, 'but I'm not sure he brought it into the city. Manchester has always been a pretty druggy place. Drugs have been a big part of the music scene there since the 1970s.

'Hooky and I originally came across E in America when it was still legal. There's actually a New Order song from that time called "Ecstasy". We discovered it because we had friends in Dallas. That was years before it made it to Britain. In Manchester, the scene grew out of clubbers going to Ibiza on holiday. Simple as that.'

Bez did, however, definitely get caught with 500 tablets of the drug. Driving an uninsured, ten-day-overdue hire car, with the Ecstasy haul in the boot, he stopped to call a copper a cunt. The short sentence he received was the least of his worries. When he got out, his suppliers were threatening to kill him.

'Bez got a good hiding for that,' says Shaun. 'I had to plead with them not to break his legs. It took a lot of talking to get him out of that.'

In the spring of 1988, New Order threw a party at Real World studios in order to celebrate the completion of *Technique*. The band bussed scores of their friends from Manchester down to Bath for the evening. Happy Mondays turned up on their own, armed with hundreds of Ecstasy tablets.

'That was one of the maddest nights of my life,' says Harper. 'The studio door was locked and everyone went on an absolutely mental drugs fest. It was so mental in fact, that at one stage, I took all my clothes off and rolled around in what I assumed to be early morning dewy grass. It turned out to be cut glass. I was so off my head I didn't feel a thing.

'It was obvious that the Mondays loved being around New Order. They liked to feel a part of their extended Factory family. New Order had a really big influence on Shaun in particular. The band's image until around 1987 had been very po-faced and serious and in some ways quite scary because of Ian Curtis's suicide. When Shaun got to know them, he realised that, rather than being doomy and gloomy, they were actually up-for-it party people. They were barking mad party people, in fact. Absolute hedonists.

'Bernard was a big influence because he showed Shaun that, regardless of your background, you could have a really ace life, travelling the world with money in your pocket and having a non-stop party. All you had to do was write some decent songs. Shaun also liked his style. Bernard was big on designer labels too.'

'Alongside The Beatles and The Stones, New Order had always been one of my favourite bands,' says Shaun. 'Barney was incredible. He'd be out all night, every night, but he was always Mr Clean And Neat.'

'I'd say Bernard was probably the closest Shaun ever got to a mentor,' says Harper. 'Of course, Bernard behaved the way he did for a very different reason. With him, that attitude masked a lot of pain. Bernard is quite a complex character, whereas Shaun is a lot more happy-go-lucky. Shaun acts the way he does because he enjoys life, not to block things out. He has more in common with Hooky in that respect. Hooky liked having the Mondays around because they were uncomplicated party people. He got on with anyone who was always up for going out and he definitely admired the Mondays as much for their attitude as for their music.'

Spending time with New Order persuaded Happy Mondays to start taking music seriously for the first time. In early summer 1988, they supported James on tour. The gigs were to prove by far the band's most coherent to date and even convinced several of their critics that they had commercial potential.

Happy Mondays' increasingly professional attitude, however, wasn't entirely down to the band themselves. It had become clear to Phil Saxe that he couldn't devote enough of his time or energy to do justice to Happy Mondays. During the group's unofficial year off,

Saxe had stepped down as their manager. In his place, Shaun had recently hired Nathan McGough, who then also looked after Factory-signed indie outfit The Bodines and a jazz-funk act called Kalima. Despite also having been in a couple of bands himself, however, Scouser McGough was best known as the son of Liverpool beat poet Roger McGough, O.B.E., who was in turn famous for having an uncool pop hit with 'Lily The Pink' as a member of The Scaffold.

Shaun first met Nathan McGough in a club in Manchester, when Nathan came up and asked him for some Rizla papers. Shaun held out a packet, Nathan took the lot. Shaun admired his front. Despite objections from Factory that Nathan was too inexperienced for the job, as soon as Happy Mondays were ready to regroup, Shaun insisted he be hired.

'I liked Nathan because he had the same attitude as us,' says Shaun. 'He was out to have a good time, all the time. It turned out he was a great manager for the Mondays. His only weakness was women.'

'Nathan was a really interesting character,' says Harper. 'He was young, but he had already had a very interesting life. Not only was his dad famous, his mum was well-known in the north-west for being quite a hip figure on the scene. I remember one rumour that Paul McCartney was Nathan's real dad. I've no idea where that came from. His mother did go out with Tony though, when Nathan was about ten. She went out with Tom Wolfe too. Apparently, she and Nathan were going to move to America to live with him. I heard they got as far as the airport before, for some reason, there was a phone call to say Tom Wolfe had changed his mind about them coming.'

Nathan McGough had first become involved with the Manchester music scene when he began promoting club nights at the Boardwalk with his friend Dave Haslam. The pair subsequently started an independent dance label called Play Hard together. Managing Happy Mondays, however, was easily his most exciting opportunity to date.

'Nathan was brilliant,' says Harper, 'a really nice bloke with bags of energy. Entertaining too. When Nathan went to meetings with Kalima, he'd wear this mad, jazzy suit. When he was seeing The Bodines, he put on a denim jacket and jeans. With the Mondays, he wore dungarees.

'Happy Mondays' whole set-up shifted up a gear when Nathan got involved. Phil had been good as well, but Nathan was just so incredibly keen. He was fearless and he really understood what was going on. He wasn't scared to give people a good kick up the arse if they weren't pulling their weight and he could turn any situation to the band's advantage. He was also a good businessman and very sharp on money. Well, for a while, at least.'

Nathan's first move as manager was to sign the band officially to Factory. Thus far, the two had exchanged no written contracts. Now, the label was legally obliged to cover Happy Mondays' future recording costs. The arrangement also suited Factory. Tony Wilson was tired of acts that his company had nurtured leaving for major labels as soon as they began to be successful, as had been the case of late with both A Certain Ratio and his great indie hope, The Railway Children.

Nathan's second suggestion for Happy Mondays, however, wasn't so well received. He had decided to ask former Joy Division and New Order producer Martin Hannett to helm the band's second album. Hannett, a former Factory director, had been locked in a bitter financial dispute with the label for the last six years. Moreover, for some time, his work had been disappointing, due without doubt to his legendary substance abuse and, in particular, a large heroin habit. For reasons both musical and social Shaun, of course, adored the idea. Wilson relented and Hannett was brought on board. Like all Happy Mondays' adventures, the outcome was destined to be either inspired or catastrophic.

In August 1988, Happy Mondays and Martin Hannett decamped to the Slaughterhouse studios in Great Driffield, East Yorkshire, to record the follow up to *Squirrel And G-Man*. Shaun would subsequently say that the band had substantially cut down their consumption of Ecstasy by then, although he reckons he was still doing three tablets a day. Certainly, the month-long recording session was approached as little more than an extended party, paid for by Factory.

Shaun had decided prior to recording that Hannett had to produce the album on E, whether he wanted to or not. He claimed that this was in order to keep Hannett off alcohol. For a number of years, the producer's work had tended to be terrible when he was drunk, and even New Order had replaced him at their helm. In truth, Shaun's decision may well have been a shrewd move to translate the party vibe of Happy Mondays at that time on to tape. Or it might have been an excuse for the band to get away with doing a minimum amount of work. It was probably a bit of both. Shaun was supposed to have written the bulk of his lyrics over the summer. In fact, he had barely started when the band first arrived at the Slaughterhouse. Three weeks on, he had lyrics for less than half the album. In the end, he had to come up with words for one entire side in only the final few days.

Getting Hannett E'd up – for whatever reason – worked wonders for Happy Mondays. Being on the same wavelength as the band helped the producer to capture much of their collective spirit, not to mention the characteristics of individual players. Although Shaun claims he had initially to stop Hannett attempting to turn his band into New Order, he admits that the producer taught him a lot about studio techniques. In fact, Hannett helped all the band put down on tape the sounds they were hearing in their heads. The results edged Happy Mondays closer to the swirling Doors territory that had for some time been their aim. Rather than lifting Shaun's vocal above the group's queer musical mélange, during post-production at Strawberry studios in Stockport, Hannett mixed it in. His production techniques also gave the songs a spacey, strangely refracted, slightly slowed down sound. In other words, they mirrored the trippy sensations of Ecstasy. Happy Mondays' second album was to be considered Martin Hannett's last great production job. Less than three years later, he was dead from a drink and drugs overdose.

'Martin was a very mercurial character,' says Harper. 'His mood swings were legendary. He would be either completely happy or completely sad, a brilliant producer or an absolutely awful one. I don't think anyone knew which came first – the drugs or the personality. I do know that Factory were very scared of him. They had been stuck in this big, sulky, Manc argument with him for years. Hannett was really bitter and twisted about it. It was all to do with the Hacienda and money. He thought Tony was wasting his time putting Factory funds into a club. He thought the money should be spent on more creative recording and building proper studios. But of course he would, he was a producer.'

'Martin was a complete drug fiend,' says Sumner. 'His idea of recording was to start at 4pm, lock yourself in the studio with heaps of drugs and booze, get off it, then stay up all night and record. That can work well for a while, until it fucks you up. With Joy Division, it helped us to record our deepest thoughts. It made us explore our fears and the corners of our minds.

'It seemed a lot like a party, but deep down it really was also work for us. I'm sure Shaun thought the same. It's no secret that Shaun gets off it all the time. What people don't realise is that he's perfectly aware that his songs are an off-the-wall product of his drug-addled mind. Shaun and drugs are like dried food and water. Neither is particularly pleasant or interesting on its own. But put them together and you get a nice soup.'

SEVEN

Swimming Through Cotton Wool

In the summer of 1988 – the so-called Second Summer Of Love – the British media went on a drugs binge. While the tabloid newspapers splashed endless Ecstasy scare stories across their front pages and Radio 1 refused to play chart hits such as D-Mob's 'We Call It Acieed', style mags reported a cultural revolution and even the guitar-obsessed music press found space for club culture. Cut-and-paste productions stuffed with hip hop samples from the likes of Coldcut and MARRS soundtracked the scene, while Bomb The Bass's Tim Simenon's smiley face gave it an emblem.

In London, the police had been regularly raiding illegal warehouse parties for months. Now they were also starting to shut down legitimate venues. The *Sun* (falsely, as it turned out) reported that Spectrum had been forced to close. In fact, it was allowed to stay open, as long as door staff meticulously body-checked everyone on their way in.

Scotland Yard instigated a clampdown on the massive outdoor raves now commonplace across the south-east of the county. Even legal gatherings such as Sunrise were infiltrated by plainclothes police. Often they left empty-handed, reluctantly admitting that they had procured no solid evidence with which to prosecute promoters. Nevertheless, the Yard didn't seem to mind recounting twisted tales of weekends spent with dangerous dealers to the tabloids come Monday morning.

The Hacienda, however, continued to thrive. If anything, the troubles down south lent the club a helping hand. The closure of several of the capital's best venues, coupled with the constant threat of a drugs raid made the prospect of a night out in Manchester unusually appealing. Besides, Ecstasy had only just caught on in the north, so the scene was still fresh.

Just as importantly, smaller cities such as Derby, Leeds and Nottingham were developing their own healthy club cultures by fusing acid house with a host of new musical influences. For the first time in over a decade, areas outside London could be considered cool. In particular, the Hacienda's Hot nights, hosted by Mike Pickering and Graeme Park – which involved the installation of a swimming pool inside the club – pioneered developments in house music that marked a move away from the omnipresent Balearic beats of 1987. Thankfully, the venue also revamped its sound system, updating it with one better suited to the club's cavernous interior.

When Happy Mondays announced that their second album, scheduled for release in November, was to be called *Bummed*, the title seemed strangely at odds with the hippy-style peace sentiments espoused by most bands at the time. In Happy Mondays' world, however, the word bummed wasn't meant to portray pissed off or unhappy.

'The title came about because, when we first started taking E,' explains Shaun, 'we didn't know how to handle it. We'd all shag anything in sight. Bummed was our word for fucking. We'd take advantage of girls on their first E and throw naughty sex parties. We gave lots of different explanations for the title when the album came out, but it was only because we knew what the reaction to the truth would be, and it wouldn't have done us any good.'

Clearly, Happy Mondays were starting to take themselves seriously as a band.

'When I started working with them,' says Harper, 'the band was just a fun way for them to waste some time. Around the recording of *Bummed*, their attitude changed. Their ideas started to gel and they actually began to care about the songs and how they sounded. They realised they had something special going on. It dawned on them that Happy Mondays really could go places if they put some effort in.

'Before *Bummed* came out, Shaun even started slagging off the band's first album, which didn't go down too well with Factory. He reckoned they shouldn't have released it because it wasn't representative of what they were about. He said the songs and the production were shit and that they hadn't known what they were doing, or cared, come to that. Of course, it could have been a press nightmare for me. If a band is in the papers mouthing off about how crap their own records are, no one in their right mind is going to go out and buy them. Fortunately, no journalists took Shaun seriously when he said that. They thought he was just trying to be controversial.'

Dave Harper was doing such a good job with Happy Mondays, in fact, that he was asked to become head of the press department at major label RCA. 'I took the job,' he says, 'but I guess I've regretted it since. Working with the Mondays was certainly an experience and I'm glad I got the chance. They are one of the very few bands that did exactly as they pleased. They didn't care about etiquette either. Looking back, they were probably a lot like Oasis when they first started out. Except that, with the Mondays, there was more trouble, more drugs, more of everything really.'

Harper handed press responsibilities for the Factory roster of acts over to Jeff Barrett, who had recently set up his own independent PR company.

'Jeff was the perfect person for the job,' says Harper. 'A real man-about-town. He came into the Mondays' camp really fresh and with a lot of enthusiasm. It was also just as things were starting to explode for the band. Jeff dealt with it all incredibly well.'

'It was baptism by bloody fire,' says Barrett. 'I wasn't that experienced at press and the Mondays really made me work. I had no idea how to deal with most of the scrapes they got into. I had already been working with Primal Scream and My Bloody Valentine, so you think I would have had some notion of what I was letting myself in for. No chance. Nothing could have prepared me for that band.

'When Harper gave me the job, New Order should have been the big attraction. I did like New Order a lot, but it was the Mondays that really got me. I knew from the start that group had a shot. A few key people had started to pick up on them, often in a weird way too. I remember I organised a gig for the Mondays in a place called Portlands, which was more or less the basement of a pub. I asked this other crappy guitar group I was doing press for to support them. The group said they would support any band in Britain but the Mondays. As far as I'm concerned, that's a fantastic thing to hear about one of your acts.

'It was hard to put your finger on what made the Mondays special. They were just so stylish. It was as though the music was secondary to their lifestyle. Their songs were the soundtrack to their lives. There was no other band at the time that had so decisively torn up the pop rulebook, chucked it in the air and picked out only the pieces they liked as their manifesto. Mark Day, who is one of the genius guitar players of all time in my opinion, had a great quote that summed them up perfectly. Someone asked him how he had developed his unique sound and he said he learnt guitar by playing along to A Certain Ratio records, but was so shit that no one had ever noticed.

'In indie circles, Primal Scream and My Bloody Valentine were important bands at the time. I had seen a lot of sad groups trying to copy them and their style. They didn't realise that anoraks and badly-played guitars alone do not punk rock make. The Mondays didn't try to act like anyone else. They were totally straight, 100 per cent themselves. They were from another planet. They were funky. They were funny – a lot of the time not knowingly so. But they were also incredibly exciting. You never knew what their next record was going to sound like, which is the greatest thing for anyone working with a band.'

Barrett's first job with Happy Mondays was to oversee the filming of a video for 'Wrote For Luck', the first single to be taken from *Bummed*. Released at the tail end of October, 'Wrote For Luck', by far the album's danciest track with its cyclic groove and sonic trippiness, saw Factory take the decision to step up their investment in the band. Happy Mondays had just supported James on tour and the strength of their shows, coupled with the crowds' reactions and several positive reviews, convinced the label that, despite appalling sales of *Squirrel And G-Man*, the band had commercial potential.

Consequently, videomakers the Bailey Brothers, who had already produced a couple of very basic, low-budget videos for 'Kuff Dam' and 'Tart Tart', were asked to deliver a promo acceptable for broadcast on TV. Their previous videos had mixed clips of live performance, shot in black and white on a shaky, hand-held camera, with shots of individual band members mucking about outside Strawberry studios, drawing chalk lines on pavements or just hanging around parked cars. Their only production techniques had been to superimpose different images on top of each other, or split the screen to show Paul Davis playing keyboards at the same time as Mark Day playing guitar.

The video for 'Wrote For Luck' was filmed in a club called Legends in Manchester, a 1970s-style disco complete with mirror balls, renowned for playing terrible R&B music.

'Two very different videos were made for that single' says Barrett. 'One featured just children and was shot in the afternoon. The other one was done at night, with a totally mad party in progress and everyone out of their minds on pills. It was ace, full of all these psychotic characters. The Mondays wanted to capture the mood of the times. It was the height of Ecstasy madness and it felt like the whole of Manchester was getting pilled up every night. The Bailey Brothers suggested that the video have this trippy, gangster vibe. Shaun in particular loved the idea, but there was no way that it was ever going to be shown on *The Chart Show*. So they decided to shoot an alternative version, a clean one with kids.'

A local community drama group was approached to supply a cast for the 'clean' video. Dozens of young teenagers spent a week in rehearsals, learning to do the 'acid dance' and making up acting roles such as the bored barmaid, the grumpy doorman and the girl being chatted up by boys all night. The parents, most of whom turned up for the shoot, were told that the video was based on the film *Bugsy Malone*. Boxes of crisps, Coke and chocolate were bought for the kids. When it came to filming, however, none of them wanted to dance to 'Wrote For Luck'. It wasn't their type of music. Eventually, the Bailey Brothers had to put on Pepsi and Shirley and Wham! for them to look like they were enjoying themselves.

'That was the first video that we took at all seriously,' says Shaun. 'For "Tart Tart", for example, I had refused to mime in time. I thought pretending to sing was a stupid idea. I'd always wanted to see someone not go along with all that promotional shit, so I was always a line behind or totally mouthing the wrong words. At the time, I thought it was funny. I later realised it was just unprofessional. I decided that, if we were going to the bother of making a video, it should be able to be shown on TV. There's no point otherwise. Besides, I didn't want to end up looking like an idiot.'

In the press, the reaction to 'Wrote For Luck' was mixed. Despite the band's growing popularity, *Melody Maker* gave the single only a couple of lines as a review, describing it as 'Happy Mondays' least irritating slab of greyness to date'. *Sounds*, on the other hand, adored the record. 'Rhythmically precise and hot as a forged tenner,' noted the paper, ' "Wrote For Luck" has an aggressive, threatening attitude. Happy Mondays are today's real northern dance happening.'

In the clubs, 'Wrote For Luck' was a surprise hit. It may have been much more of a rock than a dance record, but to those in the know, it was clearly the sound of musicians on E. Besides, at the time, clubbers were dancing to a wide mix of music.

Ecstasy had broken down barriers. For a while, even dancing to chart tunes was acceptable. Not that 'Wrote For Luck' ever looked like breaking the Top 40.

'It took most people – including most music people – a long time to get into the Mondays' music,' says Barrett. 'A huge chunk of the media were put off the band because they thought they were just thick northerners. Also, to be honest, their singles prior to 'Wrote For Luck' hadn't given much indication of their potential. Their first album had had that anonymous, white, Northern sound that was typical of Factory bands. You had to listen hard to spot that their songs did in fact have good melodies, and you had to see them to understand just how punk rock they were. If you could get on to their wavelength though, you were hooked straight away. Suddenly, what you had previously thought was just some shouting over a badly-played backing track, became the sound of a party about to go off.'

In November 1988, at Shaun Ryder's request, *Bummed* was launched as at once a rock and a dance record. The launch party began at the club Heaven in central London at 6pm on a Monday evening. Later, weekly house club Spectrum would fill the venue.

'It was originally Nathan's idea to launch the album at Spectrum,' says Barrett, 'but the club was so busy by then that it would have been impossible. So we started off at Heaven, then the band played a gig at Dingwalls in Camden, then everyone bowled back to Spectrum for the rest of the night.

'It was at the show at Dingwalls that I realised the Mondays were set to explode. The gig itself was chaos. About sixty Manc scallies had come down for the party and most of them seemed to end up on stage with the band. It was like an invasion. A lot of people definitely did their first E that night. Most of them probably bought it from the Mondays or their mates. Not many industry people or even other bands had come across E before that. It was just a club drug. At that party, people were introduced to this whole other world that they hadn't even known existed.'

NME journalist Jack Barron, one of Happy Mondays early supporters and one of the few London rock writers already into the underground club scene, saw the band live for the first time that night. 'It took me a long time to understand what the Happy Mondays were about,' says Barron. 'Dave Harper had been sending me white labels of their singles since the start, but I could never quite get my head around the music. In fact, I seem to remember slagging off their first single in print. I got a bit more interested when Harper showed me a video and said that they were all heroin addicts. Coming from a press officer, that was a little odd, to say the least. I totally fell for them though when I saw them play live. The music suddenly made sense.

'Dingwalls was an excellent gig. It was simultaneously shambolic and really tight, which I know is a contradiction, but is the best way I can describe it. Their songs seemed to incorporate something that was out with the musical context. It was rock, but it touched on contemporary culture. I don't remember many details because I was off my head on E that night. I do remember thinking that the music mirrored the rush of the drug. It was also accentuated by Bez's dancing. Shaun looked mad and was clearly off his head, which was great to watch, but the real visual pull was Bez. I'd never seen anyone dance like that before. I don't think anyone in that audience had, except of course the crew that had obviously come down from Manchester.

'I had been taken to the show by a couple of guys who later developed into Flowered Up. Some of their mates had been up to the Hacienda dealing drugs and had met Shaun and Bez. I had already met Bez at a few warehouse parties in Lewisham and pubs around Brixton. Most of the other people I recognised were from the London club scene. They definitely weren't the usual crowd at a rock gig.'

Also in the audience that night was Supertramp and Paul McCartney producer Peter Henderson.

'I had heard a bit of a buzz about Happy Mondays and wanted to find out exactly what they were about,' says Henderson. 'I hadn't even heard their music, so I had absolutely no preconceptions. I was amazed by the raw energy of the show. The guitar player in particular was fantastic. At that time, there was no one else making that funky sound that he had. It was as though he should have been playing a reggae tune, but of course he wasn't. The songs weren't typical 1980s indie music either. They were a combination of punk and funk and very exciting. The rhythm and the beat really stood out, which was very odd for an indie band.

'Dingwalls was absolutely packed. It was one of those mad, sweaty gigs where one part of the audience was determined to just go for it, no matter what, and the other part had no idea what to expect. The show started with Shaun abusing the audience. He kept saying that London was crap and that Manchester was so much better. Then he started to sing. Within half a song he had captivated the entire audience. By the second or third song, everyone was hypnotised, either by him or by Bez's dancing. People either just stood and stared or jumped about and danced. The show built up and built up throughout the set. You just didn't want it to end. The only comparison I could make was with seeing Bob Marley in the States in the late 1970s. That was probably the only other gig I've been to where I felt hypnotised by the band.

'On stage, the Mondays themselves were endearing in an odd way. They weren't good looking by any means, but they had this rough and ready appeal. Shaun clearly had a lot of charisma. He literally didn't give a shit about the crowd. He treated them with total disdain at all times and even faced the wrong way a lot of the time. The audience loved that though, they always do.

'After the show, I bumped into Bez outside in the street. He was completely off his brain. He was going on about how great the band was. It was as though he had only just realised it himself. I walked off and he was just stood there shouting how Happy Mondays were going to be the biggest band in Britain.'

Bummed was the ultimate Ecstasy test. Anyone taking the drug could instantly connect with the loose, trippy tunes and recognise the references in the song lyrics. Anyone who wasn't, tended to be baffled. 'Happy Mondays display an earthy, natural flair for music and currently reside in the foothills of genius,' said a switched-on

Sounds writer. '*Bummed* is a tripped-out, tripped-up mishmash mêlée of zonked out pop weirdness from a band that couldn't possibly contrive to sound like anything else.'

'Trying to get a grip on Happy Mondays is like trying to sculpt water,' wrote a confused, if impressed *Melody Maker* journalist. 'Trying to dance to *Bummed* reminds me of Graham Greene's description of a suicide attempt where he leapt into the swimming pool after swallowing deadly nightshade; "like swimming through cotton wool".'

Packaged in a Central Station sleeve which featured a pastel-coloured, child-like drawing of a flushed face with an open mouth on the cover and a controversial 1970s-style porn photo of a woman on the inside (the image would later stop several American stores stocking the album), *Bummed* continued Happy Mondays' passion for nicknames, made-up words and rhyming slang. The title of the sitar-steeped 'Lazyitis' was an attempt to reflect the track's melodic, breezy, laid-back tune and chiming guitars. 'Country Song', with its Grand Ol' Oprey-style piano and steel guitar, was originally called 'Some Cunt From Preston', Gaz's nickname for Country & Western. Worried that the title would be deemed offensive, the song was originally renamed 'Redneck' and then changed again to 'Country Song'.

The album was particularly noted, however, for some of Shaun's inspired one-liners. 'Wrote For Luck' had already received praise for the line 'You used to speak the truth but now you're clever', which the singer claimed had even surprised him when he realised what he had written. Other lyrics were simply poached wholesale. The track 'Brain Dead Fuckers' began with a spoken word clip – 'Young man, you're rendering that scaffolding dangerous' from *Gimme Shelter*, The Stones' Altamont festival film, while the songs 'Performance' and 'Mad Cyril' both contained samples from the Mick Jagger film *Performance*. 'Lazyitis' even borrowed (without permission) the line 'I think I did the right thing in slipping away' from The Beatles' 'Ticket To Ride', either a brave or a downright dumb idea, considering the writ issued over 'Ob-la-di Ob-la-da'. 'Lazyitis' also boasted snippets from Sly And The Family Stone's 'Family People' and David Essex's 'We're Gonna Make You A Star'.

'I went to see David Essex in *That'll Be The Day* when I was eleven or twelve,' says Shaun. 'I think I was wagging school. It had a big influence on me. After seeing films like that and *Stardust*, school seemed pretty irrelevant compared to being in a band. At the time, David Essex was young, good-looking and having the sort of fun I wanted.'

Alongside A Certain Ratio and guest DJ Mike Pickering, Happy Mondays saw out 1988 supporting New Order at their only live UK date of the year at Manchester's G-Mex. They should have been celebrating the success of their second album. However, compounded by the fact that *Bummed* had been released at a terrible time (few relatively unknown artist albums do well in the run-up to Christmas), the record was selling surprisingly slowly. Even in Manchester, *Bummed* wasn't proving nearly as popular as had been hoped. Factory were beginning to wonder if its investment in Happy Mondays had been justified. Since the release earlier in the year of Public Enemy's *It Takes A Nation Of Millions To Hold Us Back*, the music press had grown obsessed with American dance music.

Bummed barely scraped into most magazines' end of year polls. Only *NME* had the album in its Top 20.

Just as Happy Mondays themselves had started to take their music seriously, and believe for the first time that their band could be big, it seemed that other people were losing interest. In the Christmas editions of the music papers, only one person picked *Bummed* as their favourite album of the year. It was Creation Records' MD Alan McGee. Asked who he would most liked to have been during 1988, McGee made another unusual admission. He wished he had been Bez.

Part Two

EIGHT
The Future

In 1989, Happy Mondays created Madchester, The Stone Roses became the most important band in Britain and live music venues across the country fell into crisis as tens of thousands of teenagers stopped going to gigs and chose instead to spend their time in clubs and their money on drugs. Ironically, having been instrumental in proving (in London at least) that liking guitar groups and being into house music didn't have to be mutually exclusive, for much of the year, Happy Mondays found themselves caught between both camps. Their Ecstasy-addled songs alienated rock audiences, while the clubbers who did understand their music no longer attended traditional gigs.

'For months, it was going mad for the band in London and Manchester,' says Barrett, 'but nowhere else in the country got into them at all. The people who did turn up at their gigs in other cities came only out of curiosity. Most of them didn't even dance. In London, warehouse parties had been mixing up different styles of music for years, so there was an audience almost ready made for the Mondays. In Manchester, the lines between rock and dance had been blurred for some time by the likes of A Certain Ratio and a group called Laugh, which later became Intastella. So the band had this really hip club crowd in London, the flare-wearing indie students back home and virtually no one anywhere else.'

Happy Mondays was by no means the only British band fusing rock and dance. However, until the release only a year before of New Order's European disco anthem 'Blue Monday', few guitar groups had strayed from the standard indie template established by the likes of The Smiths in the early 1980s. Now records by The Shamen, The Stone Roses, KLF and The Beloved, all rooted in rock, were spilling over on to the dancefloor. Moreover, the release in February of New Order's Ibizan-influenced album *Technique* (launched with a show at Birmingham's NEC, with Happy Mondays and 808 State as support) put Manchester firmly at the centre of the scene.

'By the time *Technique* came out,' says Sumner, 'the audience at New Order gigs – in the north at least – had completely changed. We'd lost loads of the serious, spotty students from our Joy Division days and were attracting a much bigger casual crowd. Certainly in Manchester we were suddenly the band for football fans to be into. That suited us fine. It also suited the Mondays. It was obvious that that was where their big fanbase was going to be found.'

With erratic performances and notoriously short sets, Happy Mondays hardly helped to ingratiate themselves with wary audiences outside of London and Manchester. A short tour of Ireland in March won them few new fans after the band could scarcely be bothered to play even their recent singles. En route to Belfast, Bez had been detained at Manchester airport after officials discovered that he had recently spent time in prison for drugs offences. Without Bez beside him on stage, Shaun didn't enjoy the shows and cut them as short as he could.

Nevertheless, the media in London loved the idea of a band bound to both rock'n'roll tradition and contemporary street culture. In terms of music, the press in particular latched on to the more technically proficient Stone Roses. Moreover, in singer Ian Brown, Stone Roses had a frontman whose beautiful face looked good on front covers. In terms of controversial copy, however, Happy Mondays had no competition. *Bummed* may not have been a commercial success, but as a tide of drug taking literally washed over the country, the pill-popping Mondays themselves became increasingly of interest.

'Since the Summer Of Love, the press had been searching for a band to represent this incredible new youth culture,' says Barrett. 'The problem with a lot of the dance acts was that they wanted to remain faceless. They were taking all the right drugs, going to the right clubs and introducing all these exciting, new, American influences to British music, but if they talked at all, they were often pretty dull.'

To the new breed of musicians and DJs, the whole point of house was that it had come from the streets. Any kid from whatever city, perhaps without much money, could create their own house music, just for themselves or their friends if that's what they wanted. The E revolution had taken youth culture out of the hands of a posh, privileged few from central London and given it back to the masses, just as punk had promised (but failed) to do a decade earlier. The media, however, thrives on stars and the public needs recognisable faces to catch its attention. Consequently, the Mondays were perfect. They embodied the outrageous, scandal-ridden sex'n'drink'n'drugs excess of traditional rock'n'roll, but they updated it for an impending new decade. Had Happy Mondays been artificially made, they could hardly have fitted the changing times any better.

'The Mondays were so naturally right it was incredible,' says Barrett. 'Had I not been involved with them, I might have wondered if at least a little of it was contrived.'

'The way the whole drugs thing got started,' says Shaun, 'was that when we were doing our first interviews, we sat there skinning up. That was normal for us. We were used to sitting in our pubs in Manchester, smoking joints, hanging out with mates who were pissed or tripping out on acid. When the interviews came out, they were never about what we'd said. They were all about what we had done. At the time, that's just how we were living. If anyone wanted a line of speed, because of where we were from, we would chop 'em out straight away. We didn't realise journalists would be shocked and run off home to write about it. It didn't occur to us that other people didn't do exactly the same themselves.'

'From a press point of view, the Mondays had a real innocence about them,' says Barrett. 'They didn't read the music papers like other bands. Most of the indie/C86 groups around at the time were weaned on the *NME*, they had a rock heritage. The Mondays didn't care what was written about them. Shaun found it funny to read what he was supposed to have been up to, but none of them were really arsed. The only time there was a problem was when Paul Davis phoned me up one night, screaming that *Melody Maker* had referred to him as Knobhead. Of course, everyone knew him as Knobhead. He said no one called him that. He demanded that a retraction be printed the following week. Fortunately, I think he forgot about it by then.

'I turned the fact that they had such a naive attitude to our advantage. Journalists had never interviewed musicians like them before. A lot of them had never even met people from their background before. The Mondays were working-class lads on the blag and I let people be complete voyeurs to their lifestyle. I remember Bez and Shaun doing their first batch of interviews for me in a pub in Clerkenwell Road. After half a dozen or so, they came out and asked why it was only students who wanted to talk to them. As far as Shaun and Bez were concerned, journalists were as alien to them as they were to the journalists.

'When more and more drugs – and especially pills – came on the scene, I just let the press wander into the band's dressing room and watch what was going on. They couldn't believe their eyes. It was like introducing them to another world. At that time, it was really risqué even to be seen smoking spliff. I guess I was exploiting the band's naivety, but it worked.

'I'm sure that none of the Mondays were aware of the impact they had on outsiders. It was easy to forget when you got to know them, because they actually were incredibly charming, but they really did look like criminals. And maybe they were. I could also forget that seeing Bez for the first time invariably freaked the fuck out of people. They'd be like, "What is he doing? Is he dancing? Is he okay? Is he putting it on? Is he just totally deranged?" By the end of the year, of course, all the kids were copying him.

'The fact that the Mondays were in fact quite sweet, very charming individuals seemed to make the situation worse. Because of how they looked and spoke and acted, people expected them to be thick and rude and arrogant and not giving a fuck. But they were always so polite. They'd offer drinks to everyone they met. Not that they actually had any money, but they meant it none the less.'

Despite the frequent music press features and a healthy loyal following, the Happy Mondays continued to insist that the band shouldn't be taken seriously. 'Their day-to-day lifestyle hadn't changed a lot,' says Barrett. 'It was still largely scoring draw and rehearsing, then getting in a van and doing the odd gig and maybe going out to a club. But their attitude was definitely different. They never saw Happy Mondays as a career, until it obviously was, but they all clearly wanted to be in that band. They would say it was just to pass the time, but that was more than a little glib. They enjoyed it and they knew they were good. They never realised how good though, I don't think.'

For months, videomakers the Bailey Brothers had been scripting a feature-length film, tentatively titled *Mad Fuckers* and set in the not-too-distant future, about speed-crazed joyriders from Salford. For no reason other than they thought it was cool, the Bailey Brothers wanted crazed Scottish country singer Karl Denver, who had been based in Manchester for some years, to appear in their movie. To introduce Denver to the Factory set-up, it was mooted that Happy Mondays invite him to guest on their forthcoming single, a re-recorded version of 'Lazyitis'.

Shaun loved the idea. He had often asked pub singers to join him on stage because he admired their uncontrived attitude. Moreover, he had been unhappy with the version of 'Lazyitis' that had appeared on *Bummed*. Duetting with Denver on vocals, he reckoned, would give the track more of the toy pop feel he had originally hoped for. Denver agreed to collaborate with the band and, in April, he and Shaun went into a studio and literally sparred vocally over the chorus of the song, later re-titled 'Lazyitis (One Armed Boxer)'. The following month, with the single due for release, Barrett set up a feature for *NME*, in which Happy Mondays would meet up with Denver in Jersey, where the country singer was performing in a cabaret club.

'Karl was doing some spring season in Jersey, which he apparently did every year without fail,' says Barrett. 'He was an odd old bloke. He'd always stay at the same bed & breakfast that belonged to this old dear that he liked. He was very set in his ways, but also really sweet. I thought the version of "Lazyitis" that the Mondays had done with him was one of the best things they had ever recorded.

'The idea for the feature was to take *NME* out to Jersey to interview Karl and the band together and do the photos in Karl's cabaret club. The Mondays had done a show at Kilburn National Ballroom the previous night and were due to fly out a few hours before us in the morning. As soon as I arrived on the island with the journalist, I found out that Shaun had been nicked at the airport for possession. I couldn't believe it.'

On searching Shaun's luggage, a female customs official on the Channel island had discovered a small polythene bag containing traces of cocaine. Shaun was arrested immediately, but let out on bail the following day under orders to report to Swinton police station twice a week for the foreseeable future.

'It was mad,' says Barrett. 'I had no idea how to explain to the press why Shaun wasn't with the rest of the band. It was a situation I had never been in before. I no longer felt that drugs were an exploitable issue. You can't keep having fun with drugs stories when you're dealing with a working group, which is what the Mondays were by then. Drugs can start to seriously interfere with business.

'Of course the story got out, but not from me. At this stage, the Manchester press in particular were taking a big interest in the band. The guys from the *Evening News* knew they could flog on a good Mondays story to the nationals and make some money. It was a pain in the arse. I remember the bust happened on a Friday because I was supposed to be off to my brother's in Devon. Instead, I had to issue a statement on behalf of Factory and deal with all the Fleet Street and Associated News people. I think I blamed it all on Karl Denver.'

So did Shaun. In an interview recorded later for Granada TV, Shaun and Karl were asked to explain what had happened in Jersey. Shaun said he had been prepared to risk time in jail to take cocaine over to the island at Karl's request. Denver simply smiled, then claimed that he had never even taken an aspirin in his life. Nine months later, the case finally came to court. After ten minutes, the charges against Shaun were dropped after a judge ruled that the amount of cocaine left in the bag wasn't enough to warrant a guilty verdict.

Over the summer, Happy Mondays toured almost non-stop. Although still hit-and-miss and invariably shambolic, their shows were gaining in confidence. Shaun in particular had begun to feel far more comfortable in front of an audience. Sporting his latest fashion purchase – huge, round, brown-tinted sunglasses – he had taken to playing either tambourine or maracas throughout the set. He was also becoming increasingly animated on stage, dancing alongside Bez and jumping on top of other band members or hitting them over the head with his maracas.

Happy Mondays treated tours – particularly tours outside the UK – as little more than a reason to party. In July, they shared a bill at a festival in Valencia in Spain with Liverpool's The La's, baggy wannabes Inspiral Carpets and unknowns The Pop Guns.

'The Mondays had a couple of days off in Valencia,' says Barrett, 'so I went out there to join them for a bit of a holiday. It was a beautiful place and the venue for the gig was an open-roofed club that went on all night. By this stage, the band had given me a nickname. I was to be Foxhead, or Foxy or Fox, because I had long, reddish hair at the time. Having a nickname meant you were one of their mates.

'On the first night, Bez asked if I could get them any pills. I ended up scoring some mescaline instead. It was really proper, beautiful stuff.'

Shaun spent the night doing drugs, then just as the sun was rising in the morning, passed out on the beach. He woke up eight hours later, having spent the afternoon unconscious in full sunlight and temperatures of up to a hundred degrees.

Happy Mondays eventually appeared to top the British bill at the Barracas bar at 7am the next morning. They played four songs in little over ten minutes.

'Shaun was so badly burned that he couldn't move at all on stage,' says Barrett. 'He was standing trying not to let his trousers touch his skin because it was so sore. In his defence, he was doing the best he could. Midway through the show, though, Gaz somehow managed to throw himself backwards off his drum kit. He fell six feet off the stage. The rest of the band rushed over, but Shaun could only just turn around. That set him off. He really began to berate Gary. He was shouting, "Get back on stage, you fuckin' wanker," and calling him a cunt. I thought it would all end in tears, but as usual, it was just bickering, not actual scrapping. Besides, even Gaz doesn't kick a man with sunburn.'

For months, Happy Mondays worked incredibly hard without seeing any substantial increase in sales of their records.

'It was a mad, full schedule,' says Barrett. 'The band literally played wherever they were invited. Nathan was an excellent manager for them. He understood the game and was great at persuading the band that they should do certain gigs that they weren't keen on or talk to journalists that they didn't particularly like. He knew what to do because he knew what they were up to, far more than anyone else, it transpired. He was probably the only one to suss just how deep Shaun was into certain – how can I put this – stimulants.'

In late August, Happy Mondays made their second visit to America. Their first, after the release of *Squirrel And G-Man*, was a three-day trip to New York to play the Limelight Club. The band arrived on holiday visas, hired the only equipment they could afford and booked into the notorious Chelsea Hotel. The gig was so bad that they trashed the set after the show, then ended up in trouble with the police for refusing to adhere to laws against drinking in the street.

The second trip was organised by Happy Mondays' US label, Elektra, which had put together a package of its artists, lead by The Pixies, to tour club venues and visit college radio stations together. Just days after the tour began in New York, an article appeared in the *New York Times* detailing Shaun's exploits since arriving in America. Having been picked up by a record company rep at JFK airport (where he stole a leather jacket from the duty free shop), the singer had insisted on being driven to Harlem to buy some Ecstasy. The rep refused to come along and dropped both Shaun and Bez off a mile from their destination. Shaun reckoned the area would be on a par with the red-light district of Amsterdam, where he had lived for six months. He was wrong.

'In Harlem,' he says, 'they don't mug you if they want your trainers. They shoot you, then they take them. The first bloke we met there was sound. He took us to his place and introduced us to crack, which we had never tried before. We bought some gear from him, then left. Outside in the street, I was just trying to skin up when this gang of mad black kids appeared. One of them seemed to think I was spitting at him. Next thing I knew, there was a gun out and a broken Budweiser bottle at my throat. I'd have been frightened if I hadn't been so fuckin' out of it.'

The paper also reported that Shaun had almost missed the gig because he was having his stomach pumped out. His brother Paul, however, would later deny the claim, insisting that Shaun only went into hospital to have some shots for the clap.

In Cleveland, Bez returned a badly damaged hire car, which he claimed had been smashed by a gang of baseball bat-wielding dealers. In LA, an audience which included David Bowie, Axl Rose and The Beastie Boys turned up to see Happy Mondays play while stoned on weed that they likened to LSD. At the aftershow party, Gaz – by now known for his generally insulting behaviour – spent twenty minutes pointing at David Bowie and calling him a midget, before telling him to his face that he had never realised the star was such a 'shortarse'. In a downtown club later that night, Shaun was accused of stealing a girl's drink. She stormed off screaming, only to return minutes later with a dozen Puerto Rican homeboys armed with knives. Shaun, however, reckons he wasn't bothered about the gang; all of them were well under five foot tall.

'I thought I would hate LA,' says Shaun, 'but I really loved it. I've smoked some strong weed, but nothing like the Mexican gear we got there. It was instant death. You had three pulls on it and you couldn't move your arms or legs. You couldn't breathe, you were just sat there dead, a paranoid cabbage trapped inside your own head.'

As well as sampling crack for the first time, Shaun tried out PCP. 'I had a good time on PCP but I can imagine flipping out on it,' he says. 'It sent me a bit mad. I was trying to lift up cars, lift up anything in fact. I remember walking down the street and trying to snatch the gold off black kids. I could have been shot.'

By the time the tour was over, the Mondays were claiming to have corrupted their Elektra associates and turned The Pixies on to angel dust. Perhaps they should have been more careful what they said. On the band's arrival back in Britain, the Special Branch were waiting to search them at the airport.

By the autumn of 1989, the appeal of massive outdoor raves and huge acid house parties had stretched from the south to cities and their suburbs across the country. In London, however, clubbers had long since tired of huge gatherings and knew that the most happening nights now took place in tiny venues in the centre of town. Small, underground organisations such as Boy's Own, a fanzine/club/independent dance label fronted by DJs Andy Weatherall and Terry Farley, were throwing parties for only a few hundred people. They were also trying to move the scene on from house's regimented requirements such as records with a 4/4 beat and kids clad in flares. In the capital, cutting-edge clubs like Shoom, Spectrum and the Future might follow an Italian disco track with dub or Derrick May, and be as likely to end the evening with The Woodentops as they would with Bomb The Bass.

'Shaun and Bez already knew most of the people involved in the London scene at that time,' says Barrett. 'They knew the guys on the doors, the promoters, all the Boy's Own lot. It was odd because no so-called "proper" bands were really part of the club scene down south. But the Mondays always knew exactly where to go. They were like any clued-up group of lads on a night out. They gravitated towards like-minded people.'

Since Shaun had been spending so many of his nights out in the UK in London clubs, he decided to invite a DJ from the capital to make some of Happy Mondays' songs more suited to the dancefloor, rather than simply ask Factory to employ a Hacienda resident. At the suggestion of London Records A&R and radio presenter Pete Tong, the Future's Paul Oakenfold and his production partner Steve Osborne were approached to remix 'Wrote For Luck'.

'I was already aware of the Happy Mondays through Mike Pickering,' says Oakenfold. 'I liked their music, I wouldn't have agreed to work with them otherwise. I'd also noticed Bez and his crew down at Future a few Thursday nights, although I'd never seen Shaun in the club.

'I liked the Mondays as a band because they were real. For me, they were the first group from a guitar background that the new youth could relate to. Lyrically, Shaun wrote about what was happening to kids across the country right at that time. Also their image and their attitude was bang up to date. They wore the same gear as everyone else in clubland, which doesn't sound at all odd now, but back then was brand new for an indie band. The Mondays acted like any normal bunch of lads, rather than some stuck-up pop stars, which was exactly what house music was trying to stamp out at the time.

'It was Nathan McGough who actually asked me and Steve to do the track. He said Shaun wanted a version of "Wrote For Luck" that would work in the clubs. The idea I had was to merge the song with hip hop because the Mondays' sound was quite loose anyway. I knew exactly how I wanted it to sound. I had tried something similar with Cabaret Voltaire a few months earlier, but it hadn't really happened. I was sure that by strengthening the bottom end of "Wrote For Luck", we could turn it into a record that the London club crowd would go mad for. The outcome, of course, was much bigger than that. The track basically created a new form of music and kick-started the whole indie-dance scene.'

'I remember going down to the Future the second we got a test pressing of "W.F.L.",' says Jeff Barrett. 'There were only three copies of the record in existence. I gave one to Terry Farley, who was on the decks when I went into the club. He put it straight on. The crowd went absolutely mental.'

Even Oakenfold himself was stunned by the incredible reaction to his remix. Meanwhile, Factory were so pleased that they decided to put the new version out as Happy Mondays' next single. Backed by a second remix – strangely by Erasure's Vince Clarke, who was a big fan of the band – 'Wrote For Luck' was retitled 'W.F.L.' and released just as the Mondays were due back in Britain from the US.

'Happy Mondays inject disco into the jaded nervous system of guitar pop,' *NME* said of the single. 'Both mixes strip the guitars from the track and turn it into a huge, loping, lazy, demented wet dream of a hypno-dance piece. Minimal techno effects spun around a couple of mesmeric chords and Shaun's dyslexic images and hectoring tone keep things edgy. Trippy enough in its own right to keep the Columbian drug barons out of work.'

'W.F.L.' may have been well-received, but it also divided the critics into two camps – those who had taken Ecstasy and those who hadn't. One journalist, clearly E-free, equated trying to dance to 'W.F.L.' with 'moving in mucus under the influence of an opium rectal suppository'. Tellingly, the review also stated that there wasn't much to choose between Paul Oakenfold and Vince Clarke's versions. The club crowd – including Happy Mondays – opted overwhelmingly for Oakenfold's mix. By the time they could buy the record in the shops, however, London clubbers were already dancing to another Mondays' track. Called 'Hallelujah', it was the lead single from the band's forthcoming EP, 'Madchester Rave On'. It was also to give Happy Mondays their first chart hit.

NINE
Can Of What?

The word Madchester first turned up on T-shirts in the summer of 1989. Factory Records took the term from the streets, copyrighted its use, then claimed to have coined it. Madchester was seized on straight away by the press. Thanks largely to The Stone Roses, the music media had grown almost obsessed with the city. Rumour had it that record companies were sending A&R teams to the area, under instructions not to return to London until they had signed at least one new 'baggy' band. Local acts that had existed for years without any attention suddenly found themselves at the centre of a vibrant scene. Inspiral Carpets was the first band to benefit. Their single 'Move' received rave reviews, while their T-shirts – regulation baggy with a cartoon cow's head on the front – became almost as popular as Stone Roses' shirts.

When Factory suggested that Happy Mondays' forthcoming four-track EP should be titled 'Madchester Rave On' (rather than 'Rave On', as was planned), Shaun wasn't sure. Neither he nor Bez spent much of their time in the city. They certainly didn't hang out at the Hacienda any more. Now approaching the peak of its popularity, the club no longer excited Shaun. It was only smaller venues in London such as Spectrum and the Future that appealed to him these days. The Hacienda had become a cattle-market, stuffed with the sort of people he had initially gone to the club to avoid.

Shaun's second problem with the Madchester tag was that Happy Mondays didn't see themselves as part of a scene. They admired The Stone Roses and thought of them as friends, but barely knew any of the other bands. Besides, even in the days when no one had been interested in their music, Happy Mondays hadn't tried to sell themselves on the back of any other artists. Now they rather objected to barely-formed bands cashing in on their hard-earned success.

'As far as I was concerned,' says Shaun, 'the only competition the Mondays ever had with the Roses, was over who had the most expensive clothes, and what county they came from.'

Indie-dance had its day on 13 November 1989. A coincidence of scheduling saw Stone Roses and Happy Mondays simultaneously release the most significant singles of their respective careers. Stone Roses' record was the double A-sided 'Fool's Gold/What The World Is Waiting For'. Happy Mondays' 'Madchester Rave On' EP, recorded at Richard Branson's Manor studios in Oxfordshire and produced by Martin Hannett, boasted four brand new tracks: 'Hallelujah', 'Holy Ghost', 'Clap Your Hands' and 'Rave On'. It was only six weeks since Happy Mondays had put out 'W.F.L.' but, to be honest, Factory had never imagined that those remixes would prove so popular. It was 'Rave On' which was supposed to have marked the band's move into dancefloor territory.

The Stone Roses' single was guaranteed to be a hit. Despite the band's sullen, arrogant, often difficult attitude, their music had found favour with the mainstream media, due in no small part to its strong 1960s influences. When 'Rave On' broke the Top 40, however, it came as a surprise. 'Hallelujah', the EP's lead track, was the first song from the band that Factory promotions person Nicki Kefalas had managed to get on daytime radio. Happy Mondays had previously recorded two John Peel sessions for BBC Radio 1 – the first in April 1986, prior to the release of 'Freaky Dancin'' and the second shortly after *Bummed* had come out. Neither had generated much interest from other programmes. The band's only TV appearances had been a short performance almost exactly a year ago on Tony Wilson's late-night music series, *The Other Side of Midnight*, broadcast only in the north of England, plus a slot on Channel 4 youth show *Club X*.

'"Hallelujah" was the first Mondays' record that daytime radio picked up on,' says Kefalas. 'Obviously, prior to that, awareness of the band had been building and several programmers did think that the music was interesting, but none would actually stick their neck out. They all found Shaun's vocals very difficult to cope with. At the time, most guitar groups were trying to make perfect, poppy, instant radio records. It was the days of mainstream stations, including Radio 1, playing only totally straight, easily accessible singles. That was something I was quite involved in trying to change, through working with bands like the Mondays, New Order and Primal Scream. Until then, the most rebellious music on daytime would probably have been Jesus Jones.

'Since the day I started working with Factory, I had thought Happy Mondays were one of the most original bands I had ever heard. I loved a lot of the Factory roster, but the Mondays were special. They had that edge of nonconformism. Also the songs were very intelligent, which I don't think Shaun was given enough credit for. My whole attitude to plugging is that if it's really easy and obvious, I'm not that interested. Promoting the Mondays was difficult, but exciting. It took a long time to happen, but as soon as it did, it took off big time.'

One week after Happy Mondays and The Stone Roses simultaneously released singles, both bands were booked to make their debut *Top Of The Pops* appearance on the same show, alongside the likes of Jason Donovan.

'The Mondays had a party before, during and after the *Top Of The Pops* show,' says Kefalas. 'They were good mates with the Roses. There was no competition between them because they both felt that their music was going in different directions. If Shaun was nervous about the show, he never let on. He was always confident though. People thought he was cool whatever he did and the band looked incredibly sexy on stage, which very few groups do. They were just so unhinged and interesting. They put a lot of effort into how they looked, not in the same way that other people do of course.'

Backstage at *Top Of The Pops*, the only conflict between the Mondays and the Roses was what to put on the beatbox in their communal dressing room. The Roses' singer Ian Brown wanted to listen to The Beatles, but Shaun replaced his tape with The House Sound Of Chicago. There was also a matter of matching shirts. Gaz Whelan and Ian Brown had both bought the same new shirt for the show. Neither would change.

Reporting from the programme, for an article to be published in the *Face*, journalist and musician Nick Kent considered the similarities and differences between Happy Mondays and The Stone

Roses. They hung out in the same clubs, wore the same clothes and had been influenced by the same bands. In Martin Hannett, the pair had even shared the same producer. Hannett's work on an early version of 'I Wanna Be Adored', however, had disappointed The Stone Roses and he had been replaced by John Leckie.

Ultimately, Kent's observations suggested that the difference between the bands was more pronounced than the similarity. Where Happy Mondays were straightforward and upfront, the Roses were studied and secretive. Where the Mondays were open and honest, the Roses were standoffish and evasive. Bez boasted that he had been so out of it the previous evening, he had set his own bed on fire with a spliff without even noticing. Speaking on behalf of The Stone Roses, manager Gareth Evans insisted on pointing out that his charges didn't do drugs, nor were they keen to be associated with anyone who had. The most marked contrast, however, appeared to be between Shaun and Ian Brown. Shaun was simple to read. He always made his point quickly and didn't try to be clever. Brown, on the other hand, was a spiritual, complex character with an agenda which was difficult to decipher. While Shaun traded on his roots and thrived on his lack of formal education, Brown tried to play down the importance of either.

'The Happy Mondays were lumped in with The Stone Roses because of the geography and because both bands came out of the same cultural revolution,' says Barrett. 'But no one else at the time was doing what the Mondays were. They had gone from being a good group to such a fuckin' great group. Of course there were comparisons with the Roses and even Shaun would say that if he could make an album as good as The Stone Roses' debut, he would be a happy man. The Roses are one of my favourite groups of all time, but they didn't have what the Mondays had. Live, they couldn't even begin to compete. The Mondays' shows were untouchable because you never knew what was going to happen next. It was really dirty and funky and very fuckin' sexy.

'The best thing about Happy Mondays was that they came through so naturally and beautifully. Journalists would interview them and ask if they had been listening to Can. They'd say, "Can of what?" They had no idea. People said "Hallelujah" was a rip-off of "Hallelujah" by Can. The name was a coincidence. Shaun couldn't have been that contrived, even if he had tried. He might namecheck

A Certain Ratio or Orange Juice, but it would never be a band like Can.'

In order to appear on *Top Of The Pops*, Happy Mondays had to cancel two shows on their UK tour. When they were rebooked, demand for tickets had soared and new, much larger venues had to be booked. Shortly after the start of the tour in early November, photographer brothers Peter and Ian Davies had joined the band on the road.

'We were just beginning to take photos at the time,' says Ian Davies. 'Happy Mondays were the first big band we had worked with. Peter and I already knew the Ryders from school. Shaun had been three years above us at St Marks, Paul was one year above us and their aunt had taught us in primary three. Also, we had big brothers who hung out with the Carrolls, who were well-known in Swinton, which was where we lived.

'We had seen posters for *Bummed* plastered all over the city centre and there had been loads of kids wearing Happy Mondays T-shirts for ages, but we never even realised that Shaun and Paul were in the band. None of their artwork or covers ever used pictures of the band themselves, so you could be aware of the music, but have no idea what they looked like. It was only when we met Paul one night in some grotty, druggy little club in Moss Side that he mentioned he was in the Mondays. We hadn't seen either him or Shaun for two or three years before that. We'd both got on really well with Paul at school though. Peter had this boxing game that he used to bring in that Paul always wanted to play.

'A couple of days later, we contacted Nathan McGough about the possibility of doing photos. We wanted to get involved in whatever was going on in Manchester. We then went to see the band play in Wigan, just to get an idea of what the shows were like. The gig was amazing. Everyone was dancing and there was a real party vibe and a sense of excitement and occasion. It wasn't like a typical rock show at all. We found it really refreshing. We'd stopped going to big gigs when it was all stadium bands like Simple Minds who seemed to be on a different planet from the audience. The Mondays made you feel like you were as much a part of the show as they were. Afterwards, we bumped into all these people we hadn't seen for years, who were all mates of our big brothers, and Shaun said it was okay for us to join their tour.'

The first Happy Mondays gig that the Davies brothers attended as official photographers was at Manchester's Free Trade Hall, a 2000-capacity venue which had had its rock heyday in the 1970s and was now home to the city's Hallé Orchestra. Factory had asked if seats in the Free Trade Hall could be removed for the show, but the request was denied. Shaun said he hoped the crowd would just rip them out anyway. That night, before the support set from MC Buzz B, fights broke out in the queue to get in as a guestlist of 700 was torn up by the bouncers and even the press were left standing outside. The skirmishes continued when a group of lads were caught flogging bootleg band T-shirts outside the entrance. It later transpired that they were mates of the Mondays.

'Shaun quickly got wise to the fact that he could make money – a lot of money – on the side if the band got big,' says Barrett. 'I couldn't tell you exactly what he was up to. Let's just say there was a lot of people hanging around with the band who I never ever saw inside the venue before they came on stage.'

At the Free Trade Hall show, Shaun spent most of the set sitting on the edge of the drum kit. He looked shattered.

'Shaun had no stage presence whatsoever,' says Ian Davies. 'He just loped about the stage with a bottle of beer in his hand, sometimes playing the tambourine or the maracas. He was no George Michael either. His performance was all about attitude. He didn't sing, he shouted words over the music. It was rock'n'roll poetry, and it reminded me a lot of John Cooper Clarke, who was quite a big name on the Manchester scene at the time.

'Doing photos of the Mondays was a brilliant opportunity for us because access to the band was always excellent. We could wander freely wherever we wanted, even across the stage. In fact, sometimes Shaun would actually pull us up from the pit to stand beside him for a couple of songs. He'd get us to take pictures of the audience, which was a great idea because it really hyped them up.'

'On one occasion,' recalls Peter Davies, 'I was up on stage, bent over, shooting Shaun. As he moved, I started to edge backwards. What I didn't know was that I was edging straight towards this explosive device that was hidden in the bottom of a bin. It was triggered to go off near the end of the show and my backside was right over it. Suddenly, Nathan jumped up on stage and pulled me away. Literally seconds later it went off. He had got to me just in time. Any later and it would have exploded right up my arse. I still look on Nathan as someone who saved my life. Of course, it was typical of the Mondays to have something that dangerous just lying about the stage.'

A little to the band's dismay, Happy Mondays were now attracting a predominately student audience. At least, however, a substantial proportion of them were women.

'It was a mix of a club crowd and a student crowd, all fairly young,' says Ian Davies. 'There did seem to be as many screaming women as men, although it was generally the men who did all the dancing. Some of the people were completely crazy, most were heavily out of it on drugs. Our audience shots were incredible. Since then, we've been down the front at major festivals and been on stage with bands like R.E.M. We've still never photographed anything like it.'

The Free Trade Hall show was one of the few Happy Mondays' gigs attended by Shaun's mum. She watched some of the set, but spent most of the time in the dressing room downstairs with her sisters and other family relations.

'Shaun's mum did come to a couple of gigs, but only early on,' says Jeff Barrett. 'I remember that whenever she turned up, she was with loads of his aunties and cousins. They were a big Irish family. When the Mondays started to get famous, I never saw her at all, not even at the aftershows in Manchester. Derek probably didn't like her being around. I'm sure he didn't want her to see what he and the boys were up to.'

'I don't recall ever seeing Shaun's mum,' says Dave Harper. 'I spoke to her on the phone a lot though and she was always very friendly and courteous. I used to have to ring constantly to find out where either Shaun or Derek were. I could understand if Derek tried to keep her away after he became the band's road manager. When he was just mixing the sound on stage, he wasn't too bad. It was when he went off on tour with them that he started to lose it. It wasn't entirely his fault. Anyone would have ended up like that on the road all the time with the Mondays. Derek took to it like a duck to water. It was quite an amusing sight to see. Here was this little, short bloke with long grey hair, who looked sixty-five even though he wasn't, off his head on drugs, dancing about behind his son.

'What a weird situation for Shaun's mum to be in though, if she knew – and surely she must have done – that Derek and her two sons were all doing drugs together. She wouldn't have been slightly pessimistic in thinking that, at any moment, the phone would ring to say that at least one of her family was dead. I can't imagine how she got through it. Very bizarre.'

Shaun's eighteen-year-old girlfriend Trish would also be discouraged from attending a lot of the later shows.

'The better known the Mondays became,' says Barrett, 'the more the women started hanging around Shaun. He totally loved all the female attention. But it wasn't just because the band was getting famous that they liked him. Shaun has loads of charisma. He's a cool guy and quite a charmer. A lot of ladies were also attracted by the Mondays' rough working-class background, which was still unusual for a pop band at the time. They liked the fact that, on stage, this bunch of lads looked – and probably were – quite hard, but in the flesh were rather sweet and always polite, particularly to women.

'The Mondays' own set-up was always very macho though. Wherever they went, there was a bunch of lads with them, usually the biggest fuckin' motley crew you ever saw. They scared the shit out of me at first. We're talking ugly guys with major scars here. They might only have been sixteen-year-old kids, but you still didn't want to knock their drink over. I'm absolutely convinced they were dangerous people, but they were always very pleasant to me, no doubt due to my standing with the band.'

'The Mondays had dozens of dodgy hangers-on,' says Ian Davies. 'After the shows, there would be sixty or seventy people in the backstage area, all doing some sort of drug. Nigel Pivaro was around a lot too, and a few local, minor-league celebrities. There was always a party after a gig. People would be lying across the floor of the dressing room or sitting propped up against the walls, chatting and smoking. Shaun would make sure there was a ghettoblaster to hand. He played a lot of black music like Funkadelic and Sly Stone, or he'd put on acid house compilations.

'Sometimes the Mondays and their mates would all drive back from a gig to Manchester to go out clubbing, usually to the Hacienda. If we ever went with them, it was total access all the way. Whichever club they chose, you didn't pay, you didn't queue up, you just walked into VIP areas. I remember once, in the Hacienda, we were photographing Shaun and Bez just standing at the bar. Suddenly there was a real fuss and the security came over and tried to confiscate our cameras. It turned out that not only did we have shots of Shaun, but also – by accident – some major names on the Manchester drug dealing scene.'

By late 1989, hysteria over acid house in Thatcher's Britain was reaching a peak. Daily tabloid reports on the dangers of Ecstasy were encouraging authorities to make knee-jerk reactions and seemingly permitting the police to abuse their position of power. Legal, well-organised, members-only raves such as Sunrise and Back To The Future were as likely to be shut down – often before they had even begun – as illegal events. Despite the promotions company behind large-scale parties like Sunrise having already won two separate court cases against local councils to establish the fact that its organisation was operating within the law, its sold-out, end-of-year extravaganza was cancelled for apparently no reason by authorities at the eleventh hour. One month earlier, promoters of a boat party in Greenwich, at which Ecstasy was discovered during a raid, were arrested along with a drug dealer. The dealer was later sentenced to four years, while the organisers all received prison terms of up to ten years.

Across the country, writs were flying between party promoters and district councils, with both claiming to have only the interests of the kids at heart. In December, the Home Office announced proposed changes in the law to allow event organisers to receive fines of up to £140,000 and prison sentences of up to six months for any infringement of the Public Entertainments Act. A breach in the act would also entitle authorities to any profits made and allow them to seize all equipment on site, thereby making it impossible for the promoter to use an established hire company in the future. Aided by both the Home Office and the Department of the Environment, the UK's Association of District Councils issued a press release regarding what it referred to as 'the acid house party problem'. It suggested more than twenty changes to the law in order to stamp out raves, most importantly one which required private parties to be licensed in the same way as public events, ie. only with the co-operation of the local council.

Attempts by the police to infiltrate both promotions

organisations and the parties themselves had long been legendary. Sporting bandannas, smiley T-shirts and sandals a year after any self-respecting raver had moved on to more mundane fashion statements, undercover officers could scarcely have seemed more conspicuous. Now, forces throughout England were setting up their own units specifically to track down and stop any gatherings of people – almost regardless of scale – intending to dance to music with repetitive beats. According to a report in the *Sunday Telegraph*, a special intelligence unit had been set up in Gravesend, with an incident room of around twenty detectives from a dozen counties working full-time on the problem. The report also claimed that an 'acid house rapid deployment task force' of 250 officers was costing taxpayers £20,000 every Saturday night.

Writing in the *Face* on the fight for the right of young people to party, editor Sheryl Garratt interviewed the dubiously extreme right-wing MP for Luton South, Graham Bright, who had volunteered to helm a group of Tory politicians trying to push the proposed new anti-party laws through parliament as quickly as possible. Bright was best known for having helped pass strict new legislation against the distribution of video nasties, a crime he equated to the organisation of illegal raves.

'I'm always interested in protecting young people,' Bright explained to Garratt in the article. 'That is my main motive here. I've gone to pains to point out that I'm only after illegal house parties. This doesn't affect things like the tennis club barbecue or the Boy Scouts.'

Predictably, music-related activities in Manchester came under close scrutiny. With an over-eager local authority to boot, the city was one of the worst hit by the clampdowns.

'We had James Anderton in charge of our police force then,' says Bernard Sumner. 'The guy was a fanatic, determined to stamp out after-hours drinking or enjoyment of any sort. He would come down heavy even if it was only six or seven people having a party. I remember a friend of mine had a barbecue one afternoon in his back garden. There were literally half a dozen people there. The police turned up and stopped it. That is honestly how heavy it got. But Anderton's men were definitely watching certain individuals. They'd follow them around and try to infiltrate gangs. They knew everything my mates and I were doing, from where we'd meet up for a night out and at what time, to plans for birthday parties and barbecues.'

In December, the Hacienda was told to chose whether it wanted to open late on either Christmas Eve or New Year's Eve. It had to be one or the other.

'I went to a warehouse party that New Year,' says Sumner. 'There were probably only a few hundred people in there when the place was raided. Outside, the venue had been surrounded by about 500 police and there was a helicopter with searchlights hovering overhead. The clampdowns had been happening for ages, but that really did mark the end of an era. It was also the start of real violence in the city. The good times went out and the guns came in.'

TEN

To Wembley, The European Way

The British music press began a new decade obsessed with The Stone Roses. The group topped every critic's end of year poll. Not only were they dubbed best band and best live act, their debut album and the singles 'Fool's Gold' and 'She Bangs The Drum' were reckoned to be 1989's top records. They were destined to be as big as U2, everybody said so. Significantly, Happy Mondays' one end-of-year award – 'W.F.L' as best club track – was voted for not by critics, but by ordinary fans.

Madchester showed no sign of abating. A record company rush was on to sign The Charlatans, who had been together only a little over three months. Endless column inches were devoted to undeserving, barely formed bands such as Northside and The High, thanks only to the Manc connection. Bernard Sumner's new band, Electronic, a collaboration with former Smiths guitarist Johnny Marr, scored a Top 10 hit with its debut single, 'Getting Away With It'. Meanwhile, New Order were asked to write England's World Cup theme. An unsubstantiated claim that the track was titled 'E Is For England' (the lyrics were by Keith Allen, after all) later caused havoc in the tabloid press. Happy Mondays, however, continued to disassociate themselves with Manchester.

'We knew that people were bound to get sick of Manchester bands soon,' says Shaun. 'There was no danger in that for us because we had always distanced ourselves from everyone else. We started the scene, but we hadn't been a part of it since the early days.

'We didn't even get worked up over all the new bands getting massive deals because it was just too daft. It was good for the lads who hadn't had anything to do before, but at the same time it was stupid. They were being signed up for years when they had only been together a few weeks. It was obvious that only about two out of the thirty or so signed had got anything, or were going to have anything.

'I could laugh it off because I'm not a jealous person, but I hated seeing groups of kids who were a load of shit getting a deal and then their attitude totally changing. They'd get big heads and start mouthing off, thinking they were fuckin' popstars. Bands like Inspiral Carpets, they were just dickheads.'

Just one month after the release of the 'Madchester Rave On' EP, Shaun insisted that the record be deleted and replaced with 'Rave On Madchester – The Remixes'.

Following the success of Paul Oakenfold's version of 'Wrote For Luck', both he and fellow London DJ Andy Weatherall had been asked to remix tracks from the EP. With Terry Farley, Oakenfold had worked on 'Rave On'. However, it was Weatherall's take on 'Hallelujah', sub-titled 'Factory Remix The Southern Way', that dominated clubland. Weatherall, who had never before worked on a rock record, stripped away some of Shaun's vocal, beefed up the sound with a techno backing track and added snippets of Handel's *Messiah* throughout the intro and chorus. Big-name producer Steve Lillywhite was also invited to contribute a 'Hallelujah' remix to the new EP, after his wife, singer Kirsty MacColl, who contributed backing vocals to the track, was quoted in an interview saying that Happy Mondays were her favourite band. It was Weatherall's version though, that Shaun liked best. It was the only one, he said, that got him up to dance.

Because 'Rave On Madchester – The Remixes' was essentially a re-release, few music papers bothered to review the record. Writing for *NME*, however, journalist Jack Barron, who had come from the same guitar background as Happy Mondays and now hung out in the same London clubs, devoted much of his singles page to Weatherall's 'Hallelujah'.

'Youth culture quite bluntly changed in 1989 and it's so sodding exciting,' noted Barron. 'For myself and thousands of others, the change has meant being able to dance to Happy Mondays one minute, and NWA the next. Happy Mondays themselves have known about this for years. Stone Roses might sell greater quantities of records because their music is prettier and more accessible, but it is the Mondays who embody the new culture.

'This remix is an amazing first attempt by London's most groundbreaking DJ of the moment. It is also incredibly important, partly because Andrew Weatherall is from London. Right now, everyone is going overboard on anything Mancunian. The last Manc patriots you will find – despite the bluster – are Happy Mondays. The new youth culture may be more concentrated in Manchester, which explains why it has been the catalyst. But sure as eggs are fried, there is going to be an almighty explosion of rock-based music in dance clubs in London in 1990.'

For Happy Mondays, 1990 began with an offer which was to change their lives. The turn of the decade had marked the fortieth anniversary of the band's American label, Elektra. As part of its birthday celebrations, Elektra decided to compile an album of their back catalogue. Titled *Rubaiyat*, the project would consist of two boxed sets, each containing two CDs. The first set would be tracks by original artists such as The Seekers, The Doors and Queen; the second covers of their songs by contemporary signings. The Cure chose to reprise The Doors' 'Hello I Love You' and Tracy Chapman did 'House Of The Rising Sun'.

Shaun was initially set on Happy Mondays covering a Tom Waits track. However, when Elektra sent over a tape of possible material, he changed his mind. The Mondays would cover the slightly obscure 'He's Gonna Step On You', originally a No. 4 UK hit for South African artist John Kongos in 1971. Shaun had never heard the original of the song before, but he knew it was perfect. Once again, Paul Oakenfold was brought in. This time, however, he wouldn't remix a finished track, he would produce the band from the outset.

Happy Mondays' 'He's Gonna Step On You' turned out better than had been expected. A deeply funky, instantly unforgettable laid-back dance track, the song managed to be at once chart pop friendly and club cool. Before the record had even been heard by Factory, Shaun had come to a decision. The song was too good to be buried on an Elektra compilation which was only to be brought out in the US. Happy Mondays were keeping the track. It would be their next single.

'Elektra were majorly pissed off when the Mondays wouldn't give them the track,' says Eric Longley, Factory's accountant at the time. They needed the band's contribution to complete their album and they knew that it must have been good if they wanted to keep it themselves. I'm sure that soured their relationship with Elektra for the future.

'The label had really tried to push Happy Mondays in the States the previous year, when they sent them off on tour with The Pixies. Obviously it was the wrong time and the band themselves weren't into it either, but Elektra never tried again after the "Step On" incident. It's a shame because I'm sure the Mondays could have been huge there. And despite what Shaun may say, they did want to be. Shaun would have loved to play the big rock'n'roll star, with the Beverly Hills mansion and pool and shitloads of drugs.'

In the end, Happy Mondays' recorded another Kongos song, 'Tokoloshe Man', the singer's best-known hit, for *Rubaiyat*. It was good, but it wasn't 'Step On'. Not that Shaun cared. He had already collected the £1000 Omega watch he had been promised from Elektra for contributing to the album.

In late January, both Happy Mondays and The Stone Roses announced major UK dates. The Roses booked their first ever big show in the North, at Spike Island, off Widnes on Merseyside. Support DJs were to be Paul Oakenfold and the Hacienda's Dave Haslam. Happy Mondays were to play a full UK tour, culminating in a gig at London's Wembley Arena, in late March/early April. All the dates sold out instantly. The band's hometown show at the G-Mex centre oversold by 3000 and a second date was added. First, however, Happy Mondays were off to tour Europe, where their cult following was on the increase.

Combined with the energetic, adventurous new youth culture, the British government's strict anti-party action had seen trips to gigs abroad positively thrive. Once only the domain of fans of stadium acts such as Tina Turner, suddenly coach journeys to European cities simply for a show became massively popular with clubbers. When Happy Mondays arrived in Paris to play the 1000-capacity Bataclan club, literally hundreds of flare-wearing Mancunians had already descended on the city. At the end of the gig, Shaun invited them all back to the band's aftershow party at a club called La Luna.

'I remember Nathan booking the venue for that party from

Manchester,' says Eric Longley. 'He phoned up a few places we had heard of, then instead of asking what sort of music they played there, he asked what the kids' trousers looked like. He knew that if they said baggy, it was the right place to go. Nathan really understood the band and the scene at the time. That's what made him such a brilliant manager.'

The club that Nathan booked turned out to be a popular hang-out for Paris's gay community. It freaked out some of the fans, but it didn't bother the band, who partied there all night before getting back on their coach to head for Amsterdam. In fact, when in Europe, Happy Mondays often deliberately sought out predominately gay nightspots because they knew that they were bound to be wilder than the straight clubs, with better decor and more expensive sound systems.

From Holland, Happy Mondays headed to Spain, where they had been booked to do an extensive tour. Thanks to incompetent European promoters, however, some of their equipment failed to turn up at several of the venues and a number of dates were blown out. With two unexpected days off before their next show in Barcelona, the band and their entourage, all travelling on the same coach, decided to stop off in Stiges, a picturesque Spanish coastal town and resort for the rich, surrounded by mountains, which was widely regarded as the gay capital of the Mediterranean.

By the time Happy Mondays arrived in Barcelona, a large Manc contingent, most of whom just happened to be there on holiday, were already trying to blag tickets for the gig. Among them was Nigel Pivaro, clad in a pair of sixteen-inch flares and clutching a video camera, who had been taking a break at a resort nearby. Also in attendance was *NME* journalist Jack Barron, who was to meet up with the band at a studio in the afternoon for a playback of various new Oakenfold mixes of 'He's Gonna Step On You' and then travel with them throughout Europe for the following few days.

'The Mondays' show that night went off okay,' says Barron, 'although I seem to remember Bez's dancing scaring some of the Spaniards in the audience. It was after the show that the trouble started. The backstage area was raided by the police. I was just standing in the dressing room, then suddenly I was surrounded by loads of men in uniform. A number of people legged it immediately. Unfortunately, I wasn't one of them. In fact, if somebody hadn't pointed out to me that the place had been raided, I probably wouldn't have noticed. I was totally off my head. I spent several years in that state, sleep-walking basically. I don't remember if anyone was arrested on that occasion. I don't think they were.'

The following day, Happy Mondays were scheduled to shoot a video for their forthcoming single, re-titled simply 'Step On' by the time of its release. Videomakers Phil and Keith Bailey, aka the Bailey Brothers, were already on hand, having travelled with the band to Spain to do some filming for their long-delayed *Mad Fuckers* movie. Shaun insisted that everyone travel back to Stiges for the shoot.

'I never worked out why Shaun wanted to return to Stiges so much,' says Barron. 'Perhaps it was just because it's a really beautiful little town and great for discos. It was a crazy place though. There were lots of hard-looking geezers out walking their poodles and stuff like that. Totally bizarre.'

Shaun probably wanted to hook up with his old schoolfriend Nigel Pivaro, who was staying in the town's Hotel Subur Maritim. The Mondays checked into the same hotel, where the actor was waiting for them in reception, wearing a baggy sweatshirt emblazoned with the words, 'And On The Eighth Day God Created Manchester'. Barron reckoned he was starting to hallucinate, so when filming for the video began on the roof of the hotel, he opted to go into town with manager Nathan to buy some sandwiches.

'I went off in a van with Nathan and several others of the Mondays' entourage,' says Barron. 'It may have been my paranoia, but I think they were conspiring to kill me. They asked me to hold the door open all the way for absolutely no reason. Then the driver swerved wildly all over the road for miles, and eventually crashed straight into the side of a parked car. I'm sure Nathan asked him to crash on purpose. He thought it would have made for a good story.'

By the time Barron returned to the shoot (the video would later be described as a cross between a spaghetti western and *Miami Vice*), the huge neon letters spelling out HOTEL on the roof of the Subur Maritim had been vandalised. Shaun had snapped off some of the 'E' while climbing onto it for a photo. (The shot would prove to be the single most enduring image of Happy Mondays, even after their demise.) The 'L' had simply vanished. By the following morning, when the band set off to their next gig, the rest of the 'E' had gone. The sign read HOT.

'I travelled through a few European countries with the Mondays,' says Barron, 'and I have to tell you that I have never in my life been around a band that were so well sorted for whatever they wanted, whenever they wanted it, wherever they were. The Mondays put a lot of effort into having a good time, and all that that entails. Of course it helped that they had a background in dodgy mates. Actually, dodgy mates were their speciality. They were everywhere and they could literally get hold of an order in a matter of hours.

'I was amazed that the Mondays were never caught for trafficking drugs. They would be on a coach going through border patrol check-points in Europe with half of Columbia on board. They never panicked. They knew exactly where to hide the stash so that it wouldn't be found. They had probably hired experts in the field just for that purpose.'

Happy Mondays' final European tour destination before returning home for their British dates was Iceland. London's legendary Brain Club had organised a trip to the island for clubbers to coincide with the show, which was reported to be taking place at the Blue Lagoon, a well-known natural spa supposed to heal bathers of their ills with its warm waters. In fact, the gig happened in Reykjavik's local high school. It was a mess, memorable only for the sight of Shaun's dad dancing on stage in a plastic Viking helmet complete with horns. Derek's nickname temporarily morphed from Horseman to Norseman. Once again, Jack Barron was with the band.

'The show was in the school gymnasium,' he says. 'I remember most of the crowd looking totally confused. The Icelanders weren't into the drugs thing at all. As usual though, the band had brought a load of their mates with them, so it was bound to go off whatever. Before the gig even started there was bother. Some of Bez's friends had been out thieving round all the mega expensive shops in Reykjavik. I think they got chased through town by a bunch of irate sales assistants.'

The trouble continued after the show. Happy Mondays, their mates and the 100 or so Brain Club contingent from London moved on to the Moon Club, where Manchester musician A Guy Called Gerald was playing. For no apparent reason other than he looked odd, Bez was attacked on the dancefloor by three drunken Icelandic men, one of whom bit him in the thigh. By the time the band entourage had jumped in to help Bez, the rest of the locals had decided to declare war on the English.

'I think I might know what happened there,' says Barron. 'There were scores of really beautiful women in the club that the Mondays' mates couldn't keep their eyes off. Then this one woman walked past who they didn't reckon was quite up to standard. They all started shouting derogatory comments at her. To be honest, if I remember correctly, she was a bit grim. Anyway, it didn't go down too well with the men in the club. It turned out she was the reigning Miss World at the time and they were all dead proud of her.

'We all flew back to Heathrow the next morning. Even that ended in a fight. Some guy on the plane was really mithering Shaun and Muzzer asked him not to. He wouldn't, so Muzzer told him to fuck off. The bloke still wouldn't leave Shaun alone. In the end, Muzzer just walked up to him in the middle of the aisle and nutted him. There was blood everywhere. The captain threatened to land the plane in Glasgow, but as usual Shaun managed to sweet-talk his way out of any trouble.'

Happy Mondays returned to England just days before their G-Mex shows and confirmed reports that they were to headline that summer's Glastonbury festival. They didn't know, however, if rumours that The Grateful Dead were to co-headline were true, although Shaun – who claimed he had scored the best acid he had ever taken from one of their road crew in the US – said he hoped that they were.

The G-Mex centre shows, with support from 808 State, were the first big British rave events of the summer. Both sold out their 9000 capacity and even Happy Mondays were stunned by how popular they had become almost overnight. In fact, Shaun had initially tried to dissuade Factory from booking a second night at G-Mex, so convinced was he that it wouldn't sell out. After all, little over a year ago, supporting New Order at the same venue, most of the audience had hardly bothered to watch the band.

Shaun needn't have worried. Near hysteria from the fans meant that the G-Mex gigs, like the rest of the tour, were certain to be a success. Nevertheless, the band probably knew that they wouldn't be at their best. They were knackered from their weeks of non-stop dates, drug-taking and travel across Europe. Practice, however, had made them a tighter live act and there were plenty of on-stage distractions to draw attention away from Shaun, slumped for most of the set against his mike stand or reading lyrics from pieces of paper. A five-year-old 'Bez', kitted out in the same gear as the real Bez, came on stage to dance; Karl Denver sang alongside Shaun on 'Lazyitis'; and, most importantly, backing singer Rowetta, who had been brought in to sing on 'Step On', made her debut live appearance, clad in skin-tight black leather.

One of Happy Mondays' next gigs was at Newcastle Polytechnic. By now, PR Jeff Barrett was heavily involved in setting up his own record label, Heavenly, to which he would sign acts such as Manic Street Preachers, St Etienne and Flowered Up. It was his assistant, ex-*NME* photographer Jayne Houghton, who was dealing with the UK tour now. Houghton took *Melody Maker* to Newcastle to review the show. Just minutes before it was due to start, however, there was still no sign of Shaun.

'It turned out he had gone to the wrong venue,' says Houghton. 'The band had been down in London to do some press and Shaun had decided to stop over at some hotel in Bayswater. He came up to Newcastle on the train the next day, but he was terribly hungover. The band was playing the polytechnic, but Shaun went to the Town Hall by mistake. There was heavy security on the door who wouldn't let him in. Shaun was standing outside, screaming. He was going, "I'm in the fuckin' band, let me in. I can hear them soundchecking the drums, they're all waiting for me. I can hear our kid on bass."

'Eventually, he bowled past the security with all his mates, went charging into the hall and jumped straight on to the stage, in front of the mike. He started going, "One, two, one, two", trying to be all professional and pretend he wasn't dead late. Suddenly, Mick Hucknall strolls up to him. Shaun's like, "Okay mate. What are you doing here?" Mick was mad. He said, "What am I doing here? It's my bloody gig. Yours is down the road."'

A fortnight before Happy Mondays were to wind up their tour at Wembley, 'Step On' became the band's first proper post-*Bummed* single. Already a huge radio hit, the single threatened to outsell any Stone Roses' release. Despite having just played their biggest London gig to date at Alexandra Palace, the Roses had been keeping fairly quiet, except for some low-key court appearances as they struggled to free themselves from their record company.

While The Stone Roses had no new material to promote, Happy Mondays increasingly became the focus for a Manchester-mad media. *Smash Hits* ran a full-page colour pull-out of Shaun, *Elle* magazine wanted to interview him and even teen mag *Blue Jean* featured the band. Both *Sounds* and *NME* awarded 'Step On' single of the week.

'To award top prize to anything else would have been a crime against humanity, and that's an understatement,' said *Sounds*. 'In covering John Kongos' early 1970s hit, Happy Mondays have struck gold. By the time you read this, "Step On" will be etched deeply on your mind. You'll be grooving to its shimmering guitar chords on high-street strolls and whistling the delectable keyboard hook in your sleep, it's that powerful. It's hard to believe, but their creative juices are only now reaching boiling point.'

Oakenfold had done eight different mixes of 'Step On'. Four were eventually released. Before the first was even out, however, the intro of the song had already passed into pop culture. 'Call the cops' was the latest hip saying on the lips of clubbers and clued-up indie kids alike.

'We put out only the straight pop mix of the single first,' says Shaun. 'We had to. Radio 1 and British TV were still having a hard enough time trying to deal with us. They didn't get it at all. At that stage, there was no way they were going to play a ten-minute, spaced-out version of the song.'

Happy Mondays almost didn't get to perform 'Step On' on *Top Of The Pops* at all. A brief band holiday to Marbella almost ended badly when Gaz was caught coming back into the country with a small quantity of cannabis in his luggage. It was only his plea to be spared the necessary court appearance the following morning to get to the BBC on time to record the show that persuaded customs to let him off with a £50 on-the-spot fine.

'Step On' came in a Central-Station-designed sleeve which was a collage of bits of old birthday cards that the Carroll and Ryder families had sent to each other over recent years. On the back cover were thank-you credits to the various relations who had supplied the cards. The single was to give the band its first Top 5 hit.

Happy Mondays' last London show had been at the 2000-capacity Town & Country Club. It had sold out straight away and left hundreds of fans of the band desperate to get their hands on tickets. Wembley was payback time, a thank-you to those who had supported the band when the rest of the country didn't understand. It was also said to be earning the band £30,000. Nevertheless, Shaun would have liked to play there with some new songs. He was desperate to get into a studio to begin work on the follow-up to *Bummed* and bored of playing the same songs almost every night.

Tickets for the 10,000-capacity Wembley show, featuring support from Adrian Sherwood's On-U Sound Crew, announced that 'The rave is on'. Among the audience were Boy George and Primal Scream singer Bobby Gillespie.

'Wembley was bloody brilliant,' says Dave Harper. 'It's assumed you can't have a decent gig there, but the whole crowd that night was up for a good time. The atmosphere was incredible. Everyone was up dancing right the way through the set. Shaun's dad was rushing to the front of the stage every few minutes and brandishing this cardboard cut-out of a number one. He was totally off his trolley. Later on backstage, he was wheeled around unconscious.

'For me, the best moment came right at the end of the show. A massive capital E made of exploding lightbulbs came on so brightly that it lit up the entire venue. It was one of those moments you never forget. That night, the music itself almost didn't matter. That said, I'm sure there were a lot of DATs being used. I've never been able to equate Knobhead's dodgy keyboard playing with that band on stage at Wembley.'

Indeed, Paul Oakenfold played with Happy Mondays that night. 'I DJed with the Mondays quite a lot around that time, including at a few festivals,' he says. 'Wembley Arena was the highlight, though. It was fantastic. By then, I really felt like a member of the band. The Mondays were always more of a posse than your typical guitar group anyway.

'Shaun was hilarious on stage at Wembley. I always remember him starting one particular song with the second verse, instead of the first. As soon as he realised he'd got it wrong, he turned round and told the rest of the band to stop playing and start again. The crowd went absolutely mental. It was brilliant. Only Shaun could get away with that. It was a mistake, but he made it seem cool. Anyone else would have looked like an idiot.

'The Mondays were okay as musicians, to put it politely. Live, that didn't matter. It was all about getting up and having a go. Just being yourself. That's why they were the people's heroes. You had the likes of the Inspiral Carpets who took themselves very seriously and thought they were great musicians, but they didn't relate to what was happening at the time like the Roses and the Mondays did. I played with the Roses a few times too and, musician-wise, they were excellent, but the Mondays had a special vibe that no one else got near. I wouldn't compare them to any other band and I honestly don't think there can ever be another Mondays. Not only were Shaun's lyrics unique, but the songs themselves were inspired by so many different sounds, as well as the youth culture of the moment. Even if another Happy Mondays does come along in the future, there will never be another Shaun.'

ELEVEN

From Madchester With Love

In the spring of 1990, the Hacienda celebrated its eighth birthday with a party attended by Happy Mondays, New Order, A Certain Ratio, Ian McCulloch, Simply Red and Swing Out Sister. The club's birthday events made for notoriously hedonistic nights out. Two years earlier, the venue had thrown a 'haunted house' party complete with ghost trains and spooky special effects. A year ago, hundreds of Hacienda regulars decamped to Amsterdam.

This bash boasted high-tech lasers flashing figure-of-eights and dancing cartoons on the ceiling, a free barbecue and cascading balloons full of helium to inhale. Nevertheless, it was a much more muted affair than usual. Local police chief James Anderton had been trying to shut down the Hacienda for months. It was, he claimed, a drug den. The club was given until July to prove that it had cleaned up its act. Otherwise, its alcohol licence would be revoked by July and its future left in the hands of the law.

A campaign to safeguard the future of what many Manchester residents considered to be a positive part of the city (the club was reckoned to be responsible for a soaring student population) was already well underway. Letters were flooding into the local press, bulletins had been posted around the area and a petition to the council had even been organised. The Hacienda was taking action too. Manager Paul Cons had instigated strict new anti-drugs measures, such as installing security cameras and having everyone closely searched on entry.

On the night of the club's eighth birthday, it was alcohol instead of Ecstasy that kept the party going until its 2.45am curfew. (The event had been granted a rare late licence; venues usually had to shut their doors at the ridiculously early time of 1am.) Predictably, Shaun and Bez broke the Ecstasy ban, although Shaun would later claim that it was the first time he had taken the drug in months. The next morning, Happy Mondays were due to take a break from writing new material to fly to Paris for a TV show. It was cancelled, however, when only a couple of the band made it to the studio. Shaun refused to get out of bed in time to catch the flight, while Mark Day had been stranded at the airport after he nipped off to the toilet and the others accidentally left without him.

Happy Mondays were in Manchester, preparing for their gig at Glastonbury, when they met 1960s folk legend Donovan. Perhaps inspired by the peace'n'love spirit of the forthcoming festival, Shaun had recently mentioned in a radio interview that the band was planning to record a cover version of Donovan's 'Colours' as its next single. On tour in Germany, Shaun had picked up a copy of a Donovan greatest hits LP, which had since been played non-stop in the band's bus because of its trippy, mellow pop feel.

Coincidentally, at the time, Donovan, now based in Ireland, was attempting a career comeback after years out of the charts. Back in Manchester, Shaun discovered that the singer was currently on a tour of tiny clubs, which included a show at Colne Municipal Hall in nearby Burnley. When Donovan turned up at the folk club for the gig, he found Happy Mondays on the guestlist. The entire band saw his set, during which Donovan dedicated a song to them, and afterwards were introduced to the flower-power icon.

'They all came backstage at this little venue outside Manchester,' says Donovan. 'They said, "We're here to capture you and take you to the Hacie." They wanted to fill me with the best E and show me what was happening in their city. I was flattered by their interest.'

Donovan didn't go with the band to the Hacienda that night as he was due to fly back to Ireland later in the evening. He did, however, arrange to keep in touch with Shaun. A few days later, Factory announced that the proposed cover of 'Colours' was going ahead. Instead of being recorded by Happy Mondays, however, it would be sung by Shaun, but played by a mellow Electronic's Johnny Marr and Bernard Sumner.

In mid June, Happy Mondays turned up to Glastonbury with scores of Manc mates in tow. Rumour had it that they had asked for 200 complimentary guest tickets so that they could bring along some friends. When the request was denied, the band were said to have printed up as many laminates themselves, which were then sold to punters at the festival entrance.

The gig itself was poor. Since the band had finished their UK dates in April, they had been busy playing festivals in Europe and doing promotion for 'Step On'. The lack of days off, combined with the constant partying and the fact that their set still consisted mainly of tracks from *Bummed*, plus, as it transpired, a move into hard drugs for several band members, had left Happy Mondays at less than their best for the festival. It didn't help that Shaun had stayed out the previous night, caught some sleep on the coach and only woken up half an hour before he was due on stage.

The Glastonbury show was sluggish, rather than simply shambolic. The band had problems with their DAT machine – during 'Clap Your Hands' and 'Lazyitis', it switched itself off and on at random – and the tunes sounded sloppy, Shaun's vocal was weak and the belligerent attitude that usually bound their mess of influences together couldn't quite gel. Moreover, the Mondays were missing Rowetta. Although the backing singer had only just begun to perform live with the band, they were aware how much she strengthened their live sound. There were highlights – notably 'Wrote For Luck' and 'Step On' – but at under forty minutes long, the show was perceived by many critics to have been something of a sham.

Nevertheless, the bulk of the audience appeared to adore the set. Among them was guitarist Ed O'Brien, who had recently formed the group Radiohead with several of his schoolfriends. So impressed was O'Brien with the Mondays' Saturday night show, that he returned home to Oxford the next day desperate to tell the others that his ambition was now for their band to headline the main stage at Glastonbury. By then, Shaun had begun to enjoy the festival himself. He scored some opium up in the green fields, watched sets by The Cure and Hothouse Flowers and stayed on site for a full four days.

Less than a week later, despite being due imminently in the US both to tour and to appear at the city's New Music Seminar, an important annual industry event, Happy Mondays were off to Ibiza. Invited to play a special show at the island's infamous 4000-capacity

Ku Club, they had decided to treat the trip as a short but badly needed holiday. Of course, Ibiza in high season was hardly relaxing. The venue, with its stage suspended over a swimming pool, was packed with predominately British clubbers, many of whom who had flown over specially to see the show. Paul Oakenfold was there as support DJ and Rowetta sang with the band on stage, even though she had only got to Ibiza by winning the trip in a competition in a Manchester magazine.

On the night, Shaun claimed to have enjoyed the gig more than Glastonbury, and the set – dedicated to Brian Tilsley, aka *Coronation Street* actor Chris Quentin, who was in the audience – was certainly longer. Happy Mondays were paid £12,000 to appear. By the time they left, six days later, having visited almost every club on the island, Shaun reckoned they had spent more than they earned.

In the sweltering heat and stifling humidity of a New York summer, Madchester descended on the New Music Seminar. During the week-long industry event, both Factory MD Tony Wilson and Happy Mondays' manager Nathan McGough were scheduled to appear on various discussion panels. Meanwhile, five consecutive Factory-organised nights, collectively called From Madchester With Love, featuring new acts like Northside and A Guy Called Gerald, would take place in the city's Sound Factory club. Back in England, Wilson had claimed that From Madchester With Love would culminate in a huge party at Madison Square Garden with Happy Mondays, 808 State and DJs Mike Pickering, Paul Oakenfold and Graeme Park. As Wilson well knew, however, Madison Square Garden was scheduled to be shut for repairs at the time.

Along with 808 State, the DJ trio of Pickering, Park and Oakenfold were to precede the seminar with a fortnight of shows, dubbed The Hacienda Trance America Tour, in cities such as Miami, Dallas, Boston and Los Angeles. By the time Happy Mondays arrived in New York, they would already be halfway through a short US tour to promote 'Step On'. To top it all, a tour operator had even organised charter flights from Manchester to New York, so that hundreds of flare-wearing indie dance kids could watch with their own eyes as their icons broke the US. At least, that was the plan.

The New Music Seminar was founded in 1980 to showcase happening new musical talent from around the world to global industry bigwigs and international press. 1990's event was easily the biggest to date. More than 350 bands played over the five days, hotel foyers were choc-a-block with trade stalls, and sales people and experts from every related field spent their time arguing with each other on panels, some of which started as early as 9am. The only panel of any real interest to the Brits abroad that year, however, was the one hosted by Tony Wilson, cheekily titled Wake Up America, You're Dead!, which took place in a sixth-floor lecture room of the seminar's plush base at the Marriott Marquis Hotel, just off Times Square.

Wilson's chosen panelists, alongside McGough, were ground-breaking American house and techno DJs Marshall Jefferson and Derrick May, as well as comedian Keith Allen, masquerading as a supposedly world-famous doctor of psychology from Geneva.

'Welcome to the New Music Seminar,' were Wilson's opening words. 'The rest of the shit going on in this building this week is the Old Music Seminar. I'd like to begin with a quote from the Family Dog, made in 1964. "The kids just wanna dance. All you gotta do is give them somewhere to dance and everything will be okay." You used to know how to dance here. God knows how you fuckin' forgot.'

Wilson went on to trawl through the histories of British and American dance music, noting how both The Beatles and The Rolling Stones had grown out of US R&B and describing the effect that house was having in Europe. All was going well. Then Keith Allen waded in with his own personal house history.

'In 1987 in a club called Shoom,' said Allen, 'I had a load of Ecstasy, topped with a little amyl nitrate, which gave a very popular sex-inducing vibe. I would give these tablets to people and in return, they would give me £20. This made both parties very happy. I should really put this into perspective by saying that I am now the father of eight children, because as you know, when we get "on one" – as we say in England – you want to chuck it about all over the place.'

The Brits in the audience laughed at Allen's speech. The Americans were incensed by his drug references. Derrick May was so mad that he immediately threatened to leave. Wilson tried to placate the situation. He was doing okay until McGough got his say. Attempting to make Happy Mondays out as anti-hero saviours of new music, McGough played up the band's drug-dealing past. Immediately, an argument broke out over who knew what about dance music, and insults started to fly. Derrick May accused Keith Allen of being racist. Wilson reckoned Derrick was an idiot and McGough agreed. May called Wilson a 'flat-assed motherfucker'. Allen asked him what that meant. Then, Marshall Jefferson walked out in disgust and Wilson told everyone to shut up. May said Wilson should shut up instead, seconds before following Jefferson out the door.

Wilson had gone to the US wanting to make an impression. He could scarcely have done so more successfully. Two days later, however, even the Manc-induced arguments were upstaged when West Coast rapper Ice Cube made some inflammatory comments about his East Coast counterparts at another seminar in one of the Marriott Marquis's boardrooms. His remarks lead to fighting, flying furniture and finally sparked a small-scale riot in the hallway. Police were called as the feud started to spread throughout the hotel. The seminar had to be stopped and the surrounding area cordoned off until order could be restored.

That night, Happy Mondays played a stunning gig at New York's Sound Factory on the city's mid-West Side to close Wilson's From Madchester With Love event. 808 State supported, although A Guy Called Gerald and Adamski were also billed to appear, but never showed. Not that Happy Mondays noticed. They were too busy shopping. Within hours of arriving in the city, Shaun had spent £1000 in Armani. He then turned up late for the soundcheck, having decided to nip out and buy a new shirt for the gig. For the first time, Happy Mondays were making proper money from their music – they had just been offered $60,000 to play one date in Brazil – and they were determined to spend it. Not all their money, however, was strictly song-related. Bez, for example, had discovered a lucrative substitute for dealing, having just sold his story to the *News Of The World* for £8000.

The Sound Factory reminded Happy Mondays of the Hacienda. For a start, its cavernous interior was peppered with pillars. It was also full of folk from Manchester. Unlike the band's hometown club, however, Sound Factory didn't have an alcohol licence. Shaun wasn't worried that the audience wouldn't get into the gig though. He had spiked the fruit punch with twenty-five Es. Predictably, Happy Mondays went down well. There had been a buzz about their show all week. Spare tickets were simply impossible to get hold of. On the night, several thousand people queued up around the block outside, hoping desperately to either buy or blag their way in.

In front of an audience made up of a mix of trendy clubbers, industry figures and Mancs away from home, Happy Mondays basically threw a party on stage. When Shaun invited a few people to join him, hundreds crushed forward and the security were forced to wade in so that the gig could continue. It almost continued, however, without Bez, who was literally picked up and removed by one particularly burly security guard. It took intervention by Muzzer to convince the man that Bez was actually in the band. Keith Allen, crashed out on a flightcase for most of the evening, sprang to life only for the encore, leaping on stage to sing along with Shaun. The party lasted until noon the next day, when Happy Mondays had to leave to catch a flight for LA. Much to Shaun's relief, this meant blowing out a panel appearance which Wilson had arranged for him at a debate entitled 'Stars Of Tomorrow'. As far as the seminar went, however, Wilson's words may have been overshadowed by Ice Cube's antics, but Madchester still made its mark on New York.

The week after the seminar saw Wilson in Manchester fighting to save the Hacienda, while Happy Mondays began working in LA on their eagerly-awaited third album. Much to the annoyance of Elektra, the band had cancelled the last date of their Call The Cops tour in San Francisco to stay in LA to see a show by Soul II Soul.

'They wanted us to fly on to San Francisco, then back to LA to start on the album,' says Shaun. 'But when we got to LA, the vibe was top. The apartment we were in was where all the actors and movie stars who are in soap operas and shows like *Columbo* stay. It was full of videos and jacuzzis. We had already hired cars – some five-litre sports convertibles – and we really wanted to catch the Soul II Soul gig that night. We just wanted to chill out. So we sacked our own show and told the promoter in San Francisco that PD had got a big abscess in the side of his face which had leaked into his brain and we had to send him to hospital.'

Produced by Perfecto duo Paul Oakenfold and Steve Osborne, recording of Happy Mondays' third album took place over three months in the basement studios of the Capitol building by Hollywood Boulevard, which were formerly frequented by the likes of The Beatles and Frank Sinatra.

'Capitol studio is a fantastic place, easily one of the best studios in the world,' says Oakenfold. 'It was the band's decision to record in LA. I think they reckoned they could turn the sessions into a bit of a party.'

Initially, Shaun had suggested that the album be made in Amsterdam. However, he was wise enough to know that the band probably wouldn't get much done there and realised that, with The Stone Roses still tied up in court, it was essential for Happy Mondays to release new material by the end of the year.

'Shaun was great to work with,' says Oakenfold. 'He didn't start with songs already written. It was weird with that band. They had no idea about regular recording practice. Shaun would give us a dodgy demo and we'd wonder what the fuck it was all about. Usually when you get a demo, you know roughly where you're going to go with it. The Mondays' demos were too loose to make any sort of decision on. There was generally very little on them in fact. What made them special was the vibe. Very few bands can create a natural vibe. To me, if a song has that, it's halfway there already.

'Lyrically though, Shaun was bang on it. He wrote street songs that fitted the total change in mood of a generation at that time. The kids didn't want to listen to silly love songs any more, they wanted lyrics they could connect with, which is exactly what Shaun was coming up with. So the demos may have been loose, but the content was essentially there. You could just feel that the record was going to work. It was incredibly exciting. It still felt underground too, even though the band had been in the charts. That's why dance people weren't put off the Mondays. It never felt as though they were selling out.'

Oakenfold and Osborne spent twelve hours a day (from noon until midnight), six days a week in Capitol studios.

'The way we worked was that we'd get each individual player in to do their part,' says Oakenfold. 'Shaun would just come down at night and do his vocal. He wasn't actually in the studio very much. We'd spend time with Mark on guitar and Gary on drums, and get down the backing track before Shaun would even arrive. He'd do his vocal, then leave. We'd crack on with work until midnight. I think Shaun slept for most of the day, even if he hadn't been out the night before.'

Oakenfold insists that there wasn't nearly as much partying going on in LA as everyone back in Britain assumed. 'I was DJing out there at the same time as making the album,' he says. 'I had a residency in a club every Friday. That was the only night of the week that Shaun, Bez and maybe some of the others would always be out. They would come down to the club, then maybe go on to a couple of parties. It wasn't as mad as people imagined, though. Of course there was the odd crazy incident. I remember being in a car with Bez reversing up a motorway. That was slightly scary. But generally, there was such a great vibe on the record that everyone bar Shaun wanted to hang out at Capitol. You didn't need to go to a club because there was a better party going on with us in the studio.'

For months, cracks had been starting to show in Happy Mondays' once solid bond. In part, it was the pressure of their relentless workload and the hours on end they had spent together while on tour. It was also the money. With legitimate wages in their pockets for the first time, every member of Happy Mondays had their independence. They didn't need the rest of the band in order to make their own entertainment. They were also getting older and their priorities were changing. It wasn't all about having fun any more. While out in LA, Paul Ryder married Alison, his longtime girlfriend and the mother of his two children. In addition, Shaun's girlfriend Trish had announced that she was pregnant and expecting the pair's first child in February.

'Bez was the only one of the band who behaved like the archetypal party animal,' says Oakenfold. 'I seem to remember him writing off a couple of convertibles because he was trying to drive while completely off his head. But the person who did the most partying and was all over the shop was Nathan. He was never around. In fact, Nathan caused a lot more aggro than he did good. We'd be in the studio recording, then suddenly MTV would turn up and no one would know anything about it. They would tell us they had agreed it with the manager. But Shaun wouldn't be there and probably neither would most of the others. It was just Steve and me and maybe Mark Day with a full film crew. Nathan basically spent the three months partying and fucking loads of girls. If it wasn't for Steve and me pulling the whole thing together, the album would never have been made. It was a tremendous amount of pressure for the pair of us.

Apart from producing and mixing, we ended up managing the project. I would be on the phone constantly trying to get Shaun to the studio to lay down some vocals. Nathan was always impossible to find. I think he was under the false impression that he was actually a member of the band.'

While Oakenfold may have been right to think that Shaun was spending a lot of time in his room, he was wrong to assume that the singer was simply sleeping. Despite Trish having come out to LA to join him, Shaun later confessed that he had established a Mexican opium connection during the recording sessions.

'I knew that Shaun was never really straight,' says Oakenfold. 'Drug-wise, I couldn't have told you what he was doing though. There was a hell of a lot of Ecstasy around, which is why Nathan was never there. I think Shaun was getting through quite a few different kinds of drug. But the fact is, Shaun didn't have to be straight. It was the opposite in fact. We definitely got the best vocals out of him when he was off his head because he was more relaxed. I mean, Shaun isn't a regular singer. He'd come into the studio and scribble some lyrics on a scrap of paper he'd just found. His songs didn't make sense, but it didn't matter. It was more about the vibe he could create.

'Having said that, some of the lines he came out with were truly inspirational. "Call the cops" and "You're twisting my melons, man" became sayings that every clubber in England was using. "You're twisting my melons" meant "You're doing my head in". He took that from a Steve McQueen film. I remember being back in London and hearing someone else use that line for the first time. It felt so weird, like you had helped to create a new language.

'Shaun sometimes came up with his lyrics in the hotel, but usually it was on the spot in the studio. His writing was outrageous, totally brilliant. He could make me laugh or make me cry. He could tap into any emotion, but at the end of the day it was always light-hearted and funny, never ever boring. Being in LA had a huge influence, without a doubt. Shaun is very affected by where he is. He sort of soaks in his surroundings. If he's sitting at home watching a TV documentary when he should be writing, then you have a good idea of what you're going to get.'

The shift in Happy Mondays' music from chaotic, indie guitar status to slick, sample-heavy dancefloor fodder was to come under

▲ **Happy Mondays were a real gang, which is exactly what came across in the songs.** [Steve Double, 1986]

◀ **In his hood: Shaun howls at the sky for Happy Mondays' first front cover.** [Tom Sheehan, 1987]

▲ Happy Mondays looked exactly as they sounded.
It was bastardised Northern punk rock. [Tom Sheehan, 1987]

▶ Shaun had great fights with Bez, but they were
always best mates at heart. [Steve Double, 1988]

Shaun and Bez forged a strong bond. For a decade, they were inseparable.
[Tom Sheehan, 1987]

▲ **Shaun has loads of charisma. He's a cool guy and quite a charmer.**
[Tom Sheehan, 1989]

▶ **Shaun was a real Dickensian, dodgy-looking character on stage.
In fact, he was pretty much the same off stage.** [Davies & Davies, 1989]

Happy Mondays' real visual pull was Bez. People had never seen anyone dance like that before. [Davies & Davies, 1989]

Karl Denver watches Shaun and Bez misbehave on stage at Manchester's Free Trade Hall. [Davies & Davies, 1989]

▲ **Happy Mondays weren't lower working class: they were the underclass. They invented the term.** [Tom Sheehan, 1990]

▶ **One look at Shaun and it was obvious that he did shitloads of hallucinogenics.** [Tom Sheehan, 1991]

▲ **Don't bank on it: Shaun pretends to have quit the music business.** [Tom Sheehan, 1993]

▶ **The band with balls: Black Grape's Bez, Shaun and Kermit with their backs to the wall.** [Davies & Davies, 1995]

Black Grape always throw themselves full-on into whatever task is at hand.
[Tom Sheehan, 1995]

Bully boy Shaun sports a scar from his first film role.
[Deirdre O'Callaghan, 1997]

Getting higher: Shaun with Black Grape producer-turned-band-member, Danny Saber. [Steve Double, 1997]

close scrutiny. Much like Primal Scream, who had recently shed their rock skin with the aid of former Mondays' remixer Andy Weatherall on 'Loaded', the band found themselves having to fend off accusations that they no longer wrote their own songs. Many believed that Happy Mondays was now little more than a live front for the production team of Oakenfold and Osborne.

'Steve certainly had a lot to do with the instrumentation on that album,' admits Oakenfold. 'Steve is a guitarist himself. He also plays various other instruments. His expertise was central to the sound. I came up with the ideas, but it was Steve who would sit down and play them on the guitar. He could tell Mark Day exactly what we wanted. If Mark couldn't get the part right, Steve would take his guitar off him and show him what he had to do.

'It was only because of our musical background that we could deal with non-musicians. Of course, it meant a hell of a lot more effort from us, but I personally would rather work with bands that have a brilliant vibe. You can fix anything in the studio. You can make the worst musician in the world sound great. If I played you the demos of that Mondays album, which I still have, you wouldn't believe your ears. Steve really did work wonders. With The Stone Roses, who were brilliant musicians, it was simply a case of having to record them. The most you would do was fiddle with the arrangement or the song structure to get the sounds to fit right. Working with Happy Mondays, on the other hand, meant starting from scratch and basically making the record yourself.

'It was a plus in a way, of course, because we could do what we wanted. Shaun in particular trusted us. We were allowed to have a lot more input than is usual. I could tell them that the drums had to be more hip hop orientated and the drummer wouldn't ask why. I mean, Gary would still play them, but we would tell him what to play. I'd ask Paul to make the bassline heavy and reggae so that we got the right groove, rather than having that straight rock sound, and he would just do it. Other bands I've worked with, I'll suggest something and they'll have reservations. They don't trust you, even though you know it's going to work. I never had to sit down with any member of Happy Mondays for an hour and a half and talk them round, like I usually have to with rock musicians. That's why the product was so good, because we had a real mutual trust.

'Shaun understood the dance scene because he was involved in it.

I was coming from the clubs, Steve had the musicianship and Happy Mondays was an indie band. The merger worked. We all came from different backgrounds, but we all had clubs in common. Often when I work with guitar bands, they have no idea what I'm talking about.

'Looking back, I'm sure Shaun had a pretty good idea of what he wanted before we even got to LA, but he was so confident in our ability that he just let us get on with it. Listen, if Shaun hadn't been happy with what we were doing, he would have said so. Shaun is his own man. At the end of the day, I have total respect for him as a musician. It was his band and he was always in charge. If he didn't like an idea, we didn't do it. Nine times out of ten though, he was delighted.'

TWELVE
Opting Out And Cashing In

The Hacienda saw out summer 1990 in a sweat. Despite drug use within the club having been all but abolished, police insisted that the venue was still the focus for Ecstasy culture in the city. Factory hired George Karmen QC (the lawyer who had recently successfully defended Ken Dodd against the Inland Revenue) to fight for the Hacienda's right to retain its alcohol licence, but was later informed that the court case against the club had been adjourned until January. Meanwhile, Karmen went to work for ferry company Townsend Thoreson in its Zeebrugge corporate manslaughter trial.

Tabloid attacks on the Hacienda, however, continued to rage. The death the previous summer of sixteen-year-old Claire Leyton two days after collapsing inside the venue remained at the heart of the criticisms. Leyton had literally boiled to death after taking one Ecstasy tab, which triggered a reaction in her body that caused vital organs to malfunction. Nevertheless, the Hacienda's own campaign was gaining considerable support. Both the leader of the local council and the Lord Mayor's office had voiced their approval of the venue, which they knew hadn't only brought money into Manchester, but also helped to rejuvenate a run-down part of the city centre. Moreover, in the wake of the recent Strangeways riot, local authorities were eager to avoid pulling any more social issues into the public eye, particularly as they were then optimistically angling to host the 1996 Olympic games.

Factory acts such as New Order and James lent their profile to the fight by highlighting the club's pivotal role in the Manchester music scene. In addition, alongside Factory and the Hacienda, Northside and The Charlatans had T-shirts designed to encourage the Olympic bid and so ingratiate themselves with the local community. Happy Mondays, on the other hand, could scarcely have done more to scupper the Hacienda's hopes of a reprieve. Almost daily, it seemed, either Shaun or Bez was in the papers, telling tales of their wild, stimulant-soiled early life on the streets and in the clubs of Manchester. For the sake of their fee, they would often spice up the stories by adding fantastic, fabricated details. Referring to his recent cocaine bust, Shaun would say that the whole band now carried solicitors' cards with them going through customs, rather than their own drugs. He claimed he now searched his luggage before leaving the country, just to make sure that all substances had been taken out. Questioned on his use of Ecstasy, Shaun insisted that he had stopped doing the drug almost a year ago.

'The last time I did E was at a party,' he said. 'I had loads of tabs in my pocket because I was selling them. The police arrived and I ended up putting ten in my mouth at once to get rid of them. They all melted. It sent me potty and I almost had a heart attack on the Oxford Road. I collapsed and ended up in hospital. It took me weeks to recover. I couldn't move one side of my body for days.'

Drugs scandals were hardly going to help Factory in the US either. With the aid of its now world-renowned roster of DJs, the Hacienda was planning to launch weekly club nights in Chicago, Miami, LA and New York by the end of the year.

Meanwhile, Wilson was hoping to cash in on the growing American press interest in Madchester with Happy Mondays while The Stone Roses remained out of action. The Roses had postponed a scheduled debut US tour earlier that year due to the continuing dispute with their record label, Silvertone. The band, which was said to be demanding a £2 million deal, were unable to release new material until the matter was resolved. Nevertheless, the Roses' singles were receiving heavy play on American college radio and threatening to break into the mainstream charts, although the Mondays' 'Step On' was proving popular with MTV. The heavyweight US press were also taking a keen interest. Both the *New York Times* and *LA Times* had written about the scene, while even *Newsweek* had run a 'Stark Raving Madchester' story in which 'kids with bobbing Monkees' haircuts' were described as being 'stoned out of their gourds'. 'The new music,' noted *Newsweek*, 'is buoyant, almost goofy. The fashion grafts British football gear on to American hippie glad rags, with a soupçon of *Jetsons* futurism.'

Ironically, Happy Mondays – the only 'baggy' band currently in a position to break the US – had moved on from Madchester fashions several years earlier. As far back as 1987, Shaun had appeared in style mag *i-D* along with The Stone Roses' Cressa and Inspiral Carpets' Clint Boon, in an acid fashion feature on their flares, hooded tops and so-called 'Baldrick' haircuts. Moreover, with Oakenfold and Osbourne at their helm, Happy Mondays' music no longer fitted the 1960s-inspired sound that intrigued the Americans. As far as the band was concerned, Wilson could flog Madchester in the US as much as he liked, but it had little to do with them.

'Tony Wilson didn't have a clue,' says Oakenfold. 'He didn't come out to the States when we were making the album. The band didn't want him there and neither did I. Tony had come to the party really late because it was trendy. He thought he was part of the scene, but he wasn't. He knew fuck all about it. He acted like an idiot. He'd come down to clubs and embarrass himself. He'd try and talk like he knew what was happening. We'd sit there and wonder what he was on about. But he wasn't expected to be part of that scene, so I don't know why he tried. He should have just acted normal. Tony should have been taking care of business, that was his job.'

In October 1990, Happy Mondays released 'Kinky Afro', the first product from the LA sessions, and the second single and opening track from their forthcoming third album, to be entitled *Pills 'N' Thrills And Bellyaches*. Originally called 'Groovy Afro' (but changed because of The Farm's recently-released 'Groovy Train') and promoted with a video in which Shaun and Bez were flanked by a bevy of swaying models, the song was supposedly based on the Hot Chocolate hit 'Brother Louie', but actually borrowed a lot more liberally from Labelle's 1975 disco classic 'Lady Marmalade (Voulez-Vous Coucher Avec Moi Ce Soir?)'. Shaun Ryder's 'Yipee-yipee-aye-aye-ay' refrain was, in fact, a straight steal.

The mellow groove, stoned sound and spotless production of 'Kinky Afro' set the scene for *Pills 'N' Thrills And Bellyaches*. So too did Mark Day's distinctive, chiming guitar style and Shaun's smutty but brilliant lyrics, crystal clear in the mix. 'Son, I'm thirty/I only went with your mother 'cos she's dirty/And I don't have a decent bone in me', began the first verse of the song. It was to be Happy Mondays' second Top 5 hit.

Both 'Kinky Afro' and album track 'Bob's Yer Uncle' had already fallen foul of the censors. The single's sleeve was initially intended to feature a teenage Michael Jackson as its artwork. However, Elektra claimed that the image might be perceived as a reference to the lyric 'I had to crucify some brother today' and insisted that it be changed. It was Shaun himself who had censored 'Bob's Yer Uncle', the album's sexiest song, thanks in part to Rowetta's guest grunts and groans. The track, memorable for its insistent recurring clarinet sample (courtesy of Michael Nyman), had originally featured X-rated extracts from *The Exorcist* as well as snippets from various porn films. All had been removed, although Shaun promised some would resurface in the club mixes, should the song ever come out as a single. (It didn't.)

Predictably, for *Pills 'N' Thrills*, Shaun stole from a number of sources. 'Grandbag's Funeral' hinged on a stuttering riff from David Bowie's 'Diamond Dogs', 'Holiday' poached part of Lou Reed's 'Sweet Jane', and 'Dennis And Lois' started with Sound Of Philadelphia strings. Lyrically, the track 'Donovan' took the couplet 'Sunshine shines brightly through my window today/Could have tripped up quite easily but decide to stay' from its namesake's 1960s hit 'Sunshine Superman', 'God's Cop' was an off-the-wall ode to James Anderton, and 'Holiday' dealt with difficult female customs officers. The American influence came through on 'Loose Fit' – supposedly Shaun's own abstract interpretation of the Gulf War, which had dominated the US news during recording – and on 'Dennis And Lois', which referred to a couple whom the singer said had 'looked after' him in the US.

Despite the two-year gap between albums, some critics couldn't quite believe that this was the product of the same musicians who had last delivered *Bummed*. How much, they demanded to know, was Happy Mondays, and how much Oakenfold and Osborne?

'Our Paul and Mark Day were the tunes people,' says Shaun. 'They would come up with the riffs. Then the band would just start jamming and I'd tell them what bits to take out and suggest things to put in. Bez always sat in during recording too. He'd bang the bongos and make a bit of a noise. I think it's an advantage that I'm not a musical person. If I was, I wouldn't come up with half of my ideas. Oakie would always be telling me this or that was impossible. But I'd say, "Just do it," and he'd find a way.'

For 'Bob's Yer Uncle', one of the few album tracks to feature an 'outside' musician (percussionist Tony Castro, who also played on 'Loose Fit'), Oakenfold asked Shaun to make the song sound sexy.

'That's the dead dirty sex song,' says Shaun. 'I think the tune came from the *Daktari* theme music. We were in the studio and Oakie said, "Do this one sexy, for the ladies," and the words just spieled out. It's really the guitar that makes it sound sexy. My lyrics are just sick, like a schoolboy rhyme that any kid could make up. I can't write a proper sexy song, but I can write something pervy that sounds sexy. I don't know why that is.'

Despite mounting derision in the press of Bez's role in the band, Shaun insisted that his input on *Pills 'N' Thrills* was important.

'Bez was never merely a dancer,' says Shaun. 'He wasn't even on stage just for people to look at. Bez was there for us, not as a device to make the band look more interesting. Bez is great because he can spot good tunes. The press took the piss and called him a maracas player, but he was always a really important part of the music. He had a good time on stage, but he was also down there in the studio, listening to the tapes and coming up with ideas. When Bez grooved along to the sound, then we all knew it was okay.'

Pills 'N' Thrills proved to be an era-defining album, warmly received by the critics and literally stuffed full of potential singles. Mid-tempo tracks such as 'Dennis And Lois', 'Bob's Yer Uncle', 'God's Cop' and 'Loose Fit' suited the dancefloor as much for their mellow grooves as for their funky beats. But they weren't club tunes. Nor was there anything 1960s about this set of songs. What made *Pills 'N' Thrills* so special was the fact that it didn't sound like any other album. It certainly didn't slot into a scene.

'Happy Mondays are so far ahead in their disorganised progress that they have left behind the culture they represent,' noted *Sounds* in its review of the album. 'While 1990 kids sadly clamour more for sports shoes than sounds, the Mondays are – thank God – one of the last mad, bad rebel groups with a chance of infiltrating the mainstream.'

Advance sales of *Pills 'N' Thrills* (with its colourful, sweetie-wrapper collage of a sleeve) topped 150,000, remarkable for an indie album in the early 1990s and a guarantee that it would enter the UK charts at No.1. For the record's release in Europe, Factory abandoned its usual practice of licensing different labels to deal with distribution in different countries. For the first time, London Records would handle all European territories outside the UK. Factory claimed that this was simply because it made better business sense. However, the fact that German media giants BMG had just turned down the chance to distribute Happy Mondays product because of what they referred to as the band's 'interests outside of their musical output', was almost certainly an influence.

Factory had been cashing in on Happy Mondays' soaring success all year. A double A-sided single of 'Mad Cyril/Lazyitis' had come out in the summer, *Squirrel And G-Man* had been re-issued and compilation videos such as *Rave On*, *Party* and *Call The Cops* (from the band's US tour) were already in the shops for the pre-Christmas rush. The band themselves weren't doing too badly, having reputedly received £20,000 from Central TV to permit a documentary to be made about their lives. Granada TV had also been making a Mondays' programme, while Channel 4 had bought their rights to broadcast a recording of their summer show at the G-Mex centre. Like it or not, Happy Mondays had become bona fide pop stars.

A fortnight before the release of *Pills 'N' Thrills*, launched with a party at London's Regent's Park Zoo, Shaun was invited to guest on pop TV show *Juke Box Jury*, alongside Barbara Windsor (with whom he split a bottle of champagne backstage) and an actor from *Brookside*. After watching a video of The Nelson Brothers, Shaun stated – on camera – that they both looked like they could do with some sex. The pair turned out to be the programme's first secret guests. He then said that Candy Flip could do a lot better than their new single, seconds before the band made an entrance.

Having seen the show broadcast, Shaun was initially disappointed that his off-the-cuff comments concerning Paul McCartney, some small children and a load of Ecstasy had been edited out. He changed his mind a few days later, however, when McCartney was quoted in the papers as saying Happy Mondays live reminded him of The Beatles in their 'Strawberry Fields' phase. Shaun was delighted that the ex-Beatle had even heard of Happy Mondays.

Late November saw Happy Mondays back on the road, with a sold-out UK tour to promote their third album. However, all wasn't well. The band's debut date at Whitley Bay Ice Rink was overshadowed by national newspaper reports that Shaun Ryder had just spent ten days at the Priory Clinic in Hale, Cheshire, being treated for heroin addiction. Under the heading 'My Heroin Hell', the *Sun* also revealed that the singer had discharged himself early from the £160-a-day clinic, after a nurse gave him a telling-off for drinking beer in his room. Jayne Houghton, who had by now set up her own promotions company, Excess Press, to handle not only Happy Mondays, but also acts like Inspiral Carpets, The Shamen and Ned's Atomic Dustbin, was forced to admit that the stories were true.

Houghton's press release read as follows: 'It is true that Shaun was treated in a private clinic for a drug problem. He has kicked the habit. We expected the story to come out sooner or later, but just hope that it doesn't turn into a huge media circus like the Boy George fiasco of a few years back. Shaun has a lot of teenage fans and does not want them to think it is cool to use heroin. The matter is over and done with and Shaun is fine now. It was never a big problem, just something he wanted to sort out.'

'There was no point in trying to deny the rumours,' says Houghton now. 'Shaun was the most utterly upfront and honest person you could ever meet. I would have looked like an idiot had I said that the stories weren't true; Shaun would have just told the press that they were. To his credit, I think, he never ever pretended to be anything he wasn't. It was never him telling me to pretend he didn't take drugs or paint him as this squeaky clean character. It was always, "This is me. Take it or leave it. If you want to talk about sex or drugs or whatever, I will." He'd never try to deceive people. Sometimes, even I couldn't quite believe how honest he was being. I'd ring him up from a hotel lobby when he should have been down twenty minutes ago. He'd say, "Oh, I'm just finishing my wank. I'll be down in a bit." He could have pretended. He could have said he had just stepped out of the shower, but oh no, he had to tell the truth. I'd be the one turning to the tour manager and saying, "He's on his way, he's just getting dressed."'

Support on the UK leg of the Pills 'N' Thrills tour came from Donovan, who had recently contacted Shaun for the first time since their initial meeting to ask if he would be interested in the pair writing some material together. Shaun loved the idea, particularly because he had never collaborated on lyrics with anyone before.

In addition, the proposed cover of 'Colours' had failed to materialise. Both Shaun and Bernard Sumner had begun work on a vocal for the song, while Paul Oakenfold had already completed a drum track, when recording was scheduled to take place in Johnny Marr's home studio. A trip to the pub for Marr, Sumner and Shaun, however, left the trio too drunk to work. The following day, Johnny was off on tour with The The and the cover was scrapped.

At present, of course, Shaun didn't have time to write with Donovan. Besides, he had just finished months of recording Happy Mondays' material. Instead of a collaboration, Shaun decided to invite the singer to support the band on their forthcoming tour.

'I was delighted to be asked to come back with the most outrageous band of the day and do a wild tour,' says Donovan. 'I agreed to it immediately. I had been playing only acoustic solo sets for a while, so I put together an electric band for the shows. It was extraordinary to come on after a dance DJ. It was out of context, but nuts. I'm mad like that.'

By the time the tour began, Donovan had done little to ingratiate himself with hip Happy Mondays fans. In a bid for singles chart success, the singer had not only teamed up with children's TV presenters Trevor and Simon to record a comedy version of his 1960s hit 'Jennifer Juniper', but also sanctioned re-makes of another of his former singles, 'Hurdy Gurdy Man', by both The Butthole Surfers and Brix Smith. Happy Mondays had initially assumed that it would be the older members of their audience who would enjoy Donovan's set, while the younger ones mightn't get into it. Afterwards, however, Shaun reckoned it had been the other way around. The young kids liked Donovan, he said. It was the older ones who had slagged him off for being an old hippy. In fact, Donovan didn't go down well with most of the Mondays' crowd. The gigs were basically dance events, most of the kids were on E and, predictably, few appreciated a storming DJ set being stopped for a handful of folk songs.

Happy Mondays' second show of the Pills 'N' Thrills tour saw them back at Wembley Arena, this time with backing singer Rowetta (tonight clad in skintight black leather, wearing thigh-high boots and brandishing a cat o' nine tails) sharing centre-stage with Shaun. Despite the band playing adequately in front of a capacity party crowd, most of the tracks from the new album received a surprisingly muted reception. Older songs such as 'Hallelujah', 'Clap Your Hands' and 'Wrote For Luck', on the other hand, incited near hysteria. At Wembley to review the concert for *NME* was Jack Barron, who was disappointed that the stereotypical indie-dance audience preferred to hear basic 'baggy' tracks, rather than Happy Mondays' far fresher, more complex new material.

'It is tempting to dust down the old *Cynic's Handbook* when casting your eyes over an arena full of identical young men awaiting the appearance of their gurus,' said Barron in his review. 'Has all this gone too far? Has the trouser replaced the truth? Does the music matter any more? When Ian Brown sang poorly at Spike Island earlier this year, the scenery started to look very wobbly indeed.'

Happy Mondays' followed Wembley Arena with two dates at Glasgow's SECC. On the afternoon of the first show, I met Happy Mondays for the first and last time. Just out of college, I was trying to blag a job interviewing bands for BBC Radio Scotland. I had never interviewed anyone before, but was allowed to try for Happy Mondays after persuading a producer that I had access to the band. Ever since the recent revelations about Shaun's heroin habit, all press requests had been denied. I had lied about my access, but nevertheless managed to get backstage to meet the Mondays. Throughout the interview, all six sat in a circle around me, while I – equipped with BBC tape recorder and microphone – asked questions about their new album, the tour, the tabloid reports and the band's influence on their fans. When I left the dressing room twenty minutes later, I had only one short comment on tape. It was a mumbled quote from a worse-for-wear Shaun Ryder and it had something to do with my legs.

Years later, Shaun would tell me that he had spent the entire Pills 'N' Thrills tour high on heroin. He also claimed that he had fooled Donovan into thinking he was only on E.

'Did I know what Shaun was up to?' says Donovan now. 'Of course I did. I had only tried heroin once and I had never taken E, not even with the Mondays, but I had been told about the drug by my children. I guessed it was something to do with acid and I remembered speed so I presumed I had a pretty good idea what it was. It was obvious that Shaun wasn't on Ecstasy. It was also obvious that he wasn't just doing smack. Shaun was taking everything.'

THIRTEEN

Another Mars Bar Story

In 1991, the Madchester bubble burst. With no sign of new Stone Roses material and Happy Mondays music out in a league of its own, the scene was suddenly left with just bit-part players like Inspiral Carpets, Paris Angels, Northside and The High. Scarcely the sound of a revolution. Only The Charlatans, with their swirling 1960s songs and boyishly-handsome singer Tim Burgess, showed promise, albeit as a Stone Roses substitute. Moreover, Manchester itself was experiencing the party comedown. A massive increase in violence and, in particular, the use of firearms (thirty-five shootings were reported in a six-month period) saw areas of the city such as Moss Side, Hulme and Cheetham Hill nicknamed 'Gunchester', and forced clubs and music venues to step up security in order to ensure the safety of both staff and clientele. James Anderton's Draconian anti-party policies hadn't solved Manchester's drug problem, they had simply driven dealers and their phenomenally-lucrative trade further underground.

Three days into the new year, at a magistrates' court hearing, the Hacienda was granted yet another six-months' reprieve when the proposed four-week trial to revoke its drinks licence, brought by Greater Manchester Police, was adjourned until July. Despite an attendant *News Of The World* journalist eager to give evidence that he had been able to buy drugs while working undercover 'as a scally' in the venue, even the prosecution admitted that the strict body searches undertaken by the club appeared to be working. It was expected that the police would now drop their action and that the new hearing would be little more than a formality.

Nevertheless, the Hacienda's problems were far from over. Coupled with ever-increasing door prices, the searches and, inevitably, the lack of drugs, attendances were considerably down, while a lot of the atmosphere had been lost. A fortnight after the hearing, a members-only scheme was launched for the venue's notorious Nude nights in an attempt to keep gangs out of the club. However, just one week later, following an incident in which a doorman was threatened with a gun, the Hacienda was voluntarily shut down on a temporary basis by its owners.

The following statement was issued to the press by Tony Wilson: 'The Hacienda is closing its doors as of today. We are forced into taking this drastic action in order to protect our employees, our members and all our clients. We are, quite simply, sick and tired of dealing with instances of personal violence. We hope that we can reopen in a better climate. But until we are able to run the club in a safe manner, and in a way that the owners believe will guarantee the role of the Hacienda at the heart of the city's youth community, it is with great sadness that we will remain shut.'

Shaun Ryder was having almost as bad a start to the year as the Hacienda, about which he had been told by Factory to make no comment. Happy Mondays' first live performance of 1991 had been awful. Headlining the second night of the Great British Music Weekend, a three-day event at Wembley Arena organised by Jonathan King, the band followed an impressive, rapturously-received performance by James with a short, shambolic set, which began with a false start (Shaun stopped opening song 'Step On' after thirty seconds, despite the show being broadcast live on BBC Radio 1) and ended with the singer storming off. In between, Bez took frequent breaks from dancing to sit by the side of the monitors, Shaun shoved intrusive cameramen out of the way, disgruntled members of the audience threw stuff on stage and the music itself never really got going.

To add to Shaun's problems, Happy Mondays' forthcoming single, a version of 'Loose Fit' remixed by The Grid, had to be edited because of the Gulf War. Due to broadcasting restrictions, the lyric 'Gonna build an airforce base/Gonna blow up your race' was removed from the seven-inch version of the song, while the release date was delayed from February until March so that the video could also be re-cut. In addition, a TV acting role which had been all but offered to Shaun by an American production company, was given instead to Scouse actor Paul McGann. Shaun had been approached to play photographer Tim Page (whom he had met some months ago at a Happy Mondays shoot) in a three-part drama called *Frankie's House*, about the experiences of Page and fellow snapper Sean Flynn during the Vietnam War.

There was some good news though. First, Happy Mondays received two nominations for 1991's prestigious Brit Awards (for Best Group and Best Newcomer), pitting them against the likes of The Stone Roses, The Charlatans, The Beautiful South, Betty Boo and The La's. Then, on Saturday 16 February at 6.30am, Shaun watched his girlfriend Trish give birth to a perfect 10lb 10oz baby girl to the strains of Electronic's new single, 'Feel Every Beat', and The Beatles' *Rubber Soul*. Named Jael Otis Ann Ryder (Otis after Otis Redding, Ann after Shaun's grandmother), the child was said by the singer to look 'like something from outer space'. He also reckoned that Jael shared his musical taste, citing Funkadelic as her favourite.

'Shaun just stares at her and kisses her and whistles to her all the time,' Trish told *NME*, which the couple had invited to the birth. 'She goes quiet now when he whistles.'

NME also commented that Shaun hadn't fainted during the birth, nor had he touched Trish's oxygen.

Happy Mondays knew that they needed to take a break. For months, Shaun had been demanding a proper holiday. Nevertheless, barely days after the birth of his daughter, he began a European tour with the band. Moreover, he had only just returned from a week in Rio, where Happy Mondays had performed at the second Rock In Rio festival alongside such diverse acts as Guns N' Roses, Prince, George Michael, Lisa Stansfield and New Kids On The Block. The three-day event was a slightly scaled-down successor to the first Rock In Rio, which had taken place five years earlier and featured the likes of Queen and Ozzy Osbourne. Nevertheless, the local stadium's capacity crowd numbered over 200,000, twenty times the size of a Wembley Arena audience.

Although the idea of an all-expenses-paid trip to South America obviously appealed to Happy Mondays, the real incentive was their fee. *Pills 'N' Thrills And Bellyaches* may have been an instant critical and commercial success (in end-of-year polls it was unanimously voted best album of 1990 by the press and public alike), but the band themselves were still waiting to reap the financial rewards. Factory's unusual (not to mention misguidedly generous) industry contracts meant that, instead of receiving a large advance, artists shared in the profits from their output. Because recording costs had first to be recouped, however, those profits were unlikely to materialise for several more months. Meanwhile, the Mondays had increasingly expensive lifestyles to maintain. As well as new family commitments (even Bez was imminently due for fatherhood), they had developed designer tastes, not just in clothes, but in cars (BMWs all round), holidays and homes. To compound the problem, in the wake of the Hacienda's problems and the current drugs climate, there could be no more dealing or selling stories to the tabloids.

Happy Mondays arrived in Rio after a thirteen-hour flight from Heathrow to the news that the local *Evening Post* carried a front-page story claiming that the band was rumoured to be bringing 1000 Ecstasy tablets into the country for the festival. The inevitable customs search proved fruitless, however, and the Mondays and their entourage were free to go check into their rooms at the £250-a-night Intercontinental Hotel, overlooking the Copacabana Beach. Amid gossip that the Brazilian government had literally disposed of hundreds of beggars from the streets of central Rio, the following day began with a press conference attended by the world's media, most of whom had never heard of Happy Mondays.

'We're not bothered if no one knows our music,' Shaun told journalists. 'We've just come here to see what it's like and get lost.' Answering a question on what their show, scheduled for the next night, would be like, he replied, 'We've always done shit gigs because we're always stoned.'

Happy Mondays almost didn't play at all. After a fairly sedate first two days in the city (during which Shaun refused to emerge from his room until after dark and Nathan was nowhere to be seen), the band was still waiting for their keyboards and guitars to arrive from England just hours before they were due on stage. When the instruments didn't turn up, their slot was swapped with A-Ha's. They would now play at 2am on Sunday morning. On Saturday evening, however, they had already planned to attend a barbecue thrown by Great Train robber and local resident Ronnie Biggs.

'It was Piers Morgan from the *Sun* who sorted that out,' says Jayne Houghton, who had travelled to Rio with the band. 'Piers was this squeaky-clean, over-educated straight guy in a suit. He would goad Shaun into things. You could almost see his mind working on the next grubby little story. He wanted photos of Shaun and Ronnie together for the *Sun*. Naturally, Shaun was well into the idea.'

Happy Mondays arrived at Ronnie Biggs's house with a present of a box of PG Tips and a handful of £10 notes for him to sign. The tabloids – and the music press – got their shots, everyone ate some chicken and then it was on to the stadium for the show.

The band came on in a torrential downpour verging on a storm, not to mention a hail of vegetables and Coke cans from the front few rows of the audience which had never heard their songs. A handful of hits later, however, Happy Mondays had converted the crowd. 200,000 Brazilians danced in the rain to 'Hallelujah', 'Rave On' and 'Wrote For Luck' as Gaz tried desperately to stop the Ronnie Biggs autograph on his tracksuit bottoms from washing off.

After the show, the band was unable to get into the posh nightclub where both Prince and George Michael had thrown their parties. Instead, the entire Mondays entourage descended on the Copacabana's Help, South America's largest disco, where the entrance is flagged by a pair of flashing pink neon legs.

'It's a gross exaggeration to say that Shaun saved my life at that club,' says Jayne Houghton, 'but he did diffuse the situation when a prostitute tried to stab me. I remember it had taken two hours to get everyone to agree on where to go. By then, the guys from the *Sun* had decided to call it a night. I suddenly realised, way too late, that I was the only white woman in this club. A lot of the Mondays' road crew were with us, and they had all started pairing up with local women who were quite obviously prostitutes. There were hundreds of hookers in that club. I recognised several who had been hanging around outside the Intercontinental earlier. Most of the bands were staying in the same hotel, including the big American rock bands like Guns N' Roses, and even the girls who weren't prostitutes were desperate to get near Western bands and Western money.

'We were already inside the club when this associate of Ronnie Biggs, who was supposed to be looking after us, admitted that the place was basically just a pick-up joint. He told us that Western men could get a shag for about 10p, and that foreign women really weren't welcome. By now, everyone was incredibly pissed, so it was too late to go anywhere else.

'After a couple of hours in there, I noticed that this totally psychopathic-looking girl had been eyeing Shaun up for ages. He wasn't interested, so I thought I'd sit with him and it would put her off. I started talking to him, but all the time this girl was shooting me these dagger looks. When I went to the loo, she followed me in there and hauled me up against the wall. Then she pulled out a knife. It wasn't anything dramatic, just a small blade. Nevertheless, I'd never come that close to a knife wielded by a mad Brazilian prostitute before. I ran out of the toilets and headed straight back to the band because they had their security with them. I told Shaun that we had to leave straight away.

'Outside, lots of girls were chasing us to the tour bus. The security managed to fend some of them off, but there were some that the crew had brought back, who had to be allowed to come with us. Then the mad girl jumped on the bus too. I was really scared and crying. Shaun was shouting, "She's my sister. Leave her alone, she's not my girlfriend." Apparently, because I had blonde hair, I was taken to be a Dutch prostitute, who they get a lot of over there. This girl thought I'd picked up "her man". Shaun kept swearing I was his sister. Eventually, he had to take her off the bus to pacify her.

'It is an exaggeration to say that Shaun saved my life, but he certainly stopped me getting a good beating. This girl really was fierce and totally demented. A lot of the Brazilian women are quite small and not too imposing. It was just my luck to get the six-foot-something strapping one wielding a knife. It wasn't until the next morning that I realised just how serious the incident had been. They knife Westerners for simply walking down the street in Rio.'

Tales of Shaun's exploits at Rock In Rio – including freebasing cocaine while at the wheel of a car and having sex with a prostitute in a coffin – would continue long after Happy Mondays' return to Britain. If the drugs stories had only a hint of truth in their origin (the band did score coke in Rio, the same as numerous other acts at the festival), the sex stories were almost certainly fabricated, at least as far as Shaun was concerned.

'It was usually not Shaun, but all the people around him who went with women,' says Houghton. 'Not that Shaun minded people thinking that he did. It was what he thought everyone expected of him. When he was with Trish, there were one-night stands, but no big infidelities. He didn't mind having mad nights in hotels, surrounded by women, but underneath – sometimes way, way underneath – he was pretty much a moral family man. The crew and the Mondays' entourage, on the other hand, always took advantage of every situation. As far as I could see, Shaun was more concerned with the drugs and rock'n'roll than he was with the sex.

'To this day, Shaun insists that I stopped him from getting AIDS in Brazil. He says he would have gone with one of those women in the club that night and not worn a condom. He reckons I saved his life. I'm not sure about the others though. I remember at the hotel the next morning, one of the crew coming downstairs saying, "I can't believe it. The girl I spent the night with wanted me to pay her. She was a bloody prostitute. Tart! I thought she liked me." Another one of the crew was really pleased with himself because, to get out of paying his hooker, he'd given her a Mars bar from the mini-bar in his room. Apparently, she had left quite content with that.'

Happy Mondays followed their trip to Brazil with a month-long European tour, beginning in Berlin. The band had still to break big outside Britain. In the US no one understood their songs. In Europe, however, their prospects looked promising.

'We wanted to be big in places like Germany and Holland,' says Shaun. 'We weren't that bothered about commercial success in England. It would have suited us fine to make loads of money in Europe, then come back home and be able to drive nice cars, but not be associated with all the music business idiots here.'

The European tour took in two sold-out dates at a club in Paris called La Cigale and a packed album signing at a Virgin Megastore on the Champs-Elysées, throughout which Shaun sat sipping champagne. Although the usual couple of coachloads of British fans crossed the Channel for the gigs, the bulk of the audiences was French. In fact, so well received were the shows, which featured a skin-tight catsuit-clad Rowetta for half of the set, the promoter suggested that the band return soon to play a 6000-capacity venue. At last, it seemed, Happy Mondays' music was catching on outside the UK. Little progress, however, continued to be made in the US. A comprehensive tour there once again failed to establish the band or make any dent in the *Billboard* charts, despite several critically-acclaimed club-sized concerts.

At the start of the summer, when Happy Mondays returned to

Britain, Madchester had all but died. As The Stone Roses' record company tried to squeeze the last cash from the scene by re-releasing the band's eponymous debut album and former singles, the media's interest had shifted back to London. A new breed of guitar bands, led by Blur, Ride and Lush, had caught the attention of the rock music press. Predictably, they were the antithesis of Manchester's bad boys – southern, middle-class and well-educated.

Despite the 'baggy' backlash, Happy Mondays stayed in favour. A string of UK festival dates – including the Feile in Ireland, Cities In The Park in Manchester and an all-day event at Leeds' Elland Road – received glowing reviews.

'In the past, Happy Mondays have appeared boorish and scrappy, but not so today,' noted *NME* of the Elland Road show. 'Their swaggering confidence confirmed their progression from underground perverts to high street accessories to stadium fillers, and they've done it without the pomposity the previous generation of stadium-ites thrived on.'

'We treated the band as a job by then,' says Shaun. 'We had done for a while. We knew that if we didn't, people would soon get pissed off with us not turning up or whatever. At one time, we pleased ourselves. If we didn't feel like doing something, we didn't do it. But we were also aware that we were doing way too much.'

While Happy Mondays waited for their hard-earned profits to pour in, Factory couldn't spend its cash fast enough. New offices were bought and refurbished by Hacienda designer Ben Kelly at a cost of over £750,000. The building even boasted a zinc roof, of which Tony Wilson was especially proud, which no one could actually see. Accountant Eric Longley, who had now been installed as MD of the label (albeit one with little control), couldn't believe some of the business practices in progress.

'The company was run in an insane way,' he says. 'Everyone acted as though they had won the football pools. Tony in particular was intoxicated by the sudden success of Happy Mondays. The label already had New Order; now Tony thought he could keep repeating his good fortune. He thought he could score again with a new act any time he liked. What Tony didn't realise was that he was out of touch. He was over forty. The bands he liked were what other forty-year-olds liked. He'd lost the kids, he'd lost the feel. Actually, Tony had lost the plot completely. He was literally throwing money at albums which were never even going to recoup their costs. He spent £100,000 plus recording costs on the Adventure Babies. He spent £150,000 on Cath Carroll, which shifted about 3000 copies. He thought that if you chucked tons of cash at a band, they were bound to come up with a great album. 'No one at Factory seemed bothered about the business side of the operation. No one was interested. It was too uncool to be involved with money matters. Tony was fantastic with promotional ideas and he had also employed a great staff. Both Rob Gretton and Macca, who looked after Northside, were brilliant managers. I was managing the New Fast Automatic Daffodils at the time, so I could tell they were talented. But you just can't ignore business. At the time, Factory had a club that was haemorrhaging money and a bar that couldn't pay for itself. When I suggested putting the drinks prices up in the Dry Bar to cover costs, everyone was appalled. It seemed so shocking to them that someone had even made such a radical suggestion.'

In the summer of 1991, Happy Mondays put out their own bootleg live album. Recorded directly from the mixing desk of their Elland Road and Cities In The Park shows, the fourteen-track double LP, called *Baby Big Head*, featured the band's first ever live performance of 'Tokoloshe Man' (the track they had recorded for the Elektra anniversary album instead of 'Step On'). Incredibly, it wasn't an official Factory release. Said to be limited to an edition of 1000 and priced at £14.99, *Baby Big Head* was available by mail-order only. Cheques were to be sent to a Manchester address, with ten days allowed for delivery.

In a press statement on the album, Shaun Ryder said, 'The people who have done the bootleg have assured me that all profits are going to sick animals and poor children. Unlike most bootlegs, the sound quality is brilliant and so is the cover design. We have been guaranteed 100 per cent that people will receive this record.' Perhaps even more surprisingly, Factory didn't object to the release, although Shaun had noted that the label was scarcely in a position to, having calculated that it owed Happy Mondays in the region of £100,000.

'I think it is absolutely great that this bootleg is available,' Tony Wilson told the press. 'Factory are planning to release the recording officially in late autumn and negotiations for a worldwide deal are currently underway.'

'*Baby Big Head* was a truly terrible record,' says Longley. 'The Mondays were great live because of the vibe they could create. Their actual performance wasn't something you would want to listen to at home. Of course, they were so popular at the time that the album sold pretty well regardless. A few months later, Factory put it out as a proper release. Obviously, everyone who wanted it – i.e. all the hardcore fans – had already bought the pirate. Financially, it was a disaster.'

In autumn 1991, seemingly oblivious to the media's change in attitude towards sexist, laddish bands, Shaun and Bez appeared in soft-porn mag *Penthouse*. In the five-page feature, as so-called 'guest editors', the pair posed in a foam bath with three 'Penthouse Pets', including the magazine's best-known model, Linzi Drew, and revealed that they would like to corrupt Kylie Minogue by getting her stoned and giving her E.

'For better or for worse, Shaun's appearance in *Penthouse* was my idea,' says Jayne Houghton. 'I set it up. Shaun never once suggested that he wanted to be in a porn mag. It may have been totally naive of me, but it was never meant to send out a big message. If any musician could have pulled that off as a bit of light-hearted fun, it was Shaun. The idea came about because the editor loved Happy Mondays. He had come to the album launch at Regent's Park Zoo and had reviewed the record in the magazine. Obviously, *Penthouse* wasn't usually on my mailing list, but I had heard that The Farm had been featured, so I sent in a pre-release copy of *Pills 'N' Thrills*.

'At the launch party, the editor asked if the band would do something in the magazine. It wasn't as though we needed the press, I just reckoned it could be a laugh. Initially, it was going to be an interview, but the goal posts kept moving. Shaun loved the idea – partly because they were offering him a lot of money to appear – but insisted he be interviewed by one of the models. I told him it was going to be the editor. In that case, he wanted to do it where the magazine was edited. In a silly boyish farcical way, he and Bez assumed there would be loads of gorgeous, scantily-clad women wandering around the office. That was their total wank fantasy. I told them it would just be like any other office, but they didn't believe that the women whose pictures were at the top of columns didn't actually write the features.

'Shaun then decided that he wanted Linzi Drew to do the story. I asked the editor if she could at least be involved in some capacity. I also told him I didn't mind if they took pictures. I could say I completely lost control of the situation after that, but at the same time I could always have pulled the article completely. Except that of course, if I did, I would have had a mutiny on my hands from all these testosterone-fuelled Mancunians. It was the only occasion in the entire time that I did press for Happy Mondays that Shaun – and most of the rest of the band, for that matter – turned up on time for an interview. Even Muzzer started to take an interest in journalism on that occasion.

'By the time the shoot actually happened, *Penthouse* had decided that Shaun and Bez would be "guest editors" of that month's issue. They even had these daft business cards made up for the pair of them – Shaun as editor, Bez as deputy editor. Most of the band came down from Manchester specially. *Penthouse* sent a limo to pick them up at the airport. When it arrived at the magazine's offices, there were about a dozen photographers waiting outside. The second Shaun and Bez stepped out of the car, they were jumped on by Linzi Drew and two other models. Shaun's eyes were literally out on stalks. Bez's were worse.

'As far as guest-editing went, all that happened was they went into the office and posed for photographs by looking at slides and pointing at copy. The proper photo-session for the feature the following day was much more interesting. The plan was to shoot Shaun and Bez and the same three models as before together in a bubble-bath. It was very professional. *Penthouse* had booked a suite with a jacuzzi at the Holiday Inn in Swiss Cottage, north London, and employed a top photographer, who had already set up lots of lights and equipment by the time we arrived.

'At first, Bez decided he didn't want to do it. He got all shy when he realised he had to take his clothes off. So he kept his pants on and got into the jacuzzi. Shaun said he wouldn't get in at all unless the bathroom was cleared of people. By this time, Bez was really excited, messing around with the models and splashing about in the water. But all of Shaun's initial bravado had gone completely. Bez and the girls had to get out and everyone left the room.

'Ages later, we were all still waiting for Shaun to get ready. Eventually, he told us to come in. We opened the door and there he was, sitting in the jacuzzi with his vest on. Muzzer and I just burst out laughing. The vest was really grubby and baggy and off-white, like something your granddad would wear. Shaun absolutely refused to remove it though. He said he wasn't thin enough. It looked ridiculous, especially with three naked women in there with him. The photographer tried several times to cover Shaun's top half in bubbles, but it didn't work.

'In the end, it took us literally half an hour to talk Shaun out of the vest. Then the girls had to straddle both him and Bez for the shots. I kept trying to sneak off into the other room for a drink because *Penthouse* had laid on this great spread with bottles of champagne, but Shaun wouldn't let me leave. He said he had promised Trish that I would be there at all times. I got the photos back the next day. Shaun had been caught on camera with this really cheeky, dimpled grin. I swear that look didn't leave his face for about a week.'

FOURTEEN
Ghosts Of Christmas Past

Happy Mondays' self-interest, self-sufficiency and obsession with wealth saw them dubbed Thatcher's children by the Manchester media. Local magazine *City Life* concluded that the band was the Conservative leader's philosophy made hip, while staff at the Dry Bar wore T-shirts emblazoned with the question 'Who put the Tory into Factory?' It was only apt, then, that the demise of both label and band should coincide with Thatcher's downfall. Factory Records was already struggling with massive mortgage repayments on its newly-acquired, expensively-refurbished HQ when the British property boom of the past decade suddenly collapsed. In the space of three months, the Hacienda's value plummeted from over £1 million to just £300,000. The worth of the Charles Street offices and the Dry Bar similarly slumped, leaving the label literally drowning in negative equity.

For over a year, Factory had been in discussion with multi-media conglomerate Polygram in an attempt to strike up some sort of partnership. Initially, the idea of a merger was principally prompted by acts such as James and OMD, which had started out on Factory, but then signed to major labels on the brink of breaking into the charts. Wilson now realised that a deal with a major label was the only way to hang on to talent and thus reap the reward from their mainstream success. Now, however, securing major label funding increasingly appeared to be the only means of survival for Factory. As talks with Polygram went on, it became clear that the conglomerate wished to absorb Factory, rather than enter into a partnership with its directors.

Naturally, selling out wasn't what Wilson wanted. Moreover, with two of Britain's brightest bands on his label, he knew that there was room to negotiate. At least he thought there was. Aware that

Factory's famously informal contracts gave it no legal hold over its acts, Polygram needed to know with whom ownership of the bands' back catalogues lay. A thorough search through Factory's badly-kept files provided the answer. A scrap of paper signed by Wilson and his associate Alan Erasmus, the closest anyone could find to a contact, revealed that the musicians owned all rights to their own recordings. Essentially, Factory was a worthless company with mounting debts. Its only lifeline lay with its two major acts and the hope that their forthcoming albums would both be a big success. Unfortunately, neither New Order nor Happy Mondays had a new record ready to release. In fact, the pair had scarcely started work on any new material.

'By that time, New Order were more interested in their separate side projects than making another album together, despite the success of their World Cup song,' says former Factory MD Eric Longley. 'As for Happy Mondays, they were just such a difficult bunch to work with. They were so schizophrenic. Sometimes they would be incredibly lazy, sometimes very industrious. You just never knew which it was going to be, so you could never really rely on them.

'I was made MD of the company in January of that year. By spring, when there was still no sign of any albums scheduled for the autumn, I tried to instigate some ideas to cash in on the Christmas market. I wanted to put out a Happy Mondays remix album called *Substances*, which was to be eight or nine remixes of the band's best singles. It would have been the first time an entire remix album had come out. I reckoned we could have sold 40,000 of those. We could have done well with it in the States too. Tony didn't like the idea though. Instead, he decided that we were going to release a four-album compilation of assorted Factory tracks, which probably sold around 4,000 copies. I tried to tell Tony that the record was a bad idea, but of course he didn't listen.'

The compilation album – called *Palatine*, after Palatine Road, the site of Factory's first offices – was a forty-eight-song boxed set chronicling the history of the label. By the time of its release in late 1991, Longley no longer worked for Factory. Along with four other employees, the MD had been made redundant in order to cut costs. Naturally, rumours of the Factory's demise were rife. Wilson, however, issued a press statement insisting that the company was now out of trouble. He revealed that Factory had struck a distribution deal for territories outside the UK with Polygram label London Records, and claimed this had left Factory in good shape for 1992. He also admitted that he had hired a team of financial advisers to sort out the company's accounts, but said he would consider selling only a minority percentage of Factory shares, for the sole purpose of raising capital in order to expand.

'We're doing fine,' Wilson said in an interview with *NME* to promote the release of *Palatine*. 'We had a very tough summer during the recession, but we're pulling through. I had to make people redundant and there's nothing like that for reminding you that you are in business. But we have survived. I'm proud of what we've done. I'm not proud of the new offices though. It embarrasses me to have a flashy building and to have to make people redundant. If I was a great businessman, we wouldn't have had such a tough year.'

Even the Hacienda appeared to be back in business. Three months after the venue's voluntary closure, the club had been revamped and reopened in what Wilson had hoped was a less aggressive climate. Less than six weeks later, however, its future was once more thrown into doubt when a gang stormed into the club in the early hours of a Saturday morning, stabbing six doormen in the ensuing fracas. Despite repeated calls for its closure, the Hacienda stayed open and, by the autumn, had established three popular weekly nights and a number of well-attended monthly events.

Even though the music media were now dividing their attention between southern, so-called 'shoegazing' bands such as Ride and guitarless, club-born techno acts like The Prodigy and N-Joi, Wilson remained hopeful for Factory's future. He should have worried, however, about the emergence of a rejuvenated Primal Scream. With the aid of its newly-appointed producer, DJ Andy Weatherall, the band, which had always boasted a fine line in scandalous drug stories, now also oozed Happy Mondays' contemporary club cred. By late 1991, when Primal Scream's album *Screamadelica* won the first-ever Mercury Music prize, Manchester bands had all but fallen out of fashion.

'Factory will be on top form again when Northside are a monstrous group,' insisted Wilson in the *NME* interview. 'If not, I'm an idiot. But we'll see.'

Happy Mondays' first new material since the release of *Pills 'N'*

Thrills almost exactly a year earlier was an edgy, Oakenfold/ Osborne-produced single called 'Judge Fudge', which Shaun said was 'written for a film about young kids with lots of money and corrupt, pervert judges'. Over the summer, there had been rumours that the band's comeback single would be a cover of The Scaffold's 1960s hit 'Thank You Very Much', produced by Paul McCartney. Shaun was also said to be embarking on a solo career with a version of Thin Lizzy's 'Running Back', to be recorded with former Smiths bassist Andy Rourke, rather than any of the Mondays' musicians. Neither project got off the ground.

As part of promotion for 'Judge Fudge', a fortnight before its release in November, Shaun appeared on MTV. A half-hour interview with one of the station's DJs was edited down to only a few minutes. Naturally, the highlights condensed into soundbites were the singer's most contentious comments, including the usual boasts of excessive drug use and tales of outlandish band behaviour. The broadcast also included a rather dubious joke from Shaun about having once been a rent boy. 'I was making money selling my body on Sackville Street,' he jested in the interview. 'I never really wanted a proper job.' Days later, billed as a 'showbiz exclusive', the story appeared in tabloid paper *News Of The World* under the heading 'I was rent boy says Happy Mondays star'.

Accompanied by one of the *Penthouse* photos of Shaun and Bez in the jacuzzi with the three topless models, the full-page report by journalist Judy McGuire claimed that 'bad boy Shaun' had admitted to selling sex for £40-a-day before he became famous.

'I couldn't see the point in working for £40-a-week when you can make that in a day doing rent,' Shaun was quoted as saying. Comments on his current drug use were also reproduced: 'I know the hard stuff is killing me, but I need something to get me through the day. The last two years have been one long blur. I remember something about becoming a dad and being on *Top Of The Pops*, but not much else.'

It was Paul Ryder who showed Shaun the Sunday paper carrying the story. He knew that his brother would be annoyed, but didn't anticipate the fury of his reaction. Shaun later confessed that he came close to killing Paul that day. He chased him round the house, screaming that he wanted to fight because he felt Paul was laughing at him. In fact, Shaun was far more concerned that other people would be laughing. Worse still, some might even think it was true. That night, high on heroin and infuriated by the newspaper article, Shaun stormed into the Dry Bar in Manchester's Oldham Street, accompanied by Bez. He was armed with a gun, a Magnum, which he had owned for several months but never intended to use. He shot and smashed a 4' x 4' mirror on the wall in the bar, then immediately left. Two days later, the tabloids recounted the incident, claiming that Shaun had caused £1000 worth of damage. They were unaware, however, that a firearm had been used, believing that a bottle had broken the mirror. The following week, still obviously frustrated and very angry, Shaun agreed to talk to *NME* about both the rent boy story and the incident in the Dry Bar. His comments could scarcely have been more damaging to either himself or Happy Mondays.

'There was no point in going to a pub where people don't know me and causing a scene,' claimed Shaun in the interview. 'I had to go where there were heads that knew me. I got narked and smashed some mirror. I just wanted people to see that I was annoyed and also that I wasn't hiding in my house ashamed. Some people from the bar asked why I was picking on them. But I wasn't picking on anybody. I don't give a fuck though. Factory can't say anything because they owe me a hundred grand. I'm paying for nish.'

Dry Bar manager Leroy Richardson also issued a statement to the press, in which he claimed that the bar had picked up the repair bill, which came to little over £80. 'It was very clearly not a direct attack on anyone,' he insisted. 'The tabloid report saying that Shaun caused £1000 worth of damage was ridiculous. There is no problem with the band here. It was obviously an act of frustration at what had been written about him. We were sympathetic to the position.'

Shaun's reaction to the rent boy scandal was more difficult to gloss over. Although Factory's lawyers had already issued a writ against *News Of The World*, Shaun was determined to make public the strength of his hatred for journalist Judy McGuire.

'I've been really fucking pissed off since Sunday,' he said in *NME*. 'We're suing. Our lawyers think we have a good case for libel. I'm not blaming MTV, you can tell it was a joke on there. I didn't talk to the tabloids about it though. I wouldn't talk to the tabloids about that for any amount of money, and I would have wanted half a million to say I was a rent boy.

'I've said in the press hundreds of times that they can't hurt me because I'm not a pervert but they have tried to do this job on me. They know the only way to hurt any lad like me who comes from my side of town is to call them a rent boy or faggot. McGuire's shit stinks like everyone else's. There's enough corrupt politicians about, why pick on someone who is as normal as they come?

'I'm not arsed about the drugs and I don't know how it will affect the band, but it's in my head. McGuire said in the paper that my girlfriend Trish was upset. Well, Trish wasn't upset because she knows it was a load of bollocks, as do people who know me. But there's still folk out there who think that there's no smoke without fire.'

It was the word 'faggot' and the context in which it was used that caused the most damage. Shaun had revealed himself to be grossly homophobic.

Just days after the *NME* news story had been published, in a perhaps ill-advised attempt to promote the single 'Judge Fudge', Happy Mondays were interviewed for a cover story once again for *NME*. The resulting article, written by staff journalist Steven Wells, was to mark the beginning of the end for the band. In photos for the feature, Shaun looked awful. He was horribly white, his face was wide and puffy and he could hardly open his eyes. Wrapped in an expensive, zipped-up, bulky anorak, Shaun was described by Wells as resembling a 'glue-sniffing Womble'. Next to the pictures, the line didn't raise much of a laugh.

The article began as an interrogation and ended as an execution. Although Steven Wells's questions were clearly designed to antagonise, it was in fact Shaun and Bez who signed the band's death warrant.

Wells began by asking Shaun what was so bad about being called a rent boy. After all, the singer had already admitted to having been a drug dealer, which was in many ways a worse allegation.

'Lads who come from where I come from don't like being called a fuckin' faggot,' replied Shaun. 'I have nothing against them, but I have my rights and I ain't a fuckin' faggot and that's it. I ain't going to go around bashing them, they can do what they want. But where I come from, that's probably the worst thing you could call somebody.'

Wells then pointed out that being gay and being a rent boy wasn't the same thing.

'Right, all right, but I don't suck dick. Don't suck dick!' was Shaun's excruciating reply.

As the interview went on, it got worse. Shaun was baited about the sexist implications of guest-editing *Penthouse*, the discrepancy between his views of male and female prostitutes and the smallmindedness of his attitude in general. It was Bez's contribution to the conversation, however, which sealed Happy Mondays' fate.

'I hate faggots,' Bez declared. 'Anyone who is straight finds them disgusting. Faggots might find shagging pussy disgusting, but we find shagging a bloke not right. The majority of people in Britain aren't gay, are they?'

'The sad thing about the entire episode was that Bez had never once acted homophobic,' says Longley, who was by then working for Happy Mondays' manager Nathan McGough. 'He had been around people for years who he knew for a fact were gay and it hadn't bothered him. The problem was that Bez had been in jail and had seen some awful stuff in there. No one understood that. No one bothered to ask why he had that attitude. Loose words sink ships, and that's exactly what happened. The Mondays didn't honestly mean what they had said. It was quite the opposite in fact. They felt awful about it.'

'The "fag" quote was a fuckin' bad thing,' says Shaun. 'We used the word fag because that's how we talk. It wasn't really a homophobic comment, that's just how it came across. Bez was trying to say that he thought fags were all right, as long as they didn't try it on with him. Depending on where you're brought up, that can be a pretty normal thing to say.'

'The whole situation was handled very badly by everyone around the band,' says Longley. 'The general attitude was to move on and try to forget what had been said. It wasn't terribly professional. But things were starting to slip away from all sides by that stage.'

Ironically, having been in need of a holiday for so long, it was a period of relative inactivity over the summer of 1991 which saw Happy Mondays really spiral out of control. Despite assurances that the birth of his daughter had helped reduce his intake of hard drugs, and in the wake of the substance-induced death of *Bummed* producer Martin Hannett, with time on his hands, Shaun simply indulged to greater excess.

Now that he was famous, he didn't even have to finance his habit any more. Dealers were content with just the kudos of supplying Shaun Ryder.

Nevertheless, money matters were tearing Happy Mondays apart. Factory's fragile position was a huge worry, particularly as the band members were literally watching the label waste their profits. They began to squabble about who was owed what, how much input each had in the songwriting and why Bez should be paid royalties at all. When the *NME* article came out, eager to distance themselves from the homophobia outrage, Gaz Whelan and Paul Davis insisted that Bez be thrown out of the band. Just as Happy Mondays needed to pull together, they were falling apart.

Moreover, their staunch independence, which had previously served them so well, now meant that no one was on hand to help. Tony Wilson was too concerned with saving Factory. Nathan was too close to the band to be objective.

'Nathan was unlike any other manager I have ever met,' says Jayne Houghton. 'In the beginning that was great, but by the end it was very unfortunate. He was never Mr Manager in a suit, keeping an acceptable distance. The amount of drinking and drug taking he did, he might as well have been in the band. When Happy Mondays were on the up, Nathan was very good at getting things out of Shaun and fantastic at keeping schedules on course. Just the fact that he could hold together what was essentially the most dysfunctional family you could ever care to meet was amazing. On the face of it, a manager who is a mate is a bad idea. But Nathan had a remarkable knack of operating as normal in the face of total chaos and adversity.

'Nathan probably started to lose control a lot earlier, but by the time Steven Wells's story came out, it was obvious that everything was out of his hands. It was all running wild. The band was incredibly pissed off, Factory was rapidly going down, the press hated them, the new single was doing really badly, no one was talking to each other and Shaun was always out of his head. Bez's homophobic remarks just handed *NME* the rope it was going to use anyway. No way was Bez the rampant bigot he was made out to be. The guy simply isn't like that. Bez doesn't have an evil bone in his body. He's just stupid sometimes. That was the first occasion on which Happy Mondays had been badly torn apart and it couldn't have come at a worse time.

'Until then, all the middle-class music press had loved Shaun's bad boy, working-class image. It was exactly what they wanted. They actively encouraged him to act like a drug-addled nutter. They made out it was glamorous. Shaun ended up thinking that was what was expected of him. That's why he started laying it on near the end. He certainly never had a reason to give it up. No one was telling him to moderate his behaviour or suggesting that it may be out of control. Things would happen that you thought would change his lifestyle or at least help him to rein himself in a bit, like when Trish had his daughter. He did make a few half-hearted attempts to clean up, I guess, but he'd never want to talk about it. There was never a suitable time to discuss such things with Shaun. Then, before you knew it, he'd be straight back on the smack.

'Of course, the press didn't want to hear that Shaun had gone straight. A fucked-up genius makes for great copy. They were voyeurs in a really horrible way. It was like watching someone in a zoo to them. Really sick. By then, Shaun was playing the game to an extent where it wasn't a game any more. It was bound to backfire. All of a sudden, having adored him for years, everyone started scrambling to put the boot in. Steven Wells's piece did do a lot of damage, but it was really a case of sticking a pin in this balloon that was on its way down anyway.

'I remember one particularly bad interview I did with Shaun around that time. God knows how, but I had managed to get a profile piece on him in this teen magazine called *Jackie*. Some squeaky clean girl came down to Manchester from Scotland to write it. When she arrived at Factory's office, the band was midway through a totally unsuccessful press day, to which Shaun hadn't even bothered to turn up. By the time he did get there, I had ten journalists who had been waiting for hours to talk to him. It took until evening for him to finally get round to this *Jackie* girl, who had been incredibly patient and was really quite star-struck. Shaun said he wanted to do the interview back at his flat, which was only a few minutes' walk away. He said he was meeting some mates there later to go out. When we got there, he kept wandering in and out of rooms and shuffling about. He was really, really edgy. Then he disappeared for ages. I was thinking, "Please don't do anything obvious. Please don't be stupid." When he came back into the room with a piece of foil in his hand, I thought I was going to cry. I felt like shouting, "A bit of subtlety wouldn't kill you, Shaun." He threw me a knowing look and a big wink, but the girl just looked really puzzled. When he wandered off again, she asked me what he was doing. I said he'd just popped into the kitchen to bake himself a potato. She actually fell for it, thank God.'

'Judge Fudge', both musically and lyrically a rather uninspired song, became the first Happy Mondays single to bomb, as the band continued to fall out of favour. In an unfortunate coincidence, the Mondays had been booked months earlier to play at an AIDS Day benefit concert. Not surprisingly, the week before the event, they received a letter explaining that they were no longer wanted. At the time, Shaun didn't care. His only interest was in drugs. He still didn't believe that Happy Mondays were really in trouble.

'I never thought about what I wanted from the band,' says Shaun. 'The Mondays was just a way to be able to do what I wanted, when I wanted and spend what I wanted, how I wanted. We felt like we were lucky people. We'd had hard times before and come through them. It had always been pure hard times, then double good luck, then pure hard times again. It was like there was someone watching over us.

'We didn't even think that the band might be over. We never thought about the future, full stop. Never had done. It's like people would ask what our new songs were going to sound like and we never knew until we had finished them. Besides, what else could we do but be in a band? We couldn't get proper jobs. None of us had trades. The only other thing we had ever been was drug dealers and petty criminals, but we weren't much good at that. If we had been, we would have been driving big cars and living in huge houses years ago.'

It wasn't only Happy Mondays' irresponsible behaviour or the downfall of Factory, however, that had had a hand in the band's demise. In the months since *Pills 'N' Thrills And Bellyaches* had topped the charts, the musical climate in Britain had changed.

Grunge was the new indie trend, Nirvana's *Nevermind* was widely regarded as album of the year and Teenage Fanclub, who had just released *Bandwagonesque*, were being hailed the saviours of homegrown rock. Oddly, Happy Mondays' music, for all its bravado, sounded soft and powerless beside both the grunge guitar groups and the new breed of techno bands. In 1991, the Christmas issues of both *NME* and *Melody Maker* had featured Shaun Ryder on their cover. By the end of 1992, both papers were similarly obsessed with Kurt Cobain, with *Melody Maker* featuring him on the front cover. Moreover, Madchester topped the 'out' column of their in/out trends poll. Shaun, it seemed, had served his purpose.

Happy Mondays saw out the worst year of their career hanging from the gallows. The image could hardly have been more apt. Months earlier, the band had agreed to appear in a special Christmas TV show, directed by former Sex Pistols manager Malcolm McLaren. The programme, called *The Ghosts Of Oxford Street* and described by Channel 4 as 'a musical variety show', also featured artists such as The Pogues, Sinead O'Connor, Kirsty MacColl and Tom Jones. The short film gave Shaun the chance to finally have a go at acting, something he had wanted to do since being beaten to the BBC role the previous year.

'I'm not one of those people who have big ambitions to play Shakespeare,' says Shaun. 'If I make a career out of acting and I have to play a villain all the time, or a dirty, seedy, porno merchant cat burglar, that would be okay. It doesn't matter, as long as I enjoy it.'

In *The Ghosts Of Oxford Street*, which aimed to chart the 200-year history of the central London thoroughfare, Happy Mondays played convicted highwaymen. They drove down Oxford Street singing their own version of The Bee Gees' 1970s disco hit 'Stayin' Alive', before being dragged from their coach at Marble Arch (the original site of Tyburn Gallows) and strung up. While the programme ultimately fell far short of its hype, Happy Mondays claimed to be so pleased with their performance that they had decided to release 'Stayin' Alive' as their next single. Although the cover, a frankly woeful, tuneless dirge, never actually came out, its title was to prove strangely prophetic. By the end of the year, Happy Mondays had also announced that they were off to Barbados to begin recording of their fourth studio album.

FIFTEEN

The Long Goodbye

Factory Records was desperate for a new Happy Mondays album. The band itself, however, was hardly in a state to record one. No new songs had been written, no one appeared to have any new ideas and everyone was arguing. Moreover, Shaun could clearly have been better served in detox, rather then a recording studio. Financial pressures didn't help. To survive, both the band and Factory needed the album to be in the shops by autumn at the latest.

Just days into the new year, it was announced that production of Happy Mondays' fourth album proper was to begin in late January at Compass Point studios in Nassau in the Bahamas. Former Talking Heads musicians Chris Frantz and Tina Weymouth were also named as producers, a choice already causing problems. Shaun wanted Oakenfold and Osborne at the helm once again. However, the huge success of *Pills 'N' Thrills And Bellyaches* (which had won the Perfecto pair a Q award for best producers, as well as BRIT and BPI nominations) meant that their schedules were now full for months, and Factory couldn't wait. There were other factors too. Wilson was counting on the album doing well in the US as well as Europe. Frantz and Weymouth's reputation as ex-Talking Heads was certain to intrigue the American press, while their more traditional rock style would appeal to audiences which had clearly failed to fall for indie-dance. There were also financial considerations. Factory had calculated that both Happy Mondays and New Order could spend no more than £150,000 apiece on recording costs.

Thanks to bands such as Happy Mondays, Primal Scream and The Farm, demand for dance DJs as producers had soared, as had their fees. The cost of a remix had trebled in a matter of months, with the likes of Oakenfold and Andy Weatherall thought to command in the region of £2500 per track.

By the end of January, when the album sessions were scheduled to begin, Happy Mondays were still in Manchester. Meanwhile, Frantz and Weymouth had ruled out recording at Compass Point studios, which they had visited and deemed to be too basically equipped for their purposes. It was decided instead to delay the sessions until March, when Eddy Grant's Blue Wave studios in Barbados would be available.

The decision to record Happy Mondays' album in the Caribbean came originally from the band, but was credited to Factory. The official line was that studio time was cheaper there than it was in the UK or US. The location was also away from the usual distractions of a major city and would give the clearly troubled group a chance to chill out away from the prying eyes of the British press. Subsequently, Wilson would say that he had allowed Happy Mondays to go to Barbados because he believed that it would, at least temporarily, keep Shaun off smack. The island didn't have a heroin problem, nor was the singer likely to have any drug contacts in the area.

'The Mondays insisted on going to the Caribbean because they said they were making a summer album and it was still winter in the UK,' says Eric Longley. 'Factory swallowed it whole. With Tony, what the artist wanted, the artist always got. Whether the artist in question was a total genius or an absolute cunt didn't appear to come into it. No one even bothered to investigate the drugs situation in Barbados. Even if they had, I'm not sure it would have made any difference. Tony probably wouldn't have stopped to think that it may be a little unwise to pack a smackhead off to a crack-infested holiday resort with a ton of money.'

Shaun spent the first two months of 1992 trying to wean himself off heroin before recording of the album began. He had checked himself into a clinic and, by March, had switched from smack to prescription substitute methadone. Shaun's intake of the equally-addictive methadone, however, was alarming. His already substantial weekly supply of over 100ml often lasted for less than a day. For the trip to Barbados, he took 3000ml. At least, that was the plan. Before Happy Mondays had even left Britain, only a fraction of that remained.

'Barbados was a fucking disaster from beginning to end,' says Shaun. 'It all started when I dropped my methadone in the toilets at the airport. I had the lot in this one big container and it just smashed on the floor. It was madness. There were people running to the duty free shops to find any kind of container they could to rescue the stuff. They were scooping it up with glass and everything in it. I had crunchy fuckin' methadone. When we got to Barbados, someone had to filter it through this really strong linen. There was only a bit left by then. I drank that straight away.'

Happy Mondays' problems, however, had only just begun. At Blue Wave studios, it quickly became clear that opting for Frantz and Weymouth had been a mistake. The pair's clean, precise production style simply didn't suit the band's ragged songs. Worse still, they were used to working with traditionally-trained musicians who understood chords and keys and knew how to read music. And they had no idea how to deal with the Mondays, either in or out of the studio.

'Coming from the New York scene, we had worked with all kinds of freaks and weirdos,' says Weymouth. 'But it was basically a show. They had always turned out to be pretty normal people underneath. I thought that all musicians were the same. When I met the Mondays, I realised that they were different. They were real. They lived that life every day. I never knew such people existed.'

Weymouth was certainly in for a shock. While she and Frantz struggled in the studio with Happy Mondays' 'musical' members, Shaun and Bez were elsewhere on the island causing chaos.

Barely a fortnight after Happy Mondays had left Britain, Jayne Houghton was due to take *Select* magazine over to Barbados to report on the recording sessions. She flew with journalist Miranda Sawyer to New York, where they were due to catch a connecting flight for the Caribbean.

'I got news that Shaun wanted to cancel the interview,' says Houghton. 'I wasn't that worried at first. Shaun would blow out articles on a regular basis, but most of the time they would eventually get done. I once followed him round Europe for almost a week with Mary-Ann Hobbs for a feature for *NME*. I decided we should wait in New York for a few days to see if he changed his mind.

'The next thing I heard was that Bez had broken his arm really badly. It had happened on some really dubious boating trip where he had fallen into the water, apparently. Then came the news that he had turned over a couple of cars and written them off. To be honest, that wasn't entirely unexpected with Bez. By then, increasingly worse stories were coming through every couple of hours. None of the band were talking to each other, nothing had been recorded, Chris and Tina couldn't work with them and – finally – that Shaun was on crack and unable to write any lyrics. That was when we went home.'

By the time Houghton got back to Britain, Bez had crashed a total of eight vehicles. One particularly bad accident, which happened as he tried to perfect tailspins in a hire car, resulted in a collision with a tree. The smash shattered Bez's already-broken arm, which then had to be operated on. A steel rod was used to replace the bone in the upper half of his right arm, which had become diseased, and pinned into place by two rows of callipers. Bits of bone would later be sliced from Bez's hips and used to repair the damage.

Recording of the album was faring almost as badly. Only a handful of sketchy backing tracks had been completed, but with band members barely on speaking terms and producers who couldn't communicate what they wanted, the material didn't groove with Happy Mondays' trademark, ramshackle style. Worst of all, there had been no input from either Shaun or Bez.

Before arriving in the Caribbean, Shaun had taken crack only a few times in his life. It certainly wasn't his drug of choice. But without any heroin or methadone, it would have to do. As usual, Shaun wasn't needed much in the studio when recording began. While waiting for backing tracks to be laid down, he sussed out the drug scene on the island. Due to the close proximity of South America, Barbados was rife with crack. Shaun bought some, just to see him through the sessions. As far as the dealers were concerned, however, he was perfect prey: a visiting musician, obviously with money, a serious habit and no alternative supply. Shaun would later insist that it was the local dealers who cultivated his crack habit. They would post free samples through his door, he claimed, just to get him hooked. By the time Jayne Houghton was waiting in New York for him to agree to an interview, Shaun was locking himself in the studio toilets virtually all the time, smoking rock after rock of crack cocaine.

'I've read that I was supposed to be smoking fifty rocks a day, but that's well over the top,' says Shaun. 'I was buying a sixteenth at eight in the morning, and I'd smoke that by dinnertime. Then I'd buy another sixteenth and at night I'd buy an eighth. I was just buying the stuff and smoking it. Once you start, it's terrible. It's the worst, dirtiest drug in the world.

'The real trouble was that I wasn't interested in writing any music. I had no ideas. I went over there and just totally enjoyed myself. Well, I thought I enjoyed myself, but when you hit that pipe, man, you turn into a right fucker. You just don't care. I mean, everyone used to freebase coke and shit like that before, but the pipe was really bad news. By that time though, it was all fuckin' up in the air anyway. We were working for three weeks at a time on a tambourine part. Everyone was taking drugs. The whole band ended up out of their heads in different places all over Barbados.'

Shortly before Happy Mondays were due to return to Britain, Shaun stole some of the master tapes from the studio to hold as ransom. He phoned Factory and demanded that they send over £10,000 for more drugs, otherwise the tapes would be destroyed. Wilson, who claims that the sum was closer to £30,000, wired the money to a small bank on the island. Factory's finance director, Chris Smith, secured the cash with his credit card. For the next three years, says Wilson, his house was in jeopardy because of it.

'Wilson couldn't send the money himself because he simply didn't have it,' says Houghton. 'By then, there were all sorts of stories coming through about Shaun trashing apartments, getting into fights and breaking into houses and stealing stuff. I had given up trying to hide anything any more. There was no point . Before Barbados, Shaun himself had known when to draw the line. He would do hard drugs in front of his dad or the crew, for example, but never in front of journalists. Now he didn't care who knew what about him.'

With one weekend to go before Happy Mondays flew home, Chris Frantz and Tina Weymouth made a final attempt to coax some lyrics out of Shaun.

'Chris and Tina were great, considering the circumstances,' says Houghton. 'They tried very hard to stabilise Shaun. By the end, every crack dealer in Barbados was coming down to the studio because they realised there was money to be made. So Chris and Tina hired a house on the other side of the island with absolutely nothing and no one nearby. They gave Shaun no money, confiscated his watch and jewellery, took him to the house and left him there to write some lyrics. They intended to go back for him in a couple of days. The next day, however, someone spotted this little black kid on the beach outside the studio. He was swanning along in all of Shaun's clothes. That's when they realised he was beyond their help. They went back to the house and he was sitting there almost naked because he had sold all his clothes for more crack.'

In April 1992, a month after recording began in Barbados, Happy Mondays came home with just one song finished. Plans to mix the album in Miami were understandably scrapped as Shaun was admitted immediately to the Charter rehab clinic in London's Chelsea, where a six-week stay set him back over £10,000. Factory didn't care about the cost any more. Wilson was simply desperate for Shaun to recover sufficiently to add vocals to the new album. Having contracted a throat infection from his heavy crack use, he was now unable to sing at all. By late May, however, Shaun was well enough to both write some lyrics and record them with Frantz and Weymouth at Comfort studios in Surrey, amid tales that the pair were trying to help by introducing him to the I-Ching and teaching him how to dance the Peppermint Twist. There were also rumours that Rowetta was to stand in full-time for Shaun on a temporary basis, or that perhaps a singer from Prince's band would fill in for a while. Most unlikely was the story that Shaun's dad Derek would take over, simply because he had aped his son at a couple of soundchecks.

Vocals down, Shaun would spend the rest of the summer in and out of various rehab and detox centres, trying and failing to stick to whatever course of treatment was on offer. Like his weight, his willpower would fluctuate on almost a weekly basis.

'For months, I had tabloids ringing me up on a daily basis to find out what state Shaun was in,' says Houghton. 'The first shift at the *Manchester Evening News* starts at 6am. At 7am, one of its reporters would call me at home, claiming they had heard that Shaun had OD-ed in the early hours of the morning in the Hacienda. "Is it true he's dead? What hospital is he in?" I would still be half asleep, but I'd have to ring Shaun, just to be sure he was alive, which obviously pissed him off no end.

'When Shaun came out of rehab and Factory was preparing to release the album, I was putting out statements saying that the band wasn't falling apart when it quite clearly was. I'd insist that Shaun no longer had a drug problem, when it was obvious to anyone with eyes in their head that he was wasted all the time. People were still fascinated by him. They just observed him and I guess I did too. But if you showed concern, Shaun would just tell you to fuck off. I think Nathan did try a couple of times to sort him out, but with no success. Nathan had lost complete control of the situation a long time ago, while Tony Wilson had enough on his plate with the disaster that was Factory to even want to intervene. By that stage, the label was sinking even faster than the Mondays, although Tony's main concern was probably saving enough cash to get a new wardrobe for the summer.'

In July, it was revealed that Factory was set to sell a substantial, but not controlling, percentage of its shares to London Records. Wilson claimed that this meant little more than an extension of London's distribution deal with the label. The truth was that the company couldn't have been more desperate for cash. New Order's long-delayed new album was still in production at Peter Gabriel's Real World studios, where it was shaping up to be the most expensive independent LP ever made. For the time being, however, that honour lay with Happy Mondays' new album, ...*Yes Please!*, due for release in September, which had cost over £400,000, nearly three times its initial budget.

Ten months on from the flop that was 'Judge Fudge', Happy Mondays tried to kickstart their comeback with 'Stinkin' Thinkin'', the first single to be taken from the new album. Named after a term used in rehab and remixed by Stephen Hague, the track was accompanied by a hastily-made video shot at Shepherd's Bush shopping centre in west London. Slow-paced, strung-out and slightly spooky, with self-indulgent lyrics about drinking Night Nurse and the living dead, 'Stinkin' Thinkin'' sunk Shaun's weak, croaky vocals deep in the musical mix, then contrasted them sharply with Rowetta's bluesy, gospel-tinged tones. In fact, it wasn't a bad track. It was certainly far better than had been expected and was even reasonably well received by the press. The song, however, made little impression on the charts. An awful performance on *Top Of The Pops* didn't help. Bez was nowhere to be seen and Shaun looked absolutely miserable. Worse still, he decided to sing live and straight, reading his lines from a crumpled piece of paper. It sounded painful.

For months, Nathan McGough had been trying to build up interest in ...*Yes Please!*

'This album sticks two fingers up at every single critic who has tried to write off Happy Mondays,' he said in a press statement. 'When it debuts at No.1, I hope they all choke on the words they so casually spew out of their cynical mouths. Happy Mondays always will be the most important band in Britain, and the new LP is testament to this.'

Meanwhile, Wilson was insisting that the material was Factory's finest to date, while Houghton claimed that Shaun's lyrics were easily his best ever. Coupled with a batch of promising reviews, it looked briefly as though Happy Mondays may just pull through.

'Somehow, despite everything, Happy Mondays are back on the case,' declared the headline above the review in *Q* magazine, which awarded the album four marks out of five. Even the weekly press, which was itching to crucify Shaun, had to concede that ...*Yes Please!* had its highlights.

'It's actually pretty good,' revealed *Melody Maker* with more than a hint of surprise. 'At best, we're talking about the oceanic funk of late, late Can; at worst, a typically tropical soundtrack to the Mondays' expensive vacation. The sun-baked, mellow-yellow vibe is a culmination of the band's fantasy of life as an endless holiday, an eternal Ibiza.'

'Some people will never forgive Happy Mondays for what they have said in the last couple of years, and that's a perfectly cool reaction,' noted *NME*'s reviewer. 'All I'm saying is that they're back again, unflinching and honest and sick after their own shaggy fashion. And there's life in the old mung worms still.'

...*Yes Please!* fell somewhere between the brilliant album that Nathan had promised and the catastrophe that had been expected. It was a shifty, low-key comeback with a handful of stand-out tracks such as the rhythmic, bass-heavy, 'Monkey In The Family', with its electro arrangement and Arabic wails, 1970s disco tune 'Love Child', and the dark, edgy 'Angel'. There were also several awful songs like 'Cut 'Em Loose Bruce' and 'Dustman', on which Shaun simply shouted incoherently, out of tune and out of time with the music. Only 'Stinkin' Thinkin'' and 'Angel' hinted at his former talent for lyrical one-liners, while it was down to Rowetta to save mediocre, Latin-tinged funk tunes like 'Sunshine And Love', scheduled to be the album's second single. In addition, Frantz and Weymouth's methodical production had polished Happy Mondays' sleazy funk sound almost into extinction. Ramshackle had been replaced by orchestrated chaos.

Despite Nathan's boasts, ...*Yes Please!* didn't debut at No.1. It slid into the Top 10 at No.9, then slipped straight back out again. Subsequently, ticket sales for Happy Mondays' British tour dates, which had initially sold well, suddenly slowed down. Although the band was playing large indie venues rather than arenas, none of the shows sold out. Shaun appeared in the *Face* to apologise to everyone he had offended over the past year, including the gay community and Sinead O'Connor, about whom he had been quoted saying, 'She needs a fuckin' good shag.' Tickets, however, still didn't shift. Then an entire European tour had to be scrapped. Numerous reasons were given, including the highly improbable excuse that it clashed with the birth of Mark Day's child. In truth, promoters had decided that, for the number of tickets sold, putting on Happy Mondays simply wasn't worth the risk that they would either play badly or simply not turn up at all.

In interviews, Shaun seemed increasingly unsure of himself, not to mention the future of the band. Sometimes he said he claimed Happy Mondays were about to take a two-year break, other times he said they were still going strong. He didn't care about English audiences, then he did. The band was off to America, where they were destined to be big, then he hated the pop game and wanted out of music altogether.

On 10 October, Happy Mondays began their British tour in Leicester. Dressed entirely in black, Shaun stood with his back to the audience for most of the show. He was hunched up, reading all the lyrics to the new songs from pieces of paper. When he could be heard, he sounded awful. Bez, his bandaged arm in a sling, looked equally miserable. On powerful prescription morphine to kill the pain in his arm, he could hardly dance. It was Rowetta's gig. Trussed up as a schoolgirl dominatrix, cracking a whip and sporadically shoving a fluffy duck up her skirt, she not only provided the audience with a visual focus, but carried the songs with her soaring, soulful vocal. It was support group Stereo MCs, however, who really stole the show. Enjoying their first big chart hit with the single 'Connected', they were the absolute antithesis of Happy Mondays: their sound was tight, their performance captivating and full of energy.

'On that tour, you could never tell how Shaun was going to behave or where you stood with him from one minute to the next,' says Eric Longley. 'At venues, before the show started, any disabled kids with tickets were brought to the front barriers before the rest of the audience were let in. Shaun would be straight over there to talk to them and he would be charming. Then he would whinge on endlessly about having to do an interview with the local press. He would say, "I have to do all the fuckin' singing and talking to people, do I have to do fuckin' everything in this band?"

'We got around that problem by offering to give £5 to any member of the Mondays who would talk to a journalist. It was the band's money anyway. As soon as we said that though, all five of them were positively eager to give interviews. Unfortunately, that idea got them into more trouble than it was worth. The band ended up being questioned by the inland revenue about the money they made from additional ticket sales. Apparently, someone had confessed to Q magazine that all the extra tickets for shows that the band asked for, they then sold outside the venue.'

At the gig in Newcastle, a journalist and photographer from Q joined Happy Mondays to do an on-the-road feature, which involved them travelling with the band up to Glasgow.

'I was on holiday at the time,' says Jayne Houghton. 'A girl called Julie worked for me, so she went with them instead. It was her first press trip. She was very young and new to the job and had only just moved to London. I tried to brief her as well as I could, but it was like sending a lamb to the slaughter.

'I had been doing my usual press bollocks bit, insisting that the band was still together, functioning well as a unit. In the dressing room after the gig in Glasgow, Shaun sat down next to the journalist and started doing smack. Julie was freaking out. You couldn't really pretend it wasn't happening. By then, Shaun had the attitude of, "This is what I am and this is what I do, like it or not." There was absolutely no sense of restraint. Shaun was a total loose cannon and there was nothing anyone could do about it.

'During one of the last dates of that tour, at Brixton Academy in London, Shaun was chasing the dragon on the side of the stage. I mean, not even off stage or in the dressing room. All the photographers in the press pit and probably the front few rows of the crowd could see him fiddling around with pieces of foil. There was no chance of creating an effective smokescreen any more, but for some reason I was still lying to everyone that Shaun was okay and saying the band was doing fine. I think I'd just slipped automatically into denial. I had been bullshitting for so long to so many people that I'd managed to convince myself I was representing Bros.'

Two weeks after Happy Mondays' UK tour ended, 'Sunshine And Love' became the second single to be lifted from ...*Yes Please!* Backed with the Oakenfold/Osborne-produced cover of the Bee Gee's 'Stayin' Alive' and a remix of old song '24 Hour Party People' by Mike Pickering's M People, the EP was the band's first release for years not to make it on to radio playlists. It was also to be Factory's swansong. A fortnight later, after twelve years in business, the label went into receivership.

For months, it had been thought that London Records would step in and save Factory, which had debts of £3.5 million. Subsequently, rumours would suggest that London had allowed the company to collapse in order to avoid taking on its financial problems. Dozens of creditors were consequently left unpaid.

'By the time "Sunshine And Love" came out,' says Houghton, 'Factory owed me £15,000. I had only just set up my own company. Tony asked me to keep working on Happy Mondays right up until the end. But the label couldn't even get copies of the single to me. The pressing plants in England wouldn't release their stock because they were owed so much money. They were waiting for a small fortune, same as everyone else. Central Station were also owed a substantial amount. They were saying that they wouldn't do the artwork for the EP until they were paid. Everyone was pulling favours, but no one was 100 per cent sure what was happening. Plus we were all worried about the condition of Happy Mondays, not to mention the records they were putting out. I finally received preview copies of "Sunshine And Love" from some obscure place in Germany. I don't know why I even bothered to work that single. I was just spending my own money on a song that was never going to be a hit for a company that owed me thousands of pounds.

'When Factory folded, the Hacienda was saved. It wasn't part of the deal, thanks to some surprisingly astute business move by Tony.

It should have been among the assets. I wish it had been, because it was still doing okay. I know several of the creditors ended up going to the door of the club if it was having a busy night and demanding some of the takings. They might get a couple of hundred quid at a time. I tried to establish if it was worth going up to Manchester to try to get some of my money back. But for £15,000, I'd have to have made a fuckin' lot of Intercity journeys on a Saturday night. I eventually had to write off the debt and my company nearly went down. It took me four years to get a healthy cash flow again.'

Only days after Factory's HQ went up for sale, Tony Wilson was rumoured to be trying to start a new label, possibly one which would give New Order and Happy Mondays a new home. In a twist of timing, New Order had finally finished work on *Republic*, the long-delayed follow-up to *Technique*. Factory, however, now had no claim over either the recording or the band. All of its acts, in fact, were free to sign new deals with whichever label they liked, although Happy Mondays' contract was due to expire the following month anyway.

Inevitably, accusations of blame were flying fast. Wilson cited the recession and the delayed delivery of two major albums for his company's financial crisis. Happy Mondays blamed Factory for spending their money unwisely. Most of the creditors blamed Wilson for self-indulgence. The receivers claimed it was the current climate. New Order said nothing.

'I certainly didn't blame Happy Mondays for the demise of Factory,' says Bernard Sumner. 'I know that several people reckoned Shaun was responsible, but of course it wasn't his fault. It was down to whoever should have been in control of the budget. No one should have allowed the Mondays to spend nearly so much, but money was never a major concern for Factory. With Tony, the artists always got what they wanted.

'Until Happy Mondays, there was only one big act on Factory. We all thought that having two would be a good thing. We thought the label would earn twice as much and have twice the resources to plough into new projects. We didn't even think what would happen if both big acts ended up recording two very expensive albums at exactly the same time. But it is true that ...*Yes Please!* shouldn't have cost so much in the first place. It could never even recoup, never mind turn a profit. What the band needed was someone to say no to them.'

'It definitely wasn't Shaun's fault,' says Houghton. 'He had no idea what was going on in his head by then, forget record company business. It wasn't New Order's either. They had been bankrolling Factory for years. I remember Hooky going back to the offices to see what was left. The receivers had already taken all the valuable stuff, but he got all the old posters and backdrops. There were vultures and money men circling everywhere though. It was horrible.'

With Factory gone, Happy Mondays were down, but not out. While the receivers continued to sift through the company's accounts (which were in such a shambles that no one knew who was owed what, and by whom), London Records were close to closing a buyout of the Factory label. At the same time, however, Nathan McGough was negotiating his own deal with EMI. He insisted that 50,000 UK sales of ...Yes Please! plus overseas licensing deals had already recouped the album's production costs, and that Happy Mondays were free to sign with whoever they wanted. He even claimed that Factory still owed the band (which he said had kept the label going for the last two years, despite rumours that ...Yes Please! had actually sold only 10,000 copies) in the region of £40,000. In fact, it was eventually revealed that Factory owed its artists a total of just over £350,000, while £400,000 of advances remained unrecouped.

'Nathan was scrambling around to secure a solo deal for the Mondays,' says Houghton. 'When he got a meeting with EMI, I was draughted in to whitewash over the band's problems. He asked me to make out that Happy Mondays had been totally stitched up. I was supposed to try and hide all the unsupportive pieces of press and blow up big copies of any good bits of the reviews.'

While the music papers celebrated Christmas 1992 with new-found cover stars Suede (NME) and Nirvana (Melody Maker), London Records was refusing to finalise its takeover of Factory until Happy Mondays were a guaranteed part of the package. It was hardly surprising. New Order may have had an album ready to release, but it was well-known that the group was unlikely to record together again. Factory had no other big names. Even Wilson's favourites, The Adventure Babies, had found themselves a new home.

Meanwhile, however, on behalf of Happy Mondays, Nathan McGough had agreed a £1.7 million, five-album deal with EMI. The company's then head of A&R Clive Black and his associate Keith

Wozencroft (who had previously signed Supergrass and Radiohead to EMI label Parlophone) had both been persuaded that the band had a future after hearing demos of half an album's worth of brand new material, despite the fact that the tracks had yet to receive any input from Shaun. All that remained in order for the deal to go through was that contracts be signed and exchanged. A meeting between the EMI Music contingent and the band was set up to take place on 17 February 1993 at Nathan's offices in Princess Street in Manchester. Black, Wozencroft, Mark Day, Gary Whelan, Paul Davis and Paul Ryder all turned up on time. Shaun was several hours late.

'I was sat outside the office with Shaun in his car,' says Longley. 'He was totally wrecked and the car was like an ashtray. He eventually went into the meeting and just pissed off Clive Black. The contracts were all drawn up, ready to be signed, and the rest of the band were well happy. Then Shaun got up, said he was going out for a Kentucky Fried Chicken and never came back. After that, Black gave Happy Mondays a week in which to turn up together at his office in London to seal the deal. When they didn't show, EMI dropped their offer. It was a real shame. I still think EMI could have made them stars. They had great ideas about how to make it work.'

Shaun's craving for a Kentucky was his euphemism for having to score some smack. However, he now claims that drugs weren't the reason for him walking out on the deal.

'I really did go for a Kentucky,' he says. 'I didn't need to go for drugs, I had plenty of gear on me. I was hungry and I wanted a scran. I would have done anything for that band to stay together, but it was just right that it ended then. It was all over. Everyone was off doing their own thing. There was no chemistry between us any more. When the Mondays started, it was a real buzz because we all had an input in the tunes. By the end, it was, "I play drums, I play keyboards, I play bass. You sing and write lyrics and that's fuckin' all you do." Everyone had their heads up their arses. We had no respect for each other. It was just shite. I knew we were finished for good.'

'Every one of the Mondays was sick of the band by then,' says Houghton, 'but they didn't know what else to do other than sign another deal. It was probably the most dignified thing for Shaun to fuck things up with EMI. I don't think Happy Mondays could have come back. Too much had happened. Shaun was smart enough to know that. He may have pretended he was too out of it to understand, but I think deep down he knew that the self-destruct button had gone off, probably even before Barbados. None of the other band members would admit that it was the end of the line though.'

After EMI pulled their offer, which would have given Happy Mondays an instant advance of £225,000, the band members had a meeting to discuss their future. Paul Ryder was so angered by his brother's recent behaviour, however, that he refused to turn up, claiming to have quit. Nevertheless, several other offers remained on the table. London Records still wanted to sign the group, but for thousands, rather than millions. In addition, Warner Chappell was proposing a £100,000 publishing deal, while Elektra were prepared to pay £125,000 to retain licensing rights in America. The meeting, however, didn't go well.

'Mark Day kept trying to pin the whole situation on my smack habit,' says Shaun, 'but even Gaz and PD – both of whom I had fallen out with as well – knew it had fuck all to do with that. Blaming drugs was the easy option, but the drugs, even the heroin, had always been around. It wasn't anyone's fault, but they thought they had to find someone to blame, so they chose me. I remember reading one press quote later on where the rest of the band said I had to get to grips with my problems. I had a fuckin' laugh at that. I knew I had problems – always have done, even before the band started. That's one thing I've never denied.

'As far as I was concerned, three members of that band had totally changed. It had all become about money. When Factory went down, they wanted to sign a deal, any deal, just so that we'd get a load of dough. One of them was even considering pension plans. It was everything we had started the Mondays to escape from. They thought we could get the EMI deal, take the £2 million, do nothing, then meet up in ten months' time, jam some tunes and stick out another shit album. It would have been the same with any record company. The money had got to everyone.'

'Arguments over who should be paid for what had been getting worse and worse for a while,' says Eric Longley. 'The main problem was with the publishing, which is split according to who wrote what. Bez was paid like any normal member of the band when it came to royalties from records and tour earnings, but he had no discernible input into the writing of the songs. It didn't matter that they were actually on a pretty good wage. It was all about envy and greed. In the end, no one wanted to work with Shaun anyway. He was sometimes still great, but really he was a total arsehole a lot of the time. You just can't turn up for gig after gig completely out of your box and expect other people to put up with it.

'By the time the offer from London Records came in, none of the musicians in the band wanted to go on. They wouldn't work with Shaun. It was loads less money than the EMI deal, but Shaun was saying he wanted to take it. He was trying to persuade the others to pull a Sex Pistols' rock'n'roll swindle – just take the dosh and run. None of them would go for it though.'

While London Records waited to hear back from the band, on 22 February, the British tabloids reported the story that Happy Mondays had split, adding that Shaun was in such a state he could no longer perform or record. Shaun was also alleged to have fired and then reinstated Nathan McGough five times over a number of weeks. Nathan had eventually resigned, just days before the band broke up. He allegedly told colleagues he quit because he could no longer tolerate Shaun's erratic behaviour. However, it was also rumoured that he had stood to personally earn a substantial lump sum of money from EMI had Happy Mondays signed with the label, and was furious that Shaun had walked out on the deal. Nathan, however, refused to give his side of the story.

'Shaun Ryder is both the most wonderful and the most vile person I have ever known,' says Nathan. 'He is a fantastic guy who has done some despicable things. He's still the most weak-willed, pathetic and brilliant man I've ever met.'

Part Three

SIXTEEN

Secrets And Lies

Shaun Ryder had never seen himself as a musician, never mind a pop star. He hadn't needed a band to lead a cartoon-like, incident-strewn life, and, if his attitude had changed at all, it was down to having more money in his pocket, rather than the fact that he was famous. Unlike most successful singers, settling into an existence out of the limelight and off the celebrity circuit wouldn't be a problem for Shaun. After all, even during Happy Mondays' two short years of mainstream success, he had never taken in any of the back-slapping, ego-boosting accolades heaped on him 'as an artist' by the likes of Tony Wilson, Elektra executives and the fickle music media.

'I don't think I changed much through the Mondays,' says Shaun. 'I could buy flash cars and a big house, but I didn't feel special because of the band. People probably thought it had all gone to my head, but that was only because of stories in the papers, written by people who knew fuck all about me. Survival is what it was always about, however well or however badly we were doing. That never changed and nothing that happened ever surprised me. My life had always been unreal. Even when Bez and me were kids at school, we always saw ourselves as in some sort of film. Or in a really mad book, out on our own, against everyone else.'

For the first few weeks after Happy Mondays split, the various band members waged a war of words against each other via the tabloids. Paul Davis, who was in the process of forming a new band with Gary Whelan and former Smiths bassist Andy Rourke, said leaving the Mondays was the best thing he had ever done, adding that he never wanted to see Shaun Ryder again in his life. Mark Day, who was rumoured to be selling encyclopaedias for £200 a week, before reapplying for his old job back at the Post Office, told one tabloid of the hell he had been through with the drug-addled outfit. He, of course, had only ever smoked a bit of dope. Paul Ryder made it quite clear how he felt about his brother but, for the most part, refused to be drawn into the slanging match.

At first, Shaun joined in the squabbles. Then, for no apparent reason, before February was even out, he announced in the *Manchester Evening News* that Happy Mondays were to reform. The following day, both Paul Davis and Mark Day appeared in the same paper to say that they would rather go on the dole than make peace with Shaun.

'For years, Shaun had been bawling out PD, Mark and Gaz,' says Jayne Houghton. 'Shaun also had great fights with Bez and Paul, but they were always best mates at heart. If the other three ever let the side down though, they would get such a bollocking. As soon as they no longer needed Shaun, they took the opportunity to get their own back.

'I know that all of the Mondays felt massively unappreciated by Shaun. He did think of himself as the driving force and, personality-wise, it was very much the Shaun Ryder roadshow, but really it shouldn't have been because Happy Mondays was very much a sum of its parts. Having said that, Shaun has a good eye for people who are talented. He has a brilliant knack of surrounding himself with professionals who best suit his needs. Unless he was totally off his head, as long as you were doing your job well, he'd be fine. Behind the front, he really is a good bloke with a massive heart. He just won't suffer fools at all.'

As 1993 edged into spring, the other ex-Happy Mondays must have enjoyed many a laugh at Shaun's expense. The singer's first post-split public appearance was in a Manchester court. The previous July, when he was supposed to be trying to kick hard drugs before the release of *...Yes Please!* he had been arrested for drink-driving and leaving the scene of an accident. At his delayed court hearing, it was revealed that, while intoxicated, Shaun had crashed his girlfriend Trish McNamara's car into a Lada driven by a non-conformist pastor.

'That story is so typically Shaun,' says Bernard Sumner. 'When he told me about it, I remember thinking it couldn't have happened to anyone else. Apparently, he was at home, pissed up on a bottle of vodka and had to go out to score some drugs. He got in the car, drove just around the corner and collided with a Lada. The other guy got out and he was wearing a dog collar. Shaun told him he was terribly sorry, admitted it was all his fault and asked him not to call the police. He had about £500 in his pocket, which he tried to give the guy for repairs to his car. The vicar – or pastor or whatever he was – refused and insisted that they phone for the police. Shaun knew he was pissed, so he got back in his car, drove straight home and went inside. Literally a couple of minutes later, there was a knock at his door. It was the police, asking if he had been involved in an accident that evening. Shaun was going, "Oh, no officer. Hit a car? No, not me. I've been in all night." At the same time, he was wondering how the hell they tracked him down so quickly. The copper's saying, "We know it was you, Shaun. There's no point in denying it." Turns out Shaun had been driving so fast that the number plate from his car had come off and attached itself to the Lada.'

As Shaun left court after the hearing, at which he was fined £650 and banned from driving, he was photographed for the first time with his new girlfriend, Oriole Leitch, one of Donovan's daughters. A little later, the *Manchester Evening News* reported that Trish, the mother of Shaun's daughter Jael, was now living with the child in a Stretford council flat, which she shared with her sister Ursula.

Shaun's second public appearance was on Channel 4 youth show *The Word*. He put in a memorable – if highly embarrassing – brief appearance as a guest on the interview sofa. Slurring his words and looking bleary-eyed and badly wasted, Shaun announced to presenter Terry Christian that he was forming a new group called The Mondays with Bez, his brother Paul and a vocalist known as Kermit, who had previously been in Mancunian rap outfit Ruthless Rap Assassins. He also claimed to have totally forgotten the names of his three other ex band members, referring to Gary Whelan only as 'that drummer bloke'. As the studio audience watched on in a mix of amusement and amazement, Shaun then saw out the show's closing credits dancing on stage with a four-foot-tall character called Zippy, from the infants' TV programme *Rainbow*.

'I have no idea why I did that,' says Shaun. 'I was just out on a fuckin' roll, playing out in London. I met someone from the show, they asked if I'd appear, so I went along. I honestly can't even remember doing it. I was totally pissed. I think I had been drinking pints of the green liquid as well. You know, the old methadone. I've never actually seen the programme, but if someone played it to me now, I could laugh at it. Why haven't I watched it? Would you be keen to see a replay of yourself, off your box, looking like a total twat? I've probably done worse things than that though.'

Jayne Houghton was also at *The Word* studios for the recording of the show, independently of Shaun. She reckons the audience saw only a fabricated side of the singer that night.

'Shaun's appearance on *The Word* was a total act,' says Houghton. 'Ten minutes before he went live on air, I was talking to him in the dressing room and he seemed absolutely normal. He wasn't slurring his words or fucked in any way. I went out front to stand in the audience to watch the interview. I was stunned. Suddenly Shaun had turned into this gibbering, dribbling, bug-eyed character. I had never seen him do that before. Maybe it was the drugs, although I find that pretty hard to believe. The programme was the last in the series, so there was a party backstage afterwards. I talked to him again then and he was back to normal. I asked him what he had done and why he had done it. He was laughing and saying it was all a game. He said it was just what the audience expected. I told him he was selling himself short by acting like that, but he didn't think so. I was upset because he had gone on air and talked about starting this new band, which he did seem genuinely excited about. As far as I'm concerned, you have to be taken seriously when you are discussing projects that are still in the planning stages. I told Shaun he would have been much better off giving the impression that he was in complete control of his life. Obviously, he didn't agree.'

If Shaun was acting on *The Word* – he was out and about in Camden the following day looking fine – perhaps he was trying to establish in his own mind the split between the real Shaun Ryder and the public's perception of the former Happy Mondays' singer. Or maybe he just wanted to prove to himself that he could still manipulate the media. More likely, he was trying to fool everyone into believing that he was as washed up as they assumed.

'Shaun's personal lifestyle has been glamorised too much,' says Houghton. 'The truth is that no one would want him if he was really straight. Shaun knows that is part of his appeal. The problem is that he sometimes can't draw a line between his public persona – allowing people to think he is this mad, fucked-up creative genius – and letting it spill over into real life, which is when he starts to over indulge.'

'I don't think Shaun's media image is all that different to how he actually is,' says Bernard Sumner. 'What you see is what you get with Shaun. Basically, he's a dead nice guy. Sometimes, of course, too many drugs – or the wrong type of drugs – can turn you nasty. I'm sure that has happened quite a lot to Shaun because he has lost a lot of friends over the years. I know he has said and done dozens of things that have offended people, which he probably wouldn't deny. To be honest, I have heard a few terrible stories about Shaun, although he has always been absolutely fine with me. But when you take vast quantities of drugs – and Shaun's intake is well-known – you do get enormous mood swings.

'In the period after the Mondays split, most people in Manchester thought the fame had gone to Shaun's head. He stopped hanging out and didn't see a lot of his old mates. It turned out he was just trying to get clean. He didn't want to go where he knew there would be drugs. When you have been that heavily into the scene, staying well away from anyone who does any kind of drug is the only way to stop. It's doubly hard when drugs have been – or worse, still are – part of your work. It puts you in a bit of a trap. You're trying to quit, but you can't throw yourself into a new project to take your mind off it. So you sit about bored, thinking about it all the time. If you take drugs for work over a long period of time, they become like a crutch. Normality to you becomes that state of being off your head and it's being straight that feels abnormal. I'm fairly drug-free these days, but the crossover back is a very difficult thing to do. In fact, it's almost impossible. If you have no willpower, it's impossible.'

In the early months of the summer, Shaun Ryder embarked on a concerted effort to kick smack – and all other Class A drugs – which would last for a period of over a year. He felt he should at least try to be a bit more responsible. Besides, he had always promised himself that, by the age of thirty, he would no longer have a heroin habit. He was now thirty-one.

'I was pretty down with myself,' says Shaun. 'Loads of Mondays bullshit was still going on in the papers. It was all negative stuff, mostly about me. I didn't even want to answer back. I thought, "Fuck it! I'll get on with what I have to do." The more bad things I heard, the more it made me buzz. Eventually, I just stopped reading about all the crack and smack I was supposed to be taking. I wasn't bothered. I was getting down to business and getting back into making music.

'Every time I went out in Manchester, people would come over and tell me how I'd lost it. They'd say it was my own fault because I'd fucked up. They thought that just 'cos I no longer had my face on the covers of magazines or my name in the papers every other day, I was finished. The fact is, I don't need all that, never have. Having my picture plastered all over the place means fuck all to my life. I don't even like it much. It's embarrassing.'

Nevertheless, Shaun remained in Manchester, although he rarely left the house he shared with Oriole in Didsbury. On the few occasions that he was spotted out on the town, he was usually with longtime friend Nigel Pivaro and one of his Coronation Street colleagues, Kevin Kennedy, who plays Curly Watts.

'Like the rest of the Mondays, despite all the travelling and tours, Shaun never actually moved out of Manchester,' says Houghton. 'They are incredibly tight on family up there. Shaun was always giving jobs to his cousins and their cousins or someone's kid brother's best mate. He personally knew everyone involved with the band, whether they did the artwork or were security or even the roadies. He looked after the lot and not one ever took advantage. I guess it was quite grounding, particularly with all that madness going on around them.

'I also don't honestly believe that Shaun would still be alive had he gone down to London and broken away from that secure family unit. In the end, particularly because he made no secret about his heavy drug use, he was surrounded by scum. They really were like circling vultures. On the last tour, there were hundreds of people hanging around backstage who I had never seen before. It was so obvious they were dealers or spongers. He did have genuine friends there too, but he was in such a state that he couldn't tell the difference between them. When he went back to Manchester and cut himself off from everyone, his sense of perception returned. Shaun is one of the most incredibly sussed, ridiculously smart people on the planet – despite how he may act sometimes – and, believe me, he knows it. I'm quite sure he looked back on the end of the Mondays and realised that he never wanted to lose it like that again.'

Shaun's first step towards staying off smack was to start taking

Prozac. Initially prescribed to him by a doctor at one of the rehab clinics he had visited, the anti-depressant wouldn't actually take away his craving for heroin, but it would help him function from day to day for the first time in years without the aid of Class As. Had Shaun taken nothing at all, he probably wouldn't even have bothered to get out of bed in the mornings. After six weeks on Prozac, he reckoned his brain felt as though someone had taken it out of his head, given it a wash, then put it back in again. Predictably, when Shaun decided to alter his intake of drugs, he couldn't just do it the same way as everyone else. That would have been too easy, not to mention too dull. True to form, Shaun had to be different, he had to be excessive. If he was going to change his drug habit, why not change his appearance as well? In for a penny, in for a pound. For starters, he got fat.

'I saw Shaun when he was really fat,' says Tony Wilson. 'I immediately assumed it was alcohol. But his brother Paul told me it wasn't that. He said that Shaun had decided he didn't want to be a skinny junkie any more. He wanted to get some muscles, so he went out and bought all these high-protein, carbohydrate-packed food-stuffs for sportsmen. He was gobbling them down because he thought they would build him up. The trouble was, he wasn't doing any exercise at the same time.'

'I went through all these disguises,' says Shaun. 'I didn't want to look like me. I did get fat, yeah, I'll admit that. It was for a period of about six months. But I can put on weight and lose it in a week. For a while, I got dead thin too. That's when everyone said I was back on the pipe. I also grew my hair, then had the lot shaved off.'

At one stage, he even grew a rather ridiculous moustache.

'It must have been the Prozac,' says Shaun. 'That's the only explanation I have for the muzzie.'

Shaun's strangest disguise, however, was as a financial adviser-cum-bank-clerk. It was the phase he was going through in September 1993, when he gave his first full music press interview since leaving Happy Mondays.

'One of my ways to stay straight was by going on real businessy trip for a while,' says Shaun. 'I was organising things, sorting stuff out, making contacts. That was a pretty hard time for me. I didn't have a choice though. Everyone was slagging me off. I had a point to prove.'

Almost three months earlier, Shaun had spent a short afternoon in Manchester's 11th Hour studios, adding vocals to a track by local dance-pop outfit Intastella. Having stood between two huge speakers listening to an instrumental of the song for a while, Shaun had scribbled down a couple of lines of lyrics, then literally barked them incoherently to form part of a duet with Stella, the band's singer and a longtime friend of his. Beside Stella's saccharine sigh, Shaun's voice sounded rough and slightly scary. The track was titled 'Can You Fly Like You Mean It, Gungadin?' and it was to appear on the B-side of Intastella's forthcoming single, 'Drifter'. To promote the release, Shaun agreed to be interviewed with Stella for an article in *Melody Maker*. The pair appeared together on the cover of the paper. While a glamorously dolled-up Stella sported a spaghetti-strap dress, Shaun was wearing a grey business suit, white shirt and striped tie. He was also carrying a mobile phone. He looked like a middle-aged office worker.

In the interview, Shaun claimed he had quit the music business. He was clearly annoyed at the way the tide had turned against Happy Mondays. However, as a one-off, he was helping out Intastella because he believed in their music. Like many of the local acts signed at the height of Madchester – including Paris Angels, The High, World Of Twist, MC Buzz B and The Mock Turtles – Intastella had found themselves dropped as soon as the scene fell out of favour.

'I don't need to get involved with the music business or the press or anyone in England,' Shaun told *Melody Maker*. 'It bores the twat off me. I suppose it has a bit to do with my experience with the Mondays. For a few years we had good fun. Bez and I made the music business interesting. We turned it into a black comedy. But people didn't want fuckin' fun. So fuck it. It's no skin off my nose.'

In spite of his change of lifestyle, Shaun hadn't lost the travel bug. However, he could no longer visit his favourite foreign haunts such as Amsterdam and Ibiza, at least not if he wanted to keep clean. Fortunately, Oriole's father, Donovan, knew of several suitable alternatives. Shaun's new holiday destinations of choice became Ireland, Israel and Morocco.

'Morocco was the first place I went when I was getting straight,' says Shaun. 'Oriole and I stayed in the hills in the north with friends of Don's from the 1960s. Everyone there walks around with guns, but the guys that were looking after us used to look after the Stones, so it was cool. Up in the hills is where they grow all the kif. I went there to smoke all the smack out of me. I got rid of all the methadone with pure weed.'

Shaun had been introduced to Oriole by his brother Paul, who had split with his wife at the height of Happy Mondays' fame in order to go out with Astrella, Donovan's other daughter. Paul and Astrella had also formed a group together, which had recently been taken on by Donovan's manager and flown to LA to record their first sessions. Incredibly, Donovan didn't seem to mind his daughters dating the Ryders.

'Don was fine because we were always all right around him, even on tour,' says Shaun. 'I'm sure we were never shooting up or smoking rocks in front of him. I mean, it was well known there were a lot of drugs around and Don's not a dick. He's been through a lot and he's seen a lot. I think he tried more to understand what was going on, rather than just freaking. He knows that if your kids are doing mad stuff, the worst thing you can do is preach to them. If they have half a brain, they'll come through it. If they haven't, then they're finished anyway.

'Before Oriole's mother, Linda Lawrence, was married to Don, she had a son with Brian Jones. Man, Linda has seen all sorts. She went through so much shit when Brian died. I really don't think anything we could do would freak her out that much.'

With a third daughter, Ione Skye, married to Beastie Boy Adam Horowitz, and a son in his own band, Nancy Boy, Donovan was at least used to his kids hanging out with bands. Nevertheless, not many musicians have the reputation of the Ryders.

'I didn't push my children into the music scene, nor did I warn them away from it,' says Donovan. 'They chose it for themselves. I don't interfere in their lives because it doesn't help. Besides, Oriole didn't have to be anywhere near Shaun or any other musicians to find drugs. When she lived in California in the 1980s, cheap speed was everywhere. Oriole has been through that and got over it. None of my kids have ever really got hooked on anything. They saw enough of that growing up to put them off.

'I knew that both brothers had their own particular problems and, of course, you get worried. But what can you do? You just have to hope that everything works out. Paul and Astrella split up after four years; she's making music with her new boyfriend now. I really hope Oriole and Shaun stay together. I'm sure they will. She's been going out with him a lot longer than with anyone else. Oriole gives Shaun the support he needs because of where he's at and the position he's in. She can help because her mum Linda has been through it twice before – first with Brian Jones, then with me.

'Shaun comes from a culture of taking drugs from an early age, which is very different from the way I was brought up. I still think being around me and Linda and other older musicians is a good influence on him though. I hope he'll knock smack on the head, and he says he's well together with it. It's part of youth to be crazy and wild but everyone has to grow up eventually.'

SEVENTEEN

Back To The Future

Shaun Ryder never intended to stop writing songs. He just needed to take a break from the music business for a bit. Let the industry have fun with its new art-school-educated bands, if that's what it wanted. Let the press probe into Kurt and Courtney's heroin habits for a while. It would make a nice change. In fact, within a week of Happy Mondays' demise, Shaun began work on the project which was to become his second band – Black Grape. Having discovered a suitable writing partner in twenty-four-year-old rapper Paul 'Kermit' Leveridge, a former founder member of respected Mancunian hip hop outfit Ruthless Rap Assassins, Shaun was even collaborating on lyrics for the first time.

Nevertheless, the combination of Shaun and Kermit was scarcely one to inspire confidence. The pair were longtime smack buddies – allegedly Kermit had at one time been Shaun's dealer – who had bonded in a haze of heroin on the final, fateful Mondays' tour. While Bez was trying to recover from his traffic accident in Barbados, Shaun had found himself a new best friend. Kermit even joined Happy Mondays on stage several times towards the end of the tour, claiming to have suffered a stroke after one particularly drug-fuelled performance.

Brought up in Moss Side but now living in Hulme, Kermit had been into music for as long as he could remember. It was his natural interest which persuaded his parents to start him on violin lessons at the age of six. When Kermit later fell for bands such as The Specials and The Sex Pistols, he kept up the classical training, but also began his own very different musical career. He joined a local break-dance crew Broken Glass, which performed in videos for Mike Pickering's group T-Coy and appeared on several youth TV shows. It was when he got involved in the Manchester club scene, however, that Kermit really found his calling.

In the mid 1980s, funk DJ Greg Wilson ran an influential weekly Wednesday night club in Legends in the city centre. Just as Shaun had soaked up a mix of sounds in Pips as a teenager, so Kermit was introduced to new American black dance music like electro and hip hop by Wilson's innovative sets. Eventually, he was DJing himself at the club, under the monicker DJ La Freak. At the same time, he was studying for a psychology degree at Manchester Polytechnic, a course he claims to have funded by selling smack. Certainly, by his late teens, he was taking heroin on an almost daily basis. He had also taken his first steps in making his own music. Joining forces with a friend and neighbour in Hulme known as DJ Dangerous Hinds, Kermit formed Ruthless Rap Assassins. After a few months of playing at friends' parties and college clubs, they began working with Kiss AMC, female rappers who included Ann-Marie, Kermit's sister, with whom they put out the well-received twelve-inch white label 'We Don't Care'. The track caught the attention of a couple of major record companies and Ruthless Rap Assassins – now managed by Greg Wilson but split from Kiss AMC – subsequently signed with EMI. The critically-acclaimed but commercially-unsuccessful *Killer* album (which contained classic 1980s scratch singles 'And It Wasn't A Dream' and 'Justice') was the height of the band's career. *Killer* mixed serious social comment with a sense of mischief by boldly fusing electro and hip hop with 1970s rock samples, and established Ruthless Rap Assassins as one of only a handful of British acts who have ever produced proper hip hop steeped in British, rather than American culture. When follow-up LP *Think...It Ain't Illegal Yet!* also failed to break out of the underground, however, EMI lost interest and the band split in the early 1990s.

Subsequently, Kermit's drive to make music was dampened by his increasing intake of hard drugs. When he joined Happy Mondays on tour, it was hard to tell whether he or Shaun was the worse influence on the other. By the time the pair had started writing songs together, they had all but alienated most of their mates in Manchester.

'Kermit and I were totally off on our own little trip,' says Shaun. 'We were basically doing a lot of the same drugs in the same places at the same time. Eventually, no one wanted to know us. Not even our friends would talk to us.

'I guess we knew we wanted to work together at some stage, but it wasn't planned. We only started writing and rehearsing because we were staying around each other's houses after the Mondays was over. In fact, I think I may have been having a Kentucky with Kermit the day the EMI people were there.'

By the end of 1993, Black Grape was beginning to take shape. Shaun had signed up with established husband-and-wife management team Nik and Gloria Nicholl (whose clients included The Ramones and Debbie Harry), whom he had first met through Chris Frantz and Tina Weymouth. It was Weymouth who persuaded the couple that Shaun was worth taking on. Even after the nightmare that was the recording of ...*Yes Please!* she had persistently praised Shaun's natural musical talent. Much to his obvious embarrassment, she would often refer to him as 'a great modern artist'.

With any Happy Mondays' income frozen by the courts, and all of their remaining assets seized by Factory's receivers to help repay secured debts, Black Grape badly needed finance for some equipment if they wanted to attract serious record company investment. Armed with a very rough collection of demos recorded in Shaun's house, Nik and Gloria Nicholl approached numerous record companies, few of which showed any interest. Most reckoned it would be unwise to spend money on Shaun; some refused to consider having him on their label simply because of his reputation.

'Everyone warned me to stay away from Shaun Ryder,' Nik Nicholl would later say. 'Everybody I met told me he's a lunatic. They said I was a fuckin' idiot for getting involved. They said that Shaun was all over, too fucked on drugs to come up with anything interesting. But he's talented and so important – I don't think he knows how important he is.'

Eventually, the Nicholls secured Black Grape a healthy development deal with American label Radioactive, an American subsidiary of MCA, which would provide them with sufficient money to buy basic gear such as samplers and also book proper studio time. Radioactive's general manager, Brendan Bourke, who had previously worked with Perry Farrell and Billy Idol, had been a Happy Mondays fan, and was even poised to be their new American manager before the band broke up.

'I felt that Shaun was talented enough to bounce back and make another great record,' says Bourke. 'I also knew that, if he could come up with the goods, there would be a lot of people rooting for him. I was taking a big risk by getting involved with a man of his reputation, but I really believed he was worth it.'

Having tried for weeks – but ultimately failing – to persuade his brother Paul to join Black Grape, Shaun recruited Intastella members Martin Mitler (on bass) and Martin Wright (on guitar) for the band's first proper recording sessions at Drone studios in Chorlton-Cum-Hardy, south Manchester.

'At the time, we were listening to everything from The Beatles to The Orb to Scarface, Bushwick Bill, The Beastie Boys and Snoop,' says Shaun. 'We wanted to take in all those different styles, then mix up the sounds. It took Radioactive a while to get used to some of the shit, simply because it was so diverse. Finally, they gave us the go-ahead to carry on.'

Among the material eventually laid down were three stand-out tracks, one called 'Kelly's Heroes', another called 'Reverend Black Grape', and 'Yeah Brother', which had been written by Shaun for ...Yes Please! (he describes it as the sound he had originally wanted for the album), but rejected by the band. Radioactive bosses were impressed enough to make available further funds. Demoing continued into the spring of 1994 (when Oriole gave birth to Shaun's second daughter, Sean) and, when the two Martins returned to Intastella, two new band members were found in drummer Ged Lynch, who had previously worked with Ruthless Rap Assassins, and ex-Paris Angels guitarist Paul Wagstaff. Then Bez, who had decided to quit the music business, was persuaded to join too. As was the case with Happy Mondays, however, no concrete direction or album sound was established until Black Grape began to work with producers.

Shaun had initially told Radioactive's Brendan Bourke that he wanted to make a record that mixed the sound of Cypress Hill with The Rolling Stones. Consequently, Bourke called in two very different producers to help shape Black Grape's nascent, shambolic sound. The first was Steve Lironi, ex-Altered Images drummer (his wife is Clare Grogan) and songwriter for the likes of Rose Royce. Lironi's job was to give the band's songs a solid, more conventional structure. Shaun travelled down to London to meet him in June 1994. The pair spent time in a south London studio to see if they were musically compatible. They were. They even co-wrote a new track together titled 'Shake Your Money Maker'. Bourke's second choice of producer, hip hop producer Danny Saber, was sure to appeal to Shaun straight away. Saber had already worked with acts such as Cypress Hill, House Of Pain and Bobby Womack, and had remixed numerous dance and rock artists including TC Holmes and Terrorvision.

'Both Steve and Danny were multi-instrumentalists,' says Bourke. 'We felt that, together, they could accommodate the two ends of the musical spectrum that Shaun was after under one umbrella. That's certainly how it worked.'

In autumn 1994, Black Grape, Lironi and Saber all decamped to Rockfield studios in Monmouth, Wales, to record an album. Although they had initially hoped to go to Ireland (it proved too expensive), it turned out that they had chosen a more apt location. Also at the studios were The Stone Roses, incredibly still completing work on the follow-up to their debut album, made five years earlier when Happy Mondays were aiding underground DJ Paul Oakenfold's career by commissioning him to remix 'Wrote For Luck'. Already, Happy Mondays seemed to belong to another era, while Oakenfold had recently completed a world tour with U2.

Isolated from the music industry in London and away from the sniping scene in Manchester (Shaun had vanished so efficiently that someone had started signing on the dole under his name, while two other men, masquerading as him and Bez, were blagging their way into clubs and demanding free drinks), Black Grape settled into the rural lifestyle, hanging out at pubs until late afternoon, then starting recording in the evening.

'We were drinking all the time,' says Shaun. 'We became regulars at the local bar. We'd stay in there for hours, just playing tune after tune on the jukebox. We kept putting on Thin Lizzy and "Shotgun Wedding" by Rod Stewart. That made us determined to come up with some real good-time tunes ourselves.'

Three separate stints at Rockfield saw Black Grape record both rocky, guitar-driven songs and more sample-led dance tracks.

'Danny was right on our wavelength,' says Shaun. 'He's into our sort of grooves. He grew up on hip hop – he's king of that scene – but he's also open to all other kinds of music. He made the album quite poppy, which is cool. It became like a *Pin-Ups* Bowie-type record.'

'Shaun knows how to get good people around him,' says Lironi.

'He's never just shambling along without a clue. When I first met him, he wasn't in nearly as good shape as he was by the time we were recording the album, but even then he wanted to be successful, have hit records and make great pop music, rather than be an unknown cult artist. When he gets on a roll, he has a great rock'n'roll voice. Plus, he writes some of the funniest lyrics I've ever heard, not to mention the most insightful.'

When Black Grape left Rockfield towards the end of 1994, they had completed six songs and were midway through a further four. Shaun had also clocked up a night in a police cell after he and Kermit got into a fight in a pub with locals for making racist remarks. There had been other incidents reported involving the pair. Several cab drivers claimed to have picked them up lying in the middle of the road so drunk they couldn't stand. For Stone Roses' bassist Mani's birthday, they were rumoured to have got in hundreds of cheap prescription anti-depressant tablets Temazepam and ended up unconscious in a nearby field. Still, it all sounded fairly tame for Shaun.

Early 1995 marked a full year that Shaun and Kermit had successfully helped each other to stay off smack. It also began a twelve-month period of overindulgence for both. Three weeks at the Chapel studios in Lincolnshire to finish the album's remaining four tracks turned into a non-stop drinking session. A stint at Encore studios in Burbank, LA, to mix the songs with Danny Saber, involved coke-fuelled nights out at the Viper Room and various celebrity clubs about town. Shaun was even spotted out again in Manchester, albeit watching other bands. He went to an Oasis gig, where he almost got into a fight with the band's security when he wasn't allowed to watch the show from the side of the stage. He also turned up at a Paul Weller concert, after which he and Bez went backstage to try to meet the singer. For perhaps the first time, the pair were star-struck. They loitered outside Weller's dressing room door, but were too shy to go and talk to him.

By the spring of 1995, Black Grape was ready to launch itself on an audience. It was little over two years since Shaun had withdrawn from the music business, but – in the UK at least – an awful lot had changed in the charts. The suicide of Kurt Cobain had effectively ended interest in grunge and brought the focus on guitar groups back to Britain from the US. The Britpop battle between Blur and Oasis had made pop music into general front-page news for the first time in years, in the process sweeping aside long-standing MOR acts such as Dire Straits and Phil Collins. What was once called indie had become mainstream and, consequently, very big, extremely profitable business. Even cutting-edge dance acts could sell a million albums.

There were social changes too. A 1960s revival had brought so-called 'lad' culture back into fashion, as media like *Loaded* magazine celebrated all that was un-PC about a hedonistic, men-centred lifestyle. In these days, Happy Mondays' *Penthouse* pictures would have been seen as a brilliant piece of marketing, rather than a dubious publicity stunt. In addition, the north was back in fashion, thanks to Oasis, The Stone Roses' *The Second Coming*, The Charlatans' return to form, football teams like Newcastle and Manchester United, and the healthiest club scene in the country. All in all, the timing of the first Black Grape single, 'Reverend Black Grape', couldn't have been better. The madness was about to begin again, only this time it was musical.

The first sightings of Black Grape came courtesy of photographer Pennie Smith, renowned for her documentary-style coverage of the career of The Clash. Smith was asked by Gloria Nicholl, whom she had met through Mick Jones, to do the band's first press session.

Because she had worked so closely with the Roses in the late 1980s, Smith had only once photographed Happy Mondays. It was at the tail end of their career, for their final *NME* interview. Only recently back from Barbados, the band was in disarray, Bez was doubled up in pain with his twice-broken arm and Shaun was out of his head on heroin. Hardly the perfect photo-opportunity.

'I arranged to do the first Black Grape press session outside, rather than in a studio,' says Smith. 'I don't like meeting a band I don't really know in a confined space. I need to be able to run away. Thankfully, Black Grape didn't make me want to. In fact I found the lot of them really entertaining. As a pack, they look fearsome, which is great for me. The reality is that they are just a great mash of personalities. They come over more like a cartoon-strip than a pop band.

'I love photographing Shaun. Strangely, he makes for a fantastic subject. He doesn't look as though he should, but his face is really interesting. He's also very amenable. He does exactly what you ask him to. Basically, he's like an old-fashioned showman. He considers publicity as a part of the job, rather than an annoying chore which has nothing to do with making music. He is a total professional. I have to admit I was surprised by his sense of humour. Shaun is a lot funnier than he appears and also easy to get on with.

'I had to do that first shoot twice because the band forgot to bring Kermit the first time. We had arranged to do the photos next to the South Bank centre by the Thames in London. They were driving down from Manchester. I couldn't believe it when they arrived. They had come all the way before they realised that Kermit wasn't with them. In fact, they only noticed when they counted themselves out of the van. It did look like there was hundreds of them though. I'm used to shooting about four people, so it could have been a bit intimidating. But by the time they came back again the following week, to exactly the same spot, I was really looking forward to working with them.'

Smith's photo session eventually went so well that she was asked by Gloria Nicholl, at Shaun's request, to cover the making of the first Black Grape video. Shot in Manchester and directed by reggae musician and DJ Don Letts, who had been filming renegade musicians in London's Portobello area since punk broke in 1977, the video for 'Reverend Black Grape' saw Shaun and Kermit dressed up as preachers from the American mid-West, which tied in with the song's relentless religious references and celebratory, communal chorus, a straight steal from the hymn 'O Come All Ye Faithful'.

'I have this curious deal with bands that I get on with where I just hang out uncommissioned whenever they are doing something interesting,' says Smith. 'I went to the video shoot because I had enjoyed Black Grape's company so much at the photo session, which is very rare for me. The video was brilliant fun, but the band behaved like total workmen, despite the fact that dozens of their mates were there, just lying about on the grass and having a laugh. I really respected them for that. You knew that they would much rather be mucking about, but as soon as there was work to be done, they switched into super-professional mode. In that respect, Black Grape really remind me of The Clash. Whatever they do, they do absolutely thoroughly. It's a bit bizarre with Black Grape though, because they don't look like they would. Certainly, people presume that they wouldn't.

'Another reason that I admire Black Grape is that they are very much in control of what they do. I personally love bands that are masters of their own destiny – and, of course, demise in most cases. Despite being totally chaotic, they do seem to hold the reins over pretty much every aspect of their career. I'm sure it's because they are in control that they always throw themselves full-on into whatever task is at hand. I got the feeling that, if they had been ordered to do something – for example by a record company – rather than choosing to do it themselves, they just wouldn't have bothered.

'I've photographed Black Grape several times since then and, in total, Shaun has probably never said more than six words at a time to me. I go, do the job and he grunts as sort of appreciation. For some reason, I know that means he likes me and he appreciates the work that I'm doing. The band kept asking for copies of the photos anyway, so I presumed they liked them. I mean, the others would occasionally say how pleased everyone was with the shots, but Shaun would never utter a word. I guess the fact that he had me around more than once was his way of saying that he liked what I was doing. I'm not criticising though. I guess I don't talk much either. I'm pretty much known for two things: keeping my mouth shut and doing fucked, black-and-white documentary pictures. If that's what a client wants and we're compatible, that's all I need. I'm very happy to say that Shaun is one of the few people I do get on with and feel comfortable around.'

As only classic singles can, the harmonica-drenched, fun-filled, musical mish-mash that was 'Reverend Back Grape' was at once universally acclaimed (it would later be voted single of the year by several publications, including *NME*) and highly contentious. Controversy over the track initially stemmed from its lyrics. The lines 'Old Pope he got the Nazis to clean up their masses/In exchange for gold and paintings he gave them new addresses', which basically accused the Pope of war crimes, angered the Roman Catholic Church and got the song and video banned from TV in Britain. It also landed Shaun in hot water with his mum who, as a strict Catholic, was concerned that her son was in trouble with the Vatican. Less than a week later, the single attracted further criticism, this time from New York-based anti-terrorist organisation ADL (Anti-Deformation League), over its sleeve. The group attacked Black Grape for cover artwork depicting Venezuelan political terrorist Carlos The Jackal, dubbed the world's most wanted man following a long series of civilian attacks and the kidnapping in Zurich in the mid-1970s of eleven OPEC oil ministers. ADL claimed that Black Grape was elevating the terrorist to role-model status, particularly among young people. The band insisted that they had chosen the image purely because Carlos The Jackal, a solo agent who had been on the run for years, was well-known for his wealth of disguises.

Predictably, the controversy far from harmed 'Reverend Black Grape', which came out in Britain in late May and went straight into the singles chart Top 10. Its success also produced one of the most memorable *Top Of The Pops* performances for years. Shaun fronted his band's first TV appearance wearing a jumper and jeans, sporting square-framed sunglasses and a bushy beard. Rooted to the spot, he shouted his lyrics live as Kermit bounced frantically around the stage and Bez introduced the young audience to freaky dancing for the first time. You could almost hear parents sat at home complaining to their kids that this song didn't even have a tune, then watching on in horror as Shaun screamed the line, 'Go play fuckin' tennis', which should have been (but wasn't) edited out. But 'Reverend Black Grape' didn't need a tune. It had fun and energy and a sense of mischief instead. Against the odds, Shaun Ryder had made the musical comeback of the 1990s.

EIGHTEEN
Stayin' Alive

1995 was a landmark year for British pop. Albums by both guitar groups such as Pulp, Blur, Oasis and Radiohead, and dance acts like Portishead, Tricky, Chemical Brothers and Leftfield, all enjoyed mainstream success. Thanks largely to the Ecstasy-induced cultural revolution that took place at the turn of the decade, the UK's musical climate had changed almost beyond recognition. Black Grape's maverick mix of styles, samples and multi-media steals slotted easily into pop fans' increasingly-eclectic tastes. Moreover, the band was matched perhaps only by The Prodigy in its ability to combine innovative dance music with the 'personality' status normally reserved for guitar groups.

In July, Black Grape released a second single, 'In The Name Of The Father', another infectious, celebratory song literally stuffed with religious references. As with 'Reverend Black Grape', it was accompanied by a glossy mini-movie of a video, again directed by Don Letts, but this time shot in Jamaica.

A fortnight later, amid an avalanche of praise from the press, the band's debut album, *It's Great When You're Straight...Yeah!* entered the UK charts at No.1, selling over 100,000 copies in its first month. Although Shaun insisted that wilder versions of several of the songs existed, but had been replaced on the album by more straightforward rock recordings to appeal to the American market, *It's Great When You're Straight...Yeah!* still sounded a whole lot stranger than the rest of the Top 40. With its funky basslines, stuttering hip hop beats, odd noises, psychedelic effects and jubilant brass section, it was the ideal soundtrack to a demented, drug-induced, alcohol-fuelled get-together. It was the ultimate party album.

As important as the album's pick'n'mix bag of musical influences, were its lyrics, executed almost as a duel between Shaun and Kermit. While writing the songs, the pair had continually bounced ideas off one another. The same could be said of their singing. *It's Great When You're Straight...Yeah!* opened with the Kermit-delivered line 'Standing in the pews, talkin' bullshit, bullshit, bullshit', then continued with a flurry of contemporary cultural references, half-forgotten advertising slogans and famous, but often distorted quotes. Shaun's vocals were variously compared to Bart Simpson's gravel-voiced granddad (by Danny Baker) and Roland Rat (the *Independent*). The singer said both were preferable to Tony Wilson's likening of him to some dead author or poet and, besides, he agreed with any cartoon character comparisons.

Some critics reckoned *It's Great When You're Straight...Yeah!* was an updated version of Happy Mondays, only given an energy boost by Saber's injections of hip hop and Kermit's boisterous behaviour. Black Grape, however, had a far fresher feel and a much more confident, stronger sound. Naturally, it still pilfered from a vast back catalogue of Shaun's all-time favourite artists. It didn't take a second listen to spot snippets from 'Let It Be', 'Hey Jude', 'Sympathy For The Devil' and even Happy Mondays' own old album track 'Grandbag's Funeral' next to myriad classic movie moments. Less obvious were Isley Brothers' electric piano parts and the ghost of Serge Gainsbourg. Impossible to miss were relentless nods towards a bathroom cabinet stuffed with pharmaceuticals and Shaun's incessant expletives. A lot of the swearing had already been edited out for commercial reasons. Nevertheless, at the end of 'Shake Your Money', for example, Shaun descended into shouting obscenities, Tourette's Syndrome-style, to no one in particular.

In interviews, Shaun was his usual controversial self, talking openly about sex and drugs and his outlandish lifestyle. His sense of humour had returned too. Once again, he was a front-cover favourite with the press. However, Shaun had resolved to be less open and honest from now on, frequently insisting that he was off hard drugs and currently only indulged in weed and Guinness. He had become more responsible, concerned with the effect that his comments might have on his family. In addition, he was growing tired of all the sensationalist drugs headlines. Didn't anyone want to talk about the music?

Shaun even decided to stop bad-mouthing other musicians in public, including ex-Mondays members, although he was clearly pleased that none of their solo projects had been a success. He said he had gone soft, but in fact he simply couldn't be bothered to bait them any longer. Moreover, he had come to appreciate all that his former group had achieved and the opportunities that Happy Mondays' success had given him.

The acid test for Black Grape came with their live shows. Few had forgotten the sad spectacle of the final Happy Mondays tour. Moreover, no one knew if the band could recreate the madness of their songs on record live on stage – few artists score a No.1 album before playing a single gig. After a couple of low-key, unannounced warm-up dates in Ireland to which no press had been invited, Black Grape boldly made its mainland British live debut at London's Hanover Grand. Watched by an audience packed with critics, and including members of Oasis, Primal Scream, The Charlatans and Dodgy, as well as DJ Andy Weatherall, the band turned in one of the capital's most memorable pop performances for years. The concert was as manic, confusing and celebratory as the songs themselves, and the vivid spectacle made a welcome change from the motionless show put on by most of the band's guitar group peers.

Covering the gig for *The Times* was journalist David Sinclair. 'The first thing that struck me was the unlikely vitality of the performance,' said his review. 'The bug-eyed Bez lolloped with ceaseless energy about the stage. As ever, his musical role was difficult to determine, but as a dancer-cum-mascot, he was on top form. So too were the musicians, a crack squad dishing out razor-sharp funk/dance grooves on guitar, bass, drums, keyboards and saxophone. But the night belonged to Kermit and Ryder, whose bouts of shouted, rapid-fire repartee fell somewhere between the surreal conversations of Derek and Clive and the James Kelman school of literary endeavour. The rude enthusiasm of the show was infectious and there seems little doubt that Black Grape will quickly earn a place near the top of the new hierarchy of Brit-rock bands led by Oasis and Blur.'

By the band's sixth gig in Manchester, the audience knew the words to almost all of the songs, while both singles were received as standard old favourites, despite having only come out in the last couple of months. It was as though Shaun Ryder had never been away.

Over the summer, the tour took in several major UK and European festivals, including the Feile in Ireland and T In The Park in Glasgow, where Kermit accidentally broke an ankle. Having done a signing session for fans with Shaun and Bez, an excited Kermit ran out of a tent, tripped over and landed badly on his ankle. Much to the appreciation of the audience, he was later stretchered on stage, after receiving a shot of morphine. The others just took the piss out of his predicament.

While Black Grape's music was without doubt more focused and coherent than Happy Mondays', both bands shared a similarly shambolic nature and the sense that, at any second, the entire set-up could possibly collapse.

In late autumn, it looked as though that may happen to Black Grape. Kermit's accident had at first seemed like a one-off bit of bad luck. Then, just as the band was preparing to put out its third single, 'Kelly's Heroes', a writ was issued by Intastella, claiming that they had partly written not only that song, but also several others, including 'Reverend Black Grape'. Intastella had already registered the tracks as theirs and were demanding royalties from both the singles and the album. All payments to Black Grape were frozen. Shaun was furious. He said he had knocked back numerous offers to collaborate with other musicians during his short sabbatical, and had only worked with Intastella as a favour, which he now regretted.

Next, Black Grape had to cancel its first US tour after both Shaun and Bez were refused either entry visas or work permits because of criminal convictions dating back to their time in Happy Mondays. Some American publications flew journalists over to the UK to talk to the band. Others simply commissioned their overseas freelancers to do interviews. Writing for *Rolling Stone*, *The Times*'s David Sinclair met Black Grape in a bar in Hampstead, an upmarket area of north London, where Shaun had been staying for months so that he could do press and TV between tour dates.

'It was the most bizarre interview session I have ever done,' says Sinclair. 'It was supposed to be with Shaun, Kermit and Bez, but no one was able to round up all three of them in the same place at the same time. The *Rolling Stone* photographer was obviously used to a much higher standard of organisation. As the day wore on, he grew more and more frantic, fretting that the job would never get done. He was supposed to be catching a plane for Paris the following morning.

The interview was scheduled for 4pm, but I ended up doing it in bits and pieces with different members of the band over eight or so hours. When I left after midnight, the photographer and most of Black Grape were locked in a graveyard behind the bar. All the guy's gear was in there, it was pitch black and no one knew how to get out. I never found out if he made his plane.

'A really fascinating incident happened when I was interviewing Shaun. This bloke called Simon, who Shaun obviously knew pretty well, stormed into the bar and was totally freaking out. Apparently, Simon was meant to have been interviewing Shaun for Sky TV at 1pm, but Shaun hadn't bothered to show up. I think it was only for a short spot, done with a hand-held camera, but he had booked the studio time and there had been a crew waiting there for hours. It was now around 7pm. Simon had obviously spent the past few hours downing a bottle of vodka. He was belligerent and very annoyed. As soon as he came in, he started shouting, "You cunt. You fuckin' let me down," at Shaun from the other side of the bar. It was like showdown at high noon. He really was taunting Shaun.

'The entire time, Shaun never rose to it. He was sat across from me and I remember thinking that he looked like a bird. He put his hands in front of him at either side of the table and puffed his chest out. There was a sense of real violence in the air. That line from the album, "Come and have a go if you think you're hard enough," came into my head. Simon was really pushing his luck, but he was too drunk to notice for a while. In my article for *Rolling Stone*, I quoted exactly what Shaun said, "If he calls me that again ... Well, he's a big fucker, but I'll smack him and I'll knock him out."

'I had no doubt that Shaun meant every word. He certainly sounded serious and enough of a warning came to shut Simon up, even though he was plastered. To be honest, I was surprised that Shaun managed to maintain such self-control, especially considering his reputation. But people do always say that it's the really tough ones who don't get into fights, and that was definitely the vibe.

'The scene reminded me of a Mafia story I had recently read in the papers. It was an incident in a square in Milan involving two drivers. One had crashed into the other's car. The guy who had been hit started shouting and screaming and making a real fuss. The guy who had hit him stayed silent and calm. Suddenly, the loud one twigged that the other was a Mafiosi. He got straight back in his car and cleared off as fast as possible. In the bar, it was as though Simon suddenly knew that this scene wasn't going to end well for him. Shaun had psyched him out.

'Shaun is a very bright guy, but quite clearly not at all educated. There are definitely parallels between him and someone like Mohammed Ali – that natural fantastic intelligence, combined with a native wit. He was a total contrast to Bez, who appeared to have neither education nor wit. Kermit was different again, well-educated, but in the formal sense. Bez was hugely defensive about his lack of learning and he tried to cover it up by being charming, but he's clearly pretty stupid. Shaun is from a similar background to Bez, but he has a totally opposite attitude to learning. Shaun seems to pay a great deal of attention to the business of accruing knowledge. You could tell he had an intelligence that had served him well and got him to where he is now. Okay, that combined with a thuggish air. He's very deceptive and incredibly hard to read. He operates on a lot of different levels, so he is easy to underestimate.

'When I interviewed Shaun, he was going on about how he was trying to behave himself these days, act in an adult fashion. Of course, everyone had been asking him questions about whether or not he was straight, because of the album title. I didn't ask him that, but he was obviously keen to tell me how, at thirty-three, he was turning over a new leaf. It was really funny because, as he said it, he was sitting there chomping on a spliff and downing pint after pint of Guinness. Not to mention being assailed by a madman from Sky TV. The entire day was just so unbelievably chaotic that I kept wondering what it must have been like for people when Shaun wasn't trying to act adult.

'By the time I went home, I was a bit ragged, but I'd got what I wanted. I had the headache from hell because I'd been drinking all day and eaten next to nothing. I realised then that Shaun had reduced absolutely everyone there to nervous wrecks in numerous different ways, and yet it obviously all seemed fairly run-of-the-mill to him. Being around Shaun gave me that feeling of the static in the air right before a thunderstorm. There was nothing easy about being around him or Black Grape. The interview was shambolic and looked likely to disintegrate at any second. Just like their music though, it eventually came together and worked out really well. The only person I've ever met who is anything like Shaun is Tricky, in the sense that he has an inability to be anywhere as planned or to hold everyday situations together. Like Tricky, Shaun seems to make life very difficult for himself for no apparent reason.'

In late 1995, Black Grape suffered its first serious setback. Returning to England on a flight from Spain, Kermit became seriously ill. After being taken to hospital in Manchester and diagnosed with blood poisoning disease septicaemia, he went into a coma for four days. Over the following few weeks, he would lose several stones in weight and also suffer liver problems. When, in addition, a hole in his heart was discovered, it looked as though he may die. Kermit would later claim that his doctors had resigned themselves to the fact that he couldn't recover. When he did pull through, it would take him a full ten months to get over the illness.

Shaun's confession that he had immediately assumed that Kermit's problems were a result of taking too much smack somewhat contradicted the pair's claims that they were now clean of hard drugs. In fact, it turned out that the longer Black Grape was on tour, the more drugs had crept on to the agenda. Shaun insisted that he no longer had a habit, but that he had been back dabbling with heroin. The only solution was to keep the tours as short as possible.

Doubtless to Shaun's delight, Black Grape saw out 1995 in South America. Still unable to legally enter the US, the band – minus Kermit – went to Cuba, where interviews with the US press were to take place. Perhaps predictably, nothing went according to plan. Bez missed his flight out, while Shaun – who had been holidaying in Jamaica – was already ill on arrival and in no fit state to talk to dozens of journalists.

The chaos continued into 1996. In February, out at *NME* awards night The Brats, at which Black Grape won Best New Band, Shaun was stopped by police and arrested en route from the ceremony to the party. After spending a night in jail, the following morning, he phoned radio DJ Chris Evans to explain live on air what had happened. Then, with Kermit still ill, the band had to find a replacement for its forthcoming UK tour. Rapper and DJ Carl 'Psycho' McCarthy, who had initially been brought in to do drum'n'bass remixes of 'Reverend Black Grape', took Kermit's place. Less than a month later, however, Black Grape lost another member when Bez unexpectantly quit. The reasons for his leaving were at first unclear. He hadn't shown up for an MTV interview, he had fallen out with Shaun, he hadn't been getting paid and he didn't feel as though he was doing himself justice in his role as dancer were all given as explanations. The truth was a combination of several factors, not least that Bez had never been sure about joining Black Grape from day one.

'It was an accident I was in a band in the first place,' says Bez. 'In my eyes, that was a once-in-a-lifetime experience. But Shaun convinced me that, no matter what happens from now on, I'm an entertainer. That's what I got dealt in life and there's no getting away from it.'

The situation remains unresolved.

'Bez is family,' says Shaun. 'He is free to come and go as he pleases. Bez was there when we were recording the album, so he joined us on stage. It started off as fun, but nine months on, he was expected to do interviews and everything when he wasn't getting paid, so you can understand why he got fucked off. He even has to ask for his train fare. He's on strike. It's not a case of whether he'll come back. He'll never be far away as far as I'm concerned.'

Kermit returned to the fold in March 1996 for a Black Grape performance on Chris Evans' Channel 4 series *T.F.I. Friday*. A parody of tacky TV show *Stars In Their Eyes* saw a very drunk Shaun transformed into Johnny Rotten, complete with spray-painted silver hair, and Black Grape pretend to be The Sex Pistols. The band played their own version of 'Pretty Vacant', which – despite assurances that the song wouldn't contain swearing – was littered with the word 'fuck'. Subsequently, Evans' production company was given a heavy fine, while TV regulators ITC insisted that *T.F.I. Friday* no longer be broadcast live, instead committed to video and delayed for twenty minutes before it went out. Shaun had made a tiny piece of TV history. What's more, he'd done it fronting The Sex Pistols.

'The Chris Evans show was all about being in the Mondays,' says Shaun. 'I used to want to feel like that every night of my life. I couldn't give a fuck before, whereas now I try to concentrate at least some of my energy on business matters. Is that because I'm getting older? No, it's because I'm getting wiser.'

In March, after seven months of lobbying US immigration, Shaun was granted a US visa, and the next month Black Grape began a tour of the US and South America, which kicked off in Tijuana, Mexico. The band's LA gig sold out within two hours of tickets going on sale. Although Kermit was still too ill to accompany Black Grape on tour, he did fly out to the US in May to work with Shaun and Danny Saber on some new songs at a rented house in the Hollywood hills. One track from the sessions, 'Fat Neck', was completed and scheduled to be released in Britain as Black Grape's next single.

The band returned to England to headline the second Tribal Gathering over the cream of contemporary international dance acts and DJs, as if to prove that they had more to offer than their Britpop peers.

'All those bands think it's the 1960s again,' says Shaun. 'Oasis and the British invasion? Come on, we're in the 1990s now. Let's get real. Anyway, Black Grape doesn't want to be grouped with other bands; we just want to do our own thing.'

Black Grape's own thing involved supporting Oasis at their two massive outdoor gigs at Loch Lomond near Glasgow in front of audiences of 40,000, and releasing the single 'England's Irie', which they had recorded several months earlier with the aid of former Clash guitarist Joe Strummer plus old mate actor Keith Allen. The track had been written specifically for the album *The Beautiful Game*, to which artists such as Primal Scream, Simply Red and Supergrass had been asked to contribute theme songs for upcoming football competition Euro '96. Shaun was angry that the song 'Three Lions', by The Lightning Seeds and comedians Skinner and Baddiel, had been chosen as the England team's official anthem after he had been told that it would be his track. Consequently, although 'England's Irie' had already appeared on the compilation album, Black Grape reclaimed it and put it out as a single. It entered the UK charts at No.6, becoming the band's third Top 10 single.

If Black Grape was releasing records, Shaun would be in the tabloids, albeit for far less serious misdemeanours than when he was with Happy Mondays. One story claimed that hours after a *Top Of The Pops* appearance with Joe Strummer and Keith Allen, at a party at a London hotel, Shaun spent the night demanding drugs from strangers. Another told of how he was thrown out of London's Hard Rock Cafe for refusing to do up the flies of his Armani jeans, claiming that leaving them open was part of his look.

Black Grape's final UK appearance of 1996 was to prove its last for almost a year. Headlining the Saturday night of the Reading festival, the band was joined on stage by Allen, Strummer, Chris Evans and – for the first time in months – Bez, to turn in by far the best show of the weekend. The following night, The Stone Roses were all but booed off the same stage. They would split up shortly afterwards.

The bulk of the basic songs for Black Grape's second album, *Stupid, Stupid, Stupid*, were written over three separate, fortnight-long sessions at the rented house in LA, between May and December 1996. Although Danny Saber was heavily involved in the writing of the music, for the tracks to really take shape, they would have to be worked on for an intensive few months in a proper studio. By spring 1997, there was still no sign of the album being completed. Shaun wasn't worried, though. He didn't want to have to force himself to work, but would rather wait until he was in the right mood.

'We had toured the first album for ages and it was time to move on,' says Shaun. 'But it wasn't going to happen if it didn't have that fun vibe around it again. It couldn't be a chore. Everyone had to be in a good frame of mind.'

While Danny Saber disappeared to work with The Rolling Stones on their new album *Bridges To Babylon* and remix the likes of David Bowie and U2, Shaun took time off. He had just bought a farmhouse in a small village outside County Cork and was spending time with his family, sometimes sleeping all day and staying up all night smoking spliff and watching TV.

'Our biggest mistake with the Mondays,' says Shaun, 'was that we didn't take a break after *Pills 'N' Thrills*. We should have chilled out and got into having a groove instead of going straight back to recording. The Stone Roses had it sussed. They didn't fuck themselves up or wear themselves out.'

Even at home and out of the industry, however, Shaun couldn't keep away from controversy for long. Six months earlier, he had fired Black Grape management company Nicholl & Dime (Nik and Gloria Nicholl). They were now suing him for 'at least £137,070.73'. Black Grape had become big business – *It's Great When You're Straight...Yeah!* had sold over 600,000 copies worldwide – and the Nicholls claimed to have been badly and systematically ripped off by Shaun. They alleged that they weren't only still waiting to be paid for their professional services, but that they were personally owed money from the singer after they paid out £10,000 to clear his mortgage arrears in order to save his house in Manchester. The couple now claimed to be close to losing their own home.

Meanwhile, Shaun was insisting that it was he who had been ripped off by the Nicholls. Grubby stories started to fly between both parties. The Nicholls were accused of being racist and, consequently, of trying not to pay Kermit his fair share of profits. They were said to have been so tight with the band's money that they had forced Bez out by refusing to reimburse even his travel expenses to interviews and gigs, and were prepared to offer industry professionals only tiny wages for the 'opportunity' of working with the band. People close to Shaun claimed that the Nicholls had tried to alienate them from the Black Grape set-up, so that no one else ever knew exactly what was going on. One story even alleged that Nik Nicholl had tried to charge Shaun £17,000 after lending him his battered, F-registration Saab for a fortnight, then said that Shaun had written it off. Shaun was rumoured to have collated substantial evidence of malpractice against Nicholl & Dime, which was why he'd sacked the company.

Perhaps unsurprisingly, Shaun was emerging less than snowy-white from the affair himself. Various sources corroborated the story that he had somehow managed to get hold of all the gross profits from Black Grape's most recent tour, and that he had spent the money buying his farmhouse in Ireland, leaving scores of production staff and road crew unpaid.

Whatever the truth of the matter, by the time Black Grape had taken on new American management, the band's accounts were in chaos. Moreover, in order to get several key organisations worldwide to work with the band ever again, dozens of outstanding debts had to be cleared. Licensees were approached for advances on sales of Black Grape's forthcoming album in order to raise capital. Shaun, it seemed, had once again emerged all but unscathed from a dubious, rather unpleasant incident, and added at least two more to his already healthy list of aggrieved ex-associates.

Black Grape made its first public appearance of 1997 at the Phoenix festival, headlining on Thursday night to a fairly small audience, before travelling to Rotterdam to support U2 on the opening nights of their European tour. Notably without Bez, but with both Danny Saber and Kermit's former stand-in Psycho now permanent members, at Phoenix the band played several tracks from *Stupid, Stupid, Stupid* live for the first time. The album had only just been completed, following an eight-week stint at Real World studios in Bath. Shaun, however, had already been back in the public eye for several weeks, having won his first proper acting role in a movie remake of TV series *The Avengers*. Director Jeremiah Chechik had seen the singer's picture in a magazine and decided that he would make the perfect stylish thug. The film's script saw Shaun as a baddie called Bully Boy whose immediate boss was to be played by Eddie Izzard. Established actors Sean Connery, Ralph Fiennes, Uma Thurman and Patrick McNee were all to take principal parts.

On 20 October, Black Grape released 'Get Higher', the first single to be taken from their second album. The track's original intro featured the cut-up voice of ex-US president Ronald Reagan apparently extolling the virtues of drug abuse – it contained the lines 'President Bush smoked marijuana regularly' and 'Nancy and I are hooked on heroin'. Inevitably, the intro had to be removed for the single version of the song, although it was retained on the album.

Stupid, Stupid, Stupid, which came out in late November, retained the party vibe of its predecessor, but avoided any religious references, with Shaun claiming to have worked harder on the lyrics than ever before.

'All we've tried to do on the album is enjoy ourselves,' says Shaun. 'It was really important that it had a funny party feel to it. You're not supposed to listen too closely to the songs and take in every word and think it's really intense. It's just very loose.'

Stupid, Stupid, Stupid mixed P-Funk, soul, hip hop, rock and drum'n'bass beats with a buoyant brass section, bongos, scratching and the usual smattering of musical steals. Shaun named spacey trip hop single 'Marbles' as his favourite song, 'Squeaky' was a boozy cover of Frederick Knight's 1970s Stax classic 'I've Been Lonely For So Long', and 'Dadi Waz A Badi' became the band's top live track on their November UK tour. In addition, a ninety-minute documentary of the making of the album and the history of Black Grape, produced by former boxer Too Nice Tom, a friend of Shaun's, went on release.

1998 sees Shaun Ryder out of Manchester, up on the big screen, back at the top of the British charts and possibly poised to do well in America for the first time. He still stumbles into more strange situations every few months than most people would want to encounter in a lifetime. At present, his future highs seem set to be mostly musical, rather than chemical. But, as always, lows never look far away. Maybe that's what makes it exciting. Tread carefully.

Bibliography and Interview Credits

BOOK SOURCES

From Joy Division To New Order, The Factory Story by Mick Middles – Virgin (1996)
Chapters 2, 3, 5, 7, 9, 12, 13, 14, 15

Night Fever, Club Writing In The Face 1980-1997, edited by Richard Benson – Boxtree (1997). In particular, HM Government Vs Acid House by Sheryl Garratt and Chris Taggart (February 1990)
Chapters 2, 6, 7, 9

The Faber Book Of Pop, edited by Hanif Kureishi and Jon Savage – Faber and Faber (1995)
Chapters 6, 7

Meaty Beaty Big And Bouncy, Classic Rock & Pop Writing From Elvis To Oasis, edited by Dylan Jones – Hodder and Stoughton (1996)
Chapters 14, 16

Street Drugs by Andrew Tyler – Hodder and Stoughton (1986)
Chapter 6

The Dark Stuff, Selected Writings On Rock Music 1972-1993 by Nick Kent – Penguin (1994)
Chapter 9

PAPERS/MAGAZINES

NME (IPC), 1986-1997
Chapters 1-18

Melody Maker (IPC), 1987-1995
Chapters 1-15

Sounds (IPC), 1987-1991
Chapters 1-8

Vox (IPC), 1990-1995
Chapters 8, 11, 15, 16, 17, 18

Q (EMAP), 1992-1996
Chapters 1, 2, 8, 13, 14, 15, 16, 17, 18

Select (EMAP), 1995-1996
Chapters 1, 2, 6, 14, 15, 17, 18

Blah Blah Blah (Raygun), 1996
Chapters 2, 6, 16

Muzik (IPC), 1996
Chapter 2

Music Week (Miller Freeman), 1995-1997
Chapters 17, 18

The Times, 1995
Chapter 18

Guardian, 1995
Chapters 1, 16

Express, 1996
Chapters 11, 12, 16

INTERVIEWS

Peter & Ian Davies
Chapters 1, 9

Bernard Sumner
Chapters 3, 4, 5, 6, 16

Jeff Barrett
Chapters 3, 4, 5, 6, 7, 8, 9

Terry Hall
Chapter 3

Dave Harper
Chapters 3, 4, 5, 6, 7

Peter Henderson
Chapter 7

Jack Barron
Chapters 7, 10, 12

Nicki Kefalas
Chapters 4, 9

Eric Longley
Chapters 10, 12, 13, 14, 15, 16

Jayne Houghton
Chapters 8, 10, 12, 13, 14, 15, 16

Paul Oakenfold
Chapters 8, 10, 11

Donovan
Chapters 11, 12, 16

Pennie Smith
Chapter 17

David Sinclair
Chapter 18

Thank you to: All the contributors for your time and your interest, my surrogate sister Ann Scanlon, Dierdre O'Callaghan, Bernard McMahon, Mary Scanlon, Neil Perry, Jenny Parrott, Jake Lingwood at Ebury, Alfie Hitchcock, Martin Whittle and all at AVP.